Praise for *Infinite Life*

"Among the riches offered here is the insight that we do not become faceless blobs as we realize our selflessness and the infinite nature of our lives but true individualists. Liberated from a fear of death and isolation, confident that we are in a long-term relationship with life that can never be severed, we can begin to help ourselves and others to happiness."

—*Publishers Weekly* (starred review)

"Thurman delivers life-changing lessons." —*Snow Lion*

Praise for *Inner Revolution*

"An inspiring guide to incorporating Buddhist wisdom into daily life. Thurman shows how self-examination, far from miring the seeker in navel-gazing, can lead to an expanded sense of connection with others."

—*USA Today*

"This book, both testimonial and invitational, addresses in a compelling . . . argument the palpable desires of an exhausted culture eager to go on pilgrimage from 'me' to meaning."

—*The New York Times Book Review*

"Part spiritual memoir, part philosophical treatise and part religious history, Thurman's book is a passionate declaration of the possibilities of renewing the world." —*Publishers Weekly* (starred review)

"Thurman's lucid teachings infuse the concepts of liberty and happiness with cosmic significance and do much to illuminate the reasons for Buddhism's blooming in the West." —*Booklist*

ALSO BY ROBERT THURMAN

Inner Revolution: Life, Liberty, and the Pursuit of Real Happiness

The Holy Teaching of Vimalakīrti

The Central Philosophy of Tibet

The Tibetan Book of the Dead

Essential Tibetan Buddhism

Wisdom and Compassion: The Sacred Art of Tibet (with Marylin Rhie)

Worlds of Transformation: Tibetan Art of Wisdom and Compassion (with Marylin Rhie)

Mandala: The Architecture of Enlightenment (with Denise Leidy)

Circling the Sacred Mountain (with Tad Wise)

Infinite Life

Awakening to Bliss Within

Robert Thurman

RIVERHEAD BOOKS
New York

THE BERKLEY PUBLISHING GROUP
Published by the Penguin Group
Penguin Group (USA) Inc.
375 Hudson Street, New York, New York 10014, USA
Penguin Group (Canada), 10 Alcorn Avenue, Toronto, Ontario M4V 3B2, Canada
(a division of Pearson Penguin Canada Inc.)
Penguin Books Ltd., 80 Strand, London WC2R 0RL, England
Penguin Group Ireland, 25 St. Stephen's Green, Dublin 2, Ireland (a division of Penguin Books Ltd.)
Penguin Group (Australia), 250 Camberwell Road, Camberwell, Victoria 3124, Australia
(a division of Pearson Australia Group Pty. Ltd.)
Penguin Books India Pvt. Ltd., 11 Community Centre, Panchsheel Park, New Delhi—110 017, India
Penguin Group (NZ), Cnr. Airborne and Rosedale Roads, Albany, Auckland 1310, New Zealand
(a division of Pearson New Zealand Ltd.)
Penguin Books (South Africa) (Pty.) Ltd., 24 Sturdee Avenue, Rosebank, Johannesburg 2196,
South Africa

Penguin Books Ltd., Registered Offices: 80 Strand, London WC2R 0RL, England

Cover design by Andrea Ho
Book design by Michelle McMillian

PRINTING HISTORY
First Riverhead hardcover edition: February 2004
First Riverhead trade paperback edition: February 2005
Riverhead trade paperback ISBN: 1-59448-069-9

The Library of Congress has catalogued the Riverhead hardcover edition as follows:

Thurman, Robert A. F.
Infinite life : seven virtues for living well / by Robert Thurman.
p. cm.
ISBN 1-57322-267-4
1. Spiritual life—Buddhism. 2. Buddhism—Doctrines. I. Title.
BQ5660.T487 2004 2003047142
294.3'444—dc21

PRINTED IN THE UNITED STATES OF AMERICA

10 9 8 7 6 5 4 3 2 1

Acknowledgments

I deeply bow and sincerely thank all the many wonderful people who have inspired and helped me with this book. My ancestors, foremost my mother, Betsy, and father, Beverly, who gave me my body and cared for it with much love and generosity and intelligence. My spiritual ancestors in the Dharma, foremost the Buddha Shakyamuni and the great archangelic bodhisattvas, Manjushri, Tara, and company, the great sages and siddhas such as Nāgārajuna, Aryadeva, Asanga, Chandrakirti, Shantideva, and Dharmakirti, and the immortal lamas, such as Jey Tsong Khapa, who shaped my mind in ways I don't remember in previous lives and ways I somewhat remember in this life, though there seems to be no limit to the growth of my appreciation. My root teachers, formal and informal, foremost His Holiness the Dalai Lama, the Venerable Geshe Wangyal, Kyabje Ling Rinpoche, Serkhong Tsenshap Rinpoche, Tara Tulku, Locho Rinpoche, and good friend Gelek Rinpoche, who continue to instruct me, even when it is only when I remember and belatedly understand some long-past teaching, the depth of which I had not fathomed—probably still don't completely. My kind friends and capable students, such as Joel and Joe, Sarah, Bobo, Lava, and Louise, who always stir my brain and tongue to produce something more meaningful. My beloved close family, Nena, Ganden, Uma, Taya, Dechen, Mipam, Dash, Caroline, Max, Maya, and Levon, who don't even imagine how much they help me just by being there. And all my Mother Sensitive Beings, who have cared for me in countless lives and continue to help me to someday come to share with them the nexus of infinite bliss I have sensed at the core of all, in timeless moments.

On the practical level, my helpful friend Diana, my agent, Lynn Nesbit, my editors, Amy Hertz and Marc Haeringer, my editorial assistant, MeiMei Fox, and all the kind professionals at Riverhead Books.

To all of you, my main thank-you is my effort to reflect your kindness to our Mother Beings by channeling these teachings that come from higher beings while trying to minimize the channel's many imperfections. On top of that, I will not forget your kindness, and I say thank you, thank you, thank you!

To Nena

O Noble Lady, no matter how I sought you
I found no truth-substantiated certainty,
My mind-youth tortured by fabrications—
Till you bestowed upon him deep relief
In the forest hut of inexpressibility! . . .

Transcendent Wisdom, Supreme Mother of Buddhas,
Breathing out and in all that lives and stands,
Natural clear light, forever trouble-free, Truth Body Angel—
Let us all enjoy the great good fortune of the Noble Lady!

—From Pabongka Dechen Nyingpo's *Swift Path of Great Bliss*

Contents

THE DALAI LAMA

Foreword

I am very happy to introduce my old friend Bob Thurman's new book, the title of which he derives from the name of one of the buddhas, known in Tibetan as Tsepamey, meaning Infinite Life, which denotes the qualities that buddha principally embodies. He represents the Mahayana view that perfect enlightenment is not merely a peaceful state of cessation, almost like nonexistence. Buddhahood involves a state of complete awareness that finds blissful expression in a compassion that tirelessly embraces all living beings, manifesting whenever necessary to help them reach their own freedom from suffering.

Professor Thurman describes this vision in the context of the vast and extensive practices of bodhisattvas, the transcendent virtues or perfections. He also tackles an important ancillary aspect of this vision, the notion of the past and future lives of all beings. This is based on the Buddha's explanation of the principle of cause and effect, which states that no thing arises without cause, there is no uncaused cause, and no cause loses its effect. Thus, we say that consciousness is always preceded by another consciousness, and always gives rise to further consciousness, much in the manner of the continuity of physical energy. The idea that we live many lives before and many after this present one, the quality of which is affected by our own conduct and motivation, provides the context for appreciating the great rarity and value of life as a free and fortunate human being. Moreover, understanding that all beings have already lived countless lives allows us to accept our interdependence and appreciate that at some time every being has been kind to us in some way.

Most spiritual traditions relate their systems of ethics to some sense of continuity of life after death because the potential consequence of our deeds is what gives meaning to our lives. Understanding actually how this continuity works is considered to be extremely difficult, something accessible only to the mind of a buddha. On the one hand, it is difficult for us to check the existence of past and future lives for ourselves. However, a clear distinction should be made between what is not found and what is found to be nonexistent by science. What science finds to be nonexistent, we should all accept as nonexistent, but what science merely does not find is a completely different matter. On the other hand, the Buddha stated clearly that our awareness of both the impact of our previous lives on this life and the consequences of our present deeds on our future lives is an essential way to motivate a proper sense of ethical maturity and spiritual development.

The question of past and future lives can be difficult for people brought up in the modern world, used to adopting a view that accords with what can be physically proven. But even modern science still does not know with certainty what the facts of consciousness actually are, how it functions, or what its complete nature is. Therefore, I am glad to see that Bob Thurman has addressed some of these issues straightforwardly in this book with his usual vigor and wit.

July 18, 2003

Infinite Life

Introduction: Invitation to the Infinite Life

I was twenty-one years old and a novice monk studying with the Reverend Geshe Wangyal at his tiny Lamaist Buddhist Monastery of America in Freewood Acres, New Jersey. The small settlement consisted of Mongolian, Russian, and Eastern European refugees living in tract houses in the Jersey Pine Barrens. At around 10:15 on a spring morning, I was walking along East Second Street to a corner store up on Route 9, sent to buy a quart of milk for midmorning tea. I was moving briskly west, passing on my left a faded white picket fence that surrounded a small house. As I crossed the driveway, something amazing happened to me.

I experienced a disorienting sensation that I can only describe as the feeling of a push-pressure on my tailbone suddenly dislodging itself. The pressure gone, I immediately saw that I had always been feeling as if I were being pushed along from behind toward my destination, not only to the grocery store on Route 9 but to my destiny in life, to the future in general. The change in sensation gave me a pronounced feeling of relief, a sense of release. I became vividly self-aware of my posture—my brow had been clenched slightly, shoulders hunched up, torso leaning forward, pelvis retracted, and lower back arched. I spontaneously slowed my pace and straightened up my body. A ripple of relaxation moved down my frame, and I felt buoyed by the released momentum.

Looking around me as if for the first time, I noticed the flowers planted beyond the fence I had just walked past, the broader street on my right, and the blue sky filled with fluffy clouds. Then I became aware of a deeper layer of thoughts in my mind, well beneath my thinking about getting to the store, getting the milk, and getting back to Geshe-la and his guests to serve the tea. These deeper thoughts had been circling intently in my head around the Buddhist concept of "beginninglessness." I had first encountered the notion as Geshe-la read to me the Tibetan translation of Nāgārajuna's "Friendly Letter" to the South Indian King Udayi of the Shatavahana Dynasty (circa second century CE). What a funny expression, I'd thought, to talk of "from the beginninglessness." In Western books, "in the beginning" is all we ever hear about. What was this "beginninglessness," I wondered?

All at once, I grasped the concept with full clarity. "Aha!" I thought, "when we say 'in the beginning,' we implicitly assume that there is an absolute beginning behind us in time, as if our being and doings were pushing off from a back boundary. I have been driven by that sense of push my whole life, without even realizing it. Amazing! But if life is indeed beginningless, this means that my past has, in fact, been infinite. The future will be too. So there is no big rush to get somewhere. I am mistaken in my compulsion. I can take my time, and take more care, to make sure to go where I want to go. What a thrill! A bit of release, a taste of freedom, no more involuntary pressure—so this is beginninglessness."

I was delighted to begin to understand the Buddhist world I was so drawn to, and amazed to actually *feel* that understanding in my body. I experienced a physical release from a hitherto unrecognized but now obviously bothersome pressure. Returning to the business of the moment, I practically skipped to the store, each step fresh and spontaneous.

A weight was lifted from my body, a clamp removed from my heart. I had begun to break free from my inherited life of bondage to enter a new life unbound, an infinite life.

A Blissful Vacation

Is it not everyone's deepest wish to be profoundly and securely happy, joyfully and lovingly able to share that happiness with friends and neighbors as well as all the world's people and animals? To feel an inner bliss that does not depend on this or that circumstance, fortune, or success, but springs from deep within our hearts, from a place of fundamental well-being? To experience a grounding sense of the deep goodness of reality, which fills us with an unconditional joy that energizes our lives? I believe it is. Yet our culture constantly tells us that such joy is not possible, even that it is suspect. It tells us that the world is evil or inadequate and needs fixing. It tells us to think that we need this or that thing or relationship or leader or accomplishment in order to experience even a moment of contentment. They say that deep, unconditional happiness is not just unrealistic, but illegal, immoral, and unhealthy.

Often Buddhist teachings—the Dharma bequeathed to us by so many enlightened ones, which as I grow older more and more has a lifesaving effect on me every day—are misunderstood. They are falsely taught as if the Buddha agreed with all these naysayers, as if he were in fact the ultimate naysayer, the all-time champion of killjoys. "Life is suffering," he seems to have said, "so better to escape from it." How gloomy and sad!

But the truth is, the Buddha definitely did not condemn us to the unhappiness that many conventional societies and cultures, including our own, make us feel is inevitable. On the contrary, he discovered and proclaimed that total freedom from suffering—exquisite, enduring joy—is extremely possible for every sensitive being. It is only the unenlightened, self-centered, and self-constricted being who is temporarily incapable of real happiness. Most of us have a strong yet unwarranted sense of having a fixed, unchanging, limited "self" that is totally separate from all other beings. This combines with our narrow view that our existence is random and terminal; it only starts when we are born and ends abruptly when we die. Fixed and alienated, random and terminal—together these form a vicious combination. In the end, we are left feeling bereft and slightly depressed, living a life seeming to be utterly devoid of meaning. I call this "terminal living."

We can free ourselves from such a terminal existence simply by becoming aware of our misconceptions and their impact on our way of being. Once we have accepted the fact that we ourselves may be the main cause of our own unhappiness, we become determined to understand the problem fully and to solve it as soon as possible. With simple guidance, we easily discover the limiting force to be our own misunderstanding of the reality of the world and of ourselves. The first step toward true contentment lies in confronting the fundamental problem of our rigid self-sense. When we look carefully for our "self," we cannot find it. We discover the error that is the cause of our problem, and we begin to grasp the concepts of selflessness, interconnectedness to others, and infinite life. Now we can set ourselves free to experience the full satisfaction with ourselves, others, and our world that Buddhists call "enlightenment" or "awakening."

The great kindness of the Buddha (and many other enlightened beings who have shared their teachings with us) is that he created a method whereby we can use reason to get ourselves away from the imprisoning "self." That is why we sing Buddha's praises. He has invited us to join a lifelong blissful vacation from our domineering selves.

I began studying Buddhism forty years ago and became a monk precisely to go on a blissful vacation. Sometimes I wish I had spent these many years on such a retreat. Maybe after forty years, I would have actually achieved something. Who knows? As it was, I left the monastic community and returned to the U.S. to share the Buddha's message with my American *sangha,* or community. As things go in America, I've been working like a mad dog ever since.

When I came back to New York in 1965, I found there was no support for the blissful vacation I had discovered while studying to become a monk at the Dalai Lama's community in exile in India. I said, "Hey, let's have a blissful vacation." The response was, "Blissful? We've got the Vietnam War. We've got to stop the Pentagon! We've got to stop the corporations! We've got to do important things!" You know, American life. "You want to be blissful?" people asked. "Take Librium. There's no joy in this world. That's unrealistic." Isn't that our society? "Besides, you'll get to experience the bliss of being nothing when you die. Anyway, I've got to get back to work!" I get that same response from people all around the world today—I often even feel that way myself, as things go from bad to worse, when looked at from the materialistic perspective.

But we can change that, you and I. We can join the peaceful, cool, inner revolution. Why don't we have a year-round blissful vacation? We could all form big caravans and wander around, following the sun. It could be summer all the time. Gradually, more disenchanted people would join us. That's what Tibet was like before the Chinese invaded. Since 1409, they were on a blissful vacation, many people wandering on pilgrimage or staying still on retreat. They were on vacation, the whole country—I mean it. A few people had to make *mo-mo* dumplings and a few yaks were sadly sacrificed for food, and sure, some people were not very enlightened at all. It was a bit funky, of course imperfect—but it worked pretty well. With all its grime and low-tech infrastructure, it was the closest any human society so far ever came to experiencing the delightful quality of life that the Buddha tells us is our birthright, our destiny. With its inspiration we can create an even more joyous society today!

I'm writing this book because I want you to see that your blissful vacation is absolutely possible. There is a life that isn't all pointless, yet full of cell phones and deadlines and total pressure all the time. There is a life that is free, boundless, happy, and full of wisdom and natural purpose. And the great news is that you don't have to go sit by yourself on some mountaintop to gain the insights that I'm going to share with you here. I mean, sure, if you want total enlightenment on a tight schedule, then you will have to go someday to become a monk or nun or some other kind of professional evolver, an ardent retreatant. But even in the midst of my crazy, pressure-filled New York City life, I am able to experience, joyously contemplate, and discuss with others the immanence of nirvana, the blissful vacation, and relish the aura of total peace and happiness. So you can, too. When more of us do that, we get one step closer to making it real, here and now. And that is precisely what I am going to help you do.

Today—which is the day you read these words, dear reader—I invite you to enter this new realm of existence! Turn back from rushing ahead and face the facts of your life. See it bound by arbitrary limitations. Note how birth and death are imagined as concrete boundaries for no good reason: You can't remember the one and would rather not imagine the other. Take heart. Use your common sense and critical intelligence to awaken. Stop taking for granted your inherited conventional reality. Question even your habitual instincts. Take the plunge into the ocean of boundless freedom. Embrace the mystery. Discover the reality of infinite life!

The Buddha was one of the foremost planetary teachers of the human right, human ability, and human responsibility to achieve the perfect, unconditional happiness that surely is the innermost wish of most people. I follow his inspiring example and write these words for each of you, to help you learn to trust that wish, and to follow the drive of your deepest spirit of intelligent love and courageous goodwill toward a more happy life for yourself and others.

Part One

I

The Nature of Reality

When I give a talk on whatever topic, at some point I open up the infinite life dimension and invite people to join me in the year-round, lifelong blissful vacation. People often come up to me afterward. They will say, "I love what you said. I hope it's so. But, you know, I still have trouble with that future life stuff." I always say to them, as I say to you now, "The real trouble is with your sense of your present life. You tend to feel boxed in, and you don't know why. As long as you haven't come to feel as common sense, as natural, your life continuity, the reality of your own former and future lives, then you won't be able to be the happy person you really are! So move your mind away from the surface problem and try to look critically at your sense of this life, how it feels, where it comes from, how plausible is it, really?"

If you feel the infinite life perspective is a problem for you, I don't demand that you just drop everything and "believe" in it. Rather, I encourage you to go to work on the issue. I'll keep coming back to it. I more and more have come to feel that if anything positive could result from my teaching, any real benefit for any person, it should be that they get just a hint of the reality of their own former and future lives, that they diminish just the tiniest bit their usual "only this one life" sense of cosmic disconnection, loneliness, alienation, and meaninglessness. I want everyone to be able to see more clearly their culturally common belief that, "My life only began when I was born and it ends when I die. So my responsibility to the universe is limited and even my responsibility to myself is limited. Nothing really matters because we'll all be nothing in the end." If nothing else, I want to help you free yourself from that trap, that imprisoning way of thinking. To intensify your spiritual evolution, the first and most important step you must take is to embrace your boundlessness, take responsibility for your infinite continuity, and live your immortality here and now.

Religions make a big deal out of telling people, "You have an immortal soul!" The materialist scientist makes a big deal out of telling them, "You don't have any soul at all! That's only a religious superstition! You die, you're gone, full stop!" The Buddhist "inner scientist" disagrees with the religious claim: "You don't have some fixed inner essence that can be disconnected from your total you and put on a shelf in heaven, staying unchanged immortally while the rest of you rots!" And she also disagrees with the materialist scientist: "There is no full stopping of anything, it's nonsense to say something can become nothing; your consciousness is a something, just like your body! You are body and mind, spirit and soul—the whole 'you' is what is immortal! Always has been and always will be, living and dying, changing and experiencing. The question is not really whether or not you go on, but rather how are you going to enjoy it? How are your friends going to enjoy you, once you're all going to be there together forever?"

When some people hear the word "reincarnation," they automatically think that the person speaking is a nut, a weirdo, or some kind of New Age hippie. It's so ingrained in our heads by our scientific, materialistic culture that the idea is absurd. Carl Sagan thought the belief in future lives was wishful thinking by religious fanatics, an immature clinging to continuing existence by those not brave enough to face extinction. And Carl was a brave man, leaving his tenured position at Cornell to be what many considered a crackpot, running his SETI project to look for intelligent life on other planets.

Why is it so difficult for us to accept the continuation of our personal existence throughout many lives? After all, due to our educated familiarity with the theory of biological evolution, we freely embrace the concept of the evolution of life forms. We accept that we all came out of a primordial stew and that now we're these incredibly complex beings with brains, eyes, and fingers who have created communities, cultures, languages, and highly supportive habitats. We've slowly and miraculously evolved from tiny amoebas into lizards into birds into apes into Shakespeares, Mozarts, Emily Dickinsons, Einsteins, Gandhis, and all kinds of amazing human beings. If we believe that this sort of ongoing physical and mental evolution is possible, then why should it be impersonal and random, a haphazard progression of material forms? Why do we have so much trouble acknowledging a spiritual evolutionary continuum interwoven with the material genetic development? If there are material genes, why can't there be "spiritual genes"?

I'm very sorry to shake up the materialist scientist's sense of history and "progress," but long before Darwin and company, the Buddha and his contemporaries had already "discovered" evolution. He clearly saw that the life-form of the human being was not *sui generis* and was not the creation of a "God," but was evolutionarily connected with all other life-forms, had developed out of them and could also regress back into them. Only he went even further than the materialist scientists. He made evolution a *personal* matter; he acknowledged that it involves the subjective agencies of beings, intentions, and minds. It is not merely an impersonal biological process of atoms and molecules and cells. He saw that living beings do evolve—progress and regress—in a more than strictly physical sense. He taught that we are not merely passive inheritors of genetic codes. We also personally and intentionally evolve ourselves toward higher states of awareness and happiness, or deteriorate ourselves toward lesser awareness and more wretched embodiments. We do so not just in this life, or in a few lives, but over the course of billions of lives, just as it takes billions of lives for a paramecium to become a butterfly.

Why is this so hard to believe? After all, you and I and Darwin and Shakyamuni Buddha were all in the primordial soup together, little slimy creatures with no brains or eyes. And now we are here. Isn't it realistic that our continuity of mental awareness is also here with us, in the same radically transformed and transforming sense that our physical genetic codes are here with us? Why should mind be the one element of reality that is arbitrarily selected to be more nonexistent than matter? Of course, mind cannot be found by means of scientific analysis. But no one has ever found even one atom that can withstand analysis either! There is no thing that anyone has ever found that stands indivisible as a thing in itself. All things, material as well as mental, have only relational, ascribed reality. So it is sheer dogmatism, prejudice, unscientific arbitrariness to insist that matter does exist but mind does not. So an evolutionary biology that excludes the agency and continuity of beings' minds is highly unscientific, philosophically naïve, and pragmatically inaccurate.

I have a theory about why we're so reluctant even to entertain the possibility that our existences might go on: The idea just scares the pants off of us! We find the vista of infinite future lives simply terrifying. Because if we believe we will live on, it inevitably leads to anxiety about the *form* of our continued existence. Will it be good or bad? Pleasant or unpleasant? Will we be human again, angelic or maybe even divine, or insectlike, or something more terrible? When people refuse to believe in their inevitable reincarnation in whatever form their unconscious, instinctual dispositions dictate, they are emotionally trying to avoid the danger of being reborn as a spider, or even worse, in a hell—and the hellfires of the ancestral preachers are crackling away in their unconscious, now and then vividly illustrated in horror movies. That's why we are so desperate to believe that we'll be nothing after death, that the mind is just a buzz of electricity that will one day fizzle out like an old lightbulb. After all, there is a clear relief you can feel, especially when things get tough, in thinking that your life will end someday. We just want to escape.

But don't be fooled by the false promise of security in oblivion. Bars may keep the outside world away but they also imprison you within them. The denial type of defense against an uncertain yet boundless future traps you in a stagnant present. Instead, see your fear itself as the problem and allow your courage to rise as the more natural response. Feel a new kind of strength surge forth from the fullness of your sense of continuing throughout many lives. Forever changing, but forever taking responsibility for seeing that it's forever good!

We often sleep on a difficult problem when we are just too tired to deal with it at night. We all know how it feels to wake up the next morning with that problem still before us. We don't remember it at first—then it hits us. "Ugh," we think, "it's still there." Many of us feel the same way about dying. We try to push the thought away, but every once in a while it creeps into our consciousness with a giant "ugh." We feel queasiness in the pit of our stomachs. How many of us are ready to die right now? How many of us have all our projects accomplished, all the loose ends tied up? How many of us are free of any haunting guilt about negative things we've done? Or on the positive side, how many of us feel that we have already done all we possibly can for ourselves and for those we love?

Thinking along these lines brings to mind the philosopher-mathematician Blaise Pascal's famous wager, in which he establishes that a belief in the existence of God is rational. We can use his principle to support reincarnation, too. From a strictly realistic perspective, should we bet on infinite life and endless consequences to our actions? Pascal would argue that our answer must be a resounding "Yes!" We might as well assume that there will be a future continuity of our personal consciousness, however changed, however disembodied or re-embodied, however connected or disconnected we remain to the "self" we experience in this life. If we make that bet on our own future lives, then we will prepare in whatever way we can to assure that we continue in a good way, in a better embodiment and environment. We will become truly responsible for our thoughts and our acts. Even though we may not remember the previous-life self who made those preparations, we certainly will want to enjoy the results. If our bet is misplaced, and our preparations have no effect because we actually do enter oblivion at death, we will simply not exist to regret having made them. But if we wrongly bet on noncontinuity and therefore do not prepare for the future and have to face it unprepared, then we may suffer seriously in our next existence, and we will very much regret our decision. Even if we don't remember making it, don't know why we are suffering, don't know how to fault ourselves for being so unconscious in our previous life, we will still suffer and regret. Pascal's wager is therefore a very safe bet—it has a clear-cut positive outcome. Whether our personal life is really terminal at death or in fact infinite in continuity, if we bet, like Pascal, on the existence of our life after death, in whatever form, we will be in the best possible position, however things turn out.

Enlightened Theism

The perspective that life is infinite is not by any means unique to Buddhism: All great religions and spiritual traditions of the world teach the illuminating truth and energizing power of embracing the boundless nature of reality. Despite their many differences, the monotheistic religions—Judaism, Christianity, Islam, Shaivism, Shaktism, and Vaishnavism—all posit a belief that an infinite and all-powerful Being creates and maintains the world. They may or may not emphasize a person's boundlessness in the past (as in past lives), but all accept the beginningless nature of God, and all focus on the boundlessness of a person's future with (or without!) God. Each insists that the consequence of true faith and good actions will be endless positive personal continuity (heaven), just as the consequence of bad faith and bad actions will be endless negative personal continuity (hell). While followers of these traditions may be frightened by the negative vistas of infinite and eternal hells, they find the positive vistas of infinite heavenly proximity or unity with the Divine highly illuminating, motivating, and beneficial.

Thus in the grip of their faith, enlightened monotheists expand toward an infinite horizon by emphasizing their sense of connectedness and continuity with God. When they say, "I am reborn through Jesus Christ!" "Stay with me, O God of Israel!" "Allah is great!" "Lord Krishna lives in me!" "Homage to Shiva!" "Save me, O all-powerful Mother!" and so forth, they express the great release of this feeling. Unfortunately, people can get caught up in the egotistical possession of "their God" and often lose track of this sense of boundless well-being.

Secular Humanism

On the other side of the spectrum, secular humanists reject the exclusivist and literalist claims of the religious worldviews, finding meaning instead in science and reason. Nevertheless, humanists experience the infinite nature of life, too, in keeping alive their spirit of inquiry and adventure. They touch boundlessness through their curiosity and openness to the wonders of the universe, and feel connected to the vastness of evolution, the limitlessness of the cosmos, the endlessness of the future of their descendants, and the indomitable nature of the human spirit, imagination, and creativity. Think of how infinite you can feel while staring at the ocean, marveling at how those waves have continued tumbling ceaselessly, churning forth life for billions of years. Or consider the profound sense of connection with all life you gain from gazing up at a clear night sky in the wilderness, marveling at the inconceivable profusion of stars in the vast depths of space.

Those who search for the truth, strive for the good, enjoy the beautiful, and live happy and creative lives do so to the extent that their worldview avoids restricting life to a limited and concretized circle of meaninglessness. In their reality, life remains open to the infinite in time and space. Thus secular humanists also already live boundlessly to some degree, although their vision is cramped by the belief that the self's continuum does not proceed into future lives.

Consequences of Infinite Life

The Buddha taught that immense positive potential exists within each and every one of us, just waiting to be unleashed. We are naturally full of love and compassion since we have labored long and virtuously throughout many lives to become human beings. Now, with our highly advanced life-form relatively free from negative instinctual drives, we are poised and ready to pursue the path to the total bliss that is enlightenment.

The actuality of our past personal continuity is so important because it bears so strongly on our future. Where will we go from here? Our spiritual evolution, like our physical development, is an ongoing process. When you take responsibility for it, you can consciously, and therefore more accurately, aim yourself toward the achievement of a secure state of bliss for yourself and for others. You gain a sense of connectedness with all life that gives you great strength. You become determined to develop positively. You realize how tremendously meaningful is the slightest action, word, or even thought, and so you take ever more care to be virtuous in your acts of body, speech, and mind.

I call this the real "evolutionary insight"—the sense of personal involvement in your own inevitable evolutionary causality. While there is no avoiding the chance that you might experience great negativity at some point in the future, the risk is worthwhile because the evolutionary insight brings with it an infinite horizon of positivity. You benefit from a healthy alertness to the danger of evolutionary self-neglect.

When you realize the boundless nature of your self, you know your immortality and so take responsibility for its good quality. You gradually but perceptibly brighten and energize your world until you break out of your shell, opening your cocoon to spread your colorful wings and fly up into the sunlight. You no longer need fear death, as you know that you will merely pass into another life. You can experience the taste of true freedom for the first time, just as I did when I floated down that street in New Jersey years ago. You can feel confident that you will find fulfillment and empowerment, if not now then at some point in the future. When you frame your present existence in this radically transformed context, you make the shift from terminal life to infinite life, and suddenly everything becomes possible.

The Terminal Life

If the infinite life acknowledged is free and full of endless possibilities, then what is the terminal, constricted, finite life? It is just the opposite—a life limited in possibilities and human potential, a life that does not motivate us to achieve fulfillment for ourselves or for those around us. Where does the bounded life perspective come from? And how can you avoid falling prey to it?

Unfortunately, there are numerous worldviews that bind our lives in concrete finitude, but these can be boiled down to two that are most common and ruinous. One is the terminal life of bondage to nihilistic materialism. The other is the terminal life of bondage to an idolatrous interpretation of spiritualistic theism, whether monotheism or some other absolutism. There are thus both materialistic and spiritualistic forms of bondage.

Nihilistic Materialism

Being a nihilistic materialist does not mean just being materialistic, an avid consumer of material things. Someone who enjoys beautiful things is not necessarily a nihilistic materialist, for example. She may be a spiritual, kind, loving person committed to the best of all possible worlds for all beings, but one who simply wants material comforts while working on those long-term goals. (Perhaps she thinks that she'll be better able to make others happy if she's not too miserable herself along the way.) No, bondage to nihilistic materialism comes from being imprisoned in an unrealistic world-picture. Most of us with a modern education have been conditioned from an early age to accept a philosophically materialistic, so-called "scientific" worldview. This view of reality is not presented to us as a possible theory about the nature of life. Rather, it is presented dogmatically, as if it were a fact, the only thing, the one true reality. We are made to feel as if scientific geniuses had directly and comprehensively encountered this nihilistic worldview and verified it with mathematical precision using machines that produce "hard" data.

According to the nihilistic materialist construct of reality, we have no souls. Spirituality is no more than childish superstition and misplaced sentimentality based on ignorance of the true facts known to scientists. We are created at a certain moment, as yet not fully pinned down by exact measurement, out of the genetically encoded materials of the sperm and ovum of our parents. "We" are, of course, our subjectively conscious selves, whose consciousness and self-consciousness supposedly evolve at a moment when our brain matter and/or socialization reaches a certain, as yet unspecified level of complexity. Once we are conscious, we are granted the status of "persons" and allowed certain rights; our personhood is somewhat respected. However, ultimately we do not actually or substantially exist as we perceive ourselves to exist, and so it seems quite easy for the materialists to deprive us of our life once we break certain rules, fail to conform to the right ideas, or belong to the wrong clan, religion, nation, race, or gender. Killing is lamentable, but we console ourselves with the thought that once the victims are dead they no longer regret having lost their lives, since they simply cease to exist and can no longer remember that they once lived.

At death, the illusion of subjective existence is shattered when the brain ceases to function. We return from complexity and its dreams to the nothingness whence we arose. During the moments of our lives, we feel conscious (at some usually unacknowledged level) of the fact that death can instantaneously reduce us from self-sensing beings to the insensate nothingness that is our essential reality. We therefore can convince ourselves without too much difficulty, when chronic pain becomes too much for us, that suicide is a viable option, since we picture ourselves slipping quietly into a state of permanent anesthesia.

Assuming that its reality has been proven, we live in bondage to the nihilism of this worldview. We occupy ourselves with materialism rather than spirituality. We feel it is a sign of maturity to resign ourselves to the seeming fact that there is no meaning to our existence—and of course no meaning to anything else either, so we don't have to take it personally. We do have a certain kind of freedom that comes from a devil-may-care attitude about it all, since we feel that a quick exit into nothingness is the worst that can happen to us, no matter what we do or don't do. But we have no rational motivation for sustained effort at personal positive evolution, since whatever we make of ourselves will terminate at death. Nor do we have any *ultimate* motivation to treat others well or contribute to their development, since they also will simply die in the end. We live and work for results in this life only, which we know can end at any time. While we may get enthusiastic about success in some field, enjoying its limited fruits for a while, we do not feel that our efforts will be that powerful or enduring. When times are good, we may be a considerate lover, mate, parent, friend, or colleague, but in tough times we don't have any reason to make sacrifices beyond a certain point of self-interest. Ultimately unmotivated, we lack the power to give something to eternity, so to speak. The concepts of "soul mate," "spiritual friend," and so on are meaningless, although we may find "soul food" tasty.

Some may still find this worldview appealing. It seems to fit the ancient encouragement: "Eat, drink, and be merry, for tomorrow we may die" (and return to quiet nothingness!). How, you might wonder, is this a prison? Here we are with no heavy burdens or big worrisome missions, only free time on our hands. We've got to make some effort to learn how to get along and get ahead. If we're lucky we can live comfortably and then check out whenever we want. Life is no big deal. There are no consequences to our actions; no boring singing in heavenly choirs; no eternal roasting in hell. We live and love and work and play, and then end up in a state that resembles a good night's sleep that never ends. Just exactly what's the problem with this perspective?

I quite agree that things could be worse. I love a good night's sleep myself. I also have been educated to believe in this world-picture. But the question remains: Is it a true picture? Is this the reality of life, death, and the world? What is the evidence for it? How has it been confirmed? Is it a scientific discovery and a rational theory? Or is it a dogmatic fabrication and an irrational delusion? And why does it matter?

I once had a meeting with a neuroscientist about a possible project that would use sensitive machines to measure the brain patterns of experienced yogis. At one point I mentioned something about Tibetan adepts who preserved memories of out-of-body near-death and after-death states, then returned to their previous sensory bodies and brains to tell about it. The scientist, his white coat flapping with his excitement, leapt up and ran around the large hospital conference room, fiercely scolding me, "What are you talking about? Never mention such things in this place. Everyone knows there are no states of consciousness beyond brain death! It is completely confirmed: once the brain is gone, that's it. Anything else is crazy talk. Superstition. Primitive thinking." On and on he went. I was so startled by his emotional vehemence that I felt concerned for his health. I assured him I wouldn't bring it up again, that we would only consider live yogis for the project and that we would stick to meditation states. He calmed down and we completed our meeting.

A day or two later, I was in a cab riding to a different meeting when I startled the driver by bursting out laughing from a total silence. It had taken a few days, but I'd suddenly realized the flaw in my neuroscientist friend's thinking, so radically confused you could easily miss it. By definition, the *only thing* that can *never* be discovered, can never be confirmed rationally, is precisely that which he was so certain about—that is, "*nothing*." "Nothing" is the "one thing" we can be sure ahead of time that no one will ever find. No one can verify that it exists because it does not exist, simply by definition. It is not a thing. It is not a place. Nothing can come from it or enter into it. It has no size or dimension, nor can it have any location. It is not relatable to anything, and so is not really relevant to anything. It is the one word that has no referent: the word "nothing" refers to nothing by not referring to anything! Nothing is not a state of something. So our society's conviction that "nothingness" is the final state of our lives is merely an irrational assumption based on a simple confusion about and, as Wittgenstein would say, a misuse of, language.

All things in nature are *"somethings"* that constantly change into other *"somethings."* No one has ever seen anything become nothing. When wood burns, it does not disappear; rather, heat rises invisibly out of it and ashes are left behind. Ice melts into water, and water evaporates into vapor. Flowers decay into the soil, which in turn feeds the growth of new flowers. "Entropy" means that certain types of energy can become so diffuse that they cease to function in any perceptible way, but that still does not mean that they become nothing. There is, in fact, nothing scientific about our insistence on nothingness.

So where does this feeling of nothingness that seems to lie at the bottom of our lives come from? Since the Renaissance, Western scientists have been fighting to escape from the antirational, dogmatic cosmology of the church, to break the hold of the church over the minds of people. In the past, the church held the populace in thrall by convincing them that it had control over the destiny of their souls: those who refused the authority of the church would meet with eternal damnation and hellfire in the afterlife. Even in this life, the church had the power to destroy any who sought to explore the world using their own senses and reason, launching inquisitions against those who disagreed with their sanctioned worldview. They silenced Galileo and burned Giordano Bruno as well as many other scientists and philosophers. So naturally the scientists revolted. René Descartes constantly proclaimed his allegiance and faith, yet cleverly reduced the soul, consciousness, mind, and even God to a dimensionless point, effectively outside the world that "mattered." Subsequent scientists declared the exclusive existence of "matter," defining the spiritual as beyond rational consideration, reducing the soul to insignificance.

Science has enjoyed great success in the industrial age. Its discoveries, theories, and technologies have enabled us to create great machines that produce spectacular effects. And yet its practitioners have now developed in the universities something like a mother church of "scientism," or scientific materialism, along with their own sort of inquisition to maintain materialist orthodoxy. They have come to enjoy a hold over people's minds by assuring us of their control over the destiny of our souls—ultimately painless entry into guaranteed oblivion. They promise a wild ride on amazing machines while living, and a painless oblivion at the end. They offer security that there will be no hellfire or damnation. Even Hitler and Mao will never burn, though their actions burned so many others. Once dead, they escape consequences, no matter what they did.

It seems that many scientists have succumbed to the temptation of their institutional power. Like the church in days of old, they offer philosophical confusion, metaphysical dogmas, priestly jargon, mathematical magic spells, mechanical miracles, and inquisitorial intimidation to maintain the world-picture by means of which they hold us in thrall. But as we have just seen, they do not have, and by definition cannot possibly acquire, any such certain knowledge that the underlying reality of life and therefore inevitable destiny of our consciousness is nothingness. Therefore we must accept the possibility that we will have some continuum of experience after death that could, after all, be called "a soul."

Nihilists can taste a certain freedom through nothingness. After all, if everything is equally nothing when reduced to its essence, then you can feel a connection to everything in your shared essential nothingness. Nihilists can say to the world, "We share the profound fact that fundamentally we're all equally nothing." However, this kind of connection has the ultimately weak link of nothingness at its center and hence has very little impact.

Ancient Indian philosophers, probably the most sophisticated thinkers the world has yet seen, disagreed on numerous points but agreed on one thing: nihilists are the least fortunate people of all. They have no motivation to join the play of evolution wholeheartedly, no compelling reason to do anything for anyone beyond seeking immediate comfort for themselves and their loved ones in this life. This basic lack of positive drive causes them to waste the precious moments of the self-conscious, critically discerning human lifetime, the lifetime that can lead to the most miraculous achievements and the highest bliss for self and other.

Spiritualistic Absolutism

Spiritualistic absolutism refers to the belief that one's terminal and insignificant life belongs completely to an all-powerful, absolutely Other, Divine Being. While this form of bondage may seem less prevalent today, more like a pre-modern mindset, in fact huge numbers of literate persons in so-called modern societies, such as America, continue to be imprisoned by spiritualistic absolutism. It is not the real teaching of the universal religions, but is a common misinterpretation of all of them (including Buddhism).

All successful religions teach that there is a State or Being or Power which, though it may not be bound to a particular form, manifestation, or concept, is the creative force, fundamental to life, all-powerful and all-knowing, unbreakable by anything else. This Force, fortunately, is full of love, benevolently willing the welfare and happiness of all beings. The founding thrust of these religions is that they encourage humans to orient themselves toward this Ultimate Reality in order to transcend their self-centeredness, their grasping, their pride, and their tendencies to harm others, and to achieve the freedom of infinite life. Therefore, as we have seen, it is entirely possible for enlightened theists to embrace the boundlessness of existence. Religions do open the door to the infinite life perspective. But religions can also be misappropriated precisely when people *lose* their openness to the infinite and become entrenched in spiritualistic absolutism, which has proven to be immensely dangerous throughout history.

Ever since Moses' prohibition of idolatry mentioned "graven images," the Western tendency has been to think of idolatry as the worship of physical representations of gods. We assume that a "graven image" must be a thing, such as the famous golden calf, or even a statue of Jesus on a cross, a Virgin Mary with Christ-child, a buddha or a bodhisattva, a Krishna, Shiva, Vishnu, or Shakti goddess—which physical images people wrongly consider to actually be the Divine Being. But it's not that simple. Is a graven image really only an idol made of metal, stone-carved, printed in a book, or painted on a wall? Is it merely a physical image? Not at all. "Graven" may seem at first to refer only to the physical world, but are there not other ways in which we "engrave" images? Can we not engrave with our speech some verbal image of the divine to which we become attached? Are there not those whose word for "God" becomes the sacred itself, so that they feel moved to kill those who use a different word for the Divine? Can we not hold a graven image in our innermost thoughts? We know the power of the human mind. Therefore, we must count "graven images" as mental and verbal as well as physical representations. And we must define "idolatry" more broadly to mean the replacing of the infinite by a finite entity constructed by our own hands, tongues, and imaginations.

The misuse of the world religions, where their ideas and institutions have caused the most harm to individuals and whole societies, comes from just such *conceptual idolatry,* my term for this most dangerous kind. This occurs when human egotism and selfishness restrict the Divine to merely personal or tribal or national possessions, as exclusive forms, as finite entities; that is, when people conceive of the Divine as idols, whether physical (statues, paintings, mountains, rivers, sky, oceans), verbal (particular languages, sacred sounds, holy books, magic spells), or mental (specific concepts of absolute Beings or Nonbeings).

Such idolatry causes humans to proclaim: "This is *my* God!" "This is *my* divine right!" "This is *my* ultimate reality!" "My beliefs are more important than yours!" "My way is the only way!" Such idolatry lies at the heart of holy wars, crusades, and jihads, and even the secular, ideological movements of capitalist modernization and communist liberation. Such idolatry has empowered mass persecutions, witch-burnings, self-immolations, and many other kinds of religious and ideological fanaticism. Only spiritual absolutists can feel confident enough in the ultimate validity and dominance of their beliefs to kill in the name of their God, or their Reality, believing that they will be absolved and suffer no negative consequences of their actions.

Take, for example, the Muslim extremists who flew airplanes full of people into the World Trade Center towers on September 11, 2001, destroying thousands of innocent lives. Or the Irish Catholic and Protestant terrorists in the U.K., whose constant battles result in bombings that murder citizens who are just going about their daily business. Or the decades of mutual atrocities between Buddhists and Hindus in Sri Lanka. Or the Hindu–Muslim conflicts in India and Pakistan. Or the many mass killings committed by fanatical communists against religious people of various persuasions during the last century. Such religious or ideological absolutists are completely willing to sacrifice their own lives or anybody else's life to a supposedly better, bigger cause—the defense of the absolute dominance of their Gods, their religion, their ideology, or their way of life. Who among us would say that their actions contribute to bringing humanity a step closer to nirvana? Who would argue that they have done anything to help us find happiness and harmony? These are very real examples of the sort of damage that can, and does, result from absolutism still today.

Trapped in a tightly bounded worldview, such conceptually idolatrous spiritual absolutists feel their own lives to be essentially an absolute nothingness. They envision all being, reality, destiny, power, and knowledge to belong in the hands of the all-powerful, absolute Deity. They believe that we were nothing before conception or birth, when our inner essence, a mere spark of the great fire of the One, was created from the One. At death, we will return back to the One, where we will again be nothings in ourselves, will no longer have individual continuity or self-awareness apart from the Great One.

People who hold this view lose all sense of freedom because they see themselves as absolutely dependent, the enslaved subjects of the One. They perceive no aim in life other than to obey the orders of those people whom they consider to represent the One, usually sacred texts and high priests but sometimes monarchs, premiers, or presidents. Such people are captured by a paradoxical sense of both utter personal worthlessness as individual selves, and absolute personal power and authority as part of the One. They see themselves as agents and instruments of the will of the One. Since they do not participate in evolution as individuals, they are no longer responsible for the consequences of their thought, speech, or physical actions, nor can they count on good results coming from good deeds. Thus they are disempowered in any pursuit of personal development, transformation, or liberation. Like the materialistic nihilists, these spiritual absolutists are in a subliminal sense disconnected from their own lives. They consider any tangible evidence of themselves to be, ultimately, nothing, feeling the fundamental core of things to be an obliterating light, just as the nihilists look forward to an obliterating darkness.

Spiritualistic absolutism does have a good side to it, of course, a liberating interpretation, just as does materialistic nihilism. After all, absolutists believe that something greater than they is what is truly real. Depending on their religious background, they may believe in their own endless future continuity, either in heaven or in hell. They may be motivated to act in a way that ensures they enjoy the benefits of the former and avoid the horrors of the latter, and hence behave in a manner that is generous, kind, and gentle to other beings.

Furthermore, it is possible that spiritual absolutists can experience some sense of the infinite life. They tend to think of themselves as having been created by the One, which allows them to feel they are part of the Divine. The more they emphasize this tie, the more they are able to enter the boundless life, connecting with the infinite through the One's connection to everything.

A very important point I'd like to emphasize again here is that this critique of idolatrous spiritual absolutism is not a critique of theistic world religions in general, but rather a critique of the misunderstanding and misuse of these religions. All the world religions share in common ethical precepts about love and mercy, wisdom, compassion, generosity, altruism, and so forth. What matters most is that spiritual persons can believe in whomever they want with all their hearts, and yet at the same time take the prohibition against idolatry seriously enough to avoid viewing their conception of the Ultimate Reality as exclusive of what others believe it to be. The statements in many of the world religions' scriptures about how "this way is the only way" to salvation or liberation can be understood as hyperbolic affirmations expressing strong emotional commitment in a specific context, rather than as dogmatic statements valid for all time and for everyone on the planet. The transcendent, infinite Being or Power simply must not be imprisoned within any particular absolutized belief system.

No living person holds exactly any of the worldview types described above. We all have a bit of the spiritualistic absolutist, a bit of the nihilistic materialist, a bit of the open-minded theist, and a bit of the secular humanist within us. And yet when we understand the two primary types of extremism that can enslave us in the terminal life, we are able to free ourselves from the materialistic or spiritualistic bonds that can lock us in the prison of stagnation, insignificance, and evolutionary aimlessness, devoid of boundless horizons. We can break out of delusional confinement by tribal conventions into the infinite life of opportunity and creativity that awaits us.

A New Reality

In encouraging you to accept your life as infinite, I am asking you to transform your concept of reality. I am calling on you to deepen your natural insight. I am empowering your plain common sense. I am encouraging you to open your heart to a new understanding of yourself and your world.

It is always best to live in tune with reality. It is strenuous to live in denial. When we strain to preserve wishful thinking, we must hold off the pressure of the real by investing more and more energy in the unreal. We all know how trying to maintain even a white lie can be confusing and exhausting. Realism is simply practical: it is the essential adaptive quality of human beings and all successful animals, and so it can be cultivated limitlessly without fear of going too far. Why try to deny it? Why not embrace the reality of infinite life?

In inviting you to shift your perspective, I am similar to the rebel leader Morpheus in the popular movie *The Matrix,* when he offers Neo, his latest recruit in the battle to free humanity, a new perspective on life. Neo must choose between a red pill, which will allow him to discover the truth, or a blue pill, which will return him to his ignorant, imprisoning, yet familiar reality. Like Morpheus, I am offering you a new way of looking at the world. Will you take the red pill or the blue pill? Will you choose to expand your concept of reality? Or will you choose to be "safe," to continue to live with your preconceived notions despite the fact that they may be false and thus will radically constrict your ability to improve your situation and that of those around you?

Let me be crystal clear from the very beginning that this movement from terminal existence to infinite living, from bound to free personhood, does not require a "conversion" to some sort of religion, either Buddhism or any other. You can accept this new reality within the context of your existing worldview or religion. I am sort of a lax Buddhist myself, that happens to be my way. It doesn't have to be yours. Most Buddhists do not seek followers. They do not try to convert the world to one particular religion, as much as they may love the Buddha's Dharma themselves. They are more like psychologists, scientists, or educators—they want people of all religions or no religion to become more aware, to think critically, to understand reality better, and so allow themselves to be more happy and helpful to others.

In my case, I enthusiastically chime in with the Dalai Lama's call for the leaders of all world religions to abandon once and for all their campaigns to convert everybody. The time is past for religious institution-building, religious competition for market share, and religious imperialism. It has caused great violence and harm in the past, and, if continued with the modern machinery of mass communication and coercion, could cause untold misery in the future. None of the founders of the great religions wanted to cause any injury to anyone. Their belief systems are radically misunderstood and cruelly misused when harm is done in their names.

No, you are free to keep your current belief system, whether it happens to be religious or secular humanist. Within whatever chosen tradition, there is a broad range of interpretations, some more realistic than others. Your imperative is simply to choose the most realistic view.

All spiritual traditions, as well as secular humanism, are based on a specific picture of reality. Yet they all make room for mutual inquiry, constructive criticism, creative reevaluation, and liberal reinterpretation in light of scientific discovery. For example, most great historical spiritual founders, including the Buddha, Isaiah, Mahavira, Zoroaster, Lao-tzu, Confucius, Plato, Jesus, and Muhammad, in order to communicate with the people of their times, seemed to accept the conventional ancient view that the world is flat. Today, most of their followers are still capable of great faith and devotion but feel no need to deny that the world is, in fact, round. They have changed their view of reality in this respect, departing from that of their prophet or teacher. Yet they remain faithful members of their traditions. They still value the relevant information those teachers imparted—insights about the human heart, mind, and soul, which seem true and useful even now.

So please, remain a faithful and observant Jew, Christian, Muslim, Vaishnava, Shaiva, or Shakta, simply expanding your joy and tolerance by focusing on the infinite dimensions of your deity. Or remain a liberated secular humanist, recognizing that your sense of the boundless mystery of the universe is what makes you feel free and enables you to find meaning in your life, while increasing your tolerance of your own spiritual urges and those of overtly religious people. There is no need for anyone to become a Buddhist. Whatever your belief system, this book is for you.

I invite you to embrace a new reality. It is not a matter of religion—it is a matter of fact, a matter of science, a matter of experiment, and a matter of awareness. I invite you to awaken to the infinite life you already have, no matter what your worldview. I invite you to take up responsibility for your own evolutionary destiny. I invite you to take advantage of your priceless human opportunity to make a definitive turn toward ultimate security, complete freedom, and unbounded happiness.

Conceiving the Spirit of Enlightenment

The invitation to the infinite life is not controversial in the sense that it is universally beneficial and therefore can be neither extended too casually nor accepted too prematurely. Embracing the reality of infinite life does not mean making a leap off a cliff or involving yourself in a dangerous experiment. On the contrary, it is the most obvious, practical, commonsensical, realistic decision you can make.

However, the invitation does have a further implication that might seem daunting at first. So I am going to present it as optional for the time being. I'd rather have you shy away from this aspect of infinite living until you feel more comfortable with your new perspective than deny yourself the benefits altogether. Worse yet, you may enthusiastically embrace this principle, but then, due to lack of appropriate preparation, fall back in discouragement and become cynical, rejecting the entire premise of continuous existence. Be forewarned.

The further implication is as follows: *Embracing infinite life means embracing infinite interconnection with all other beings.* If life is beginningless and endless, and death nothing but a swift transition from one existence to the next, then you and everyone else have already been living together forever. Therefore, you have had endless different relationships with them—as they have had with you. We have all been each other's mothers, fathers, lovers, best friends, and worst enemies, and we will continue to be everything to each other throughout time. So in order for our lives to become completely actualized in enlightened happiness, all other beings must also experience their lives as full of happiness. We can leave out no single being. Like the Three Musketeers, we are "all for one and one for all." We cannot liberate just ourselves from suffering, because it is impossible to achieve fully perfect bliss if anyone is excluded from it. Infinite interconnection logically mandates infinite responsibility.

I offer the following analogy when I speak to audiences about the concept of interconnection, though it is perhaps most meaningful to New Yorkers. Imagine that you are seated in a subway car. Other people are riding in the car, too. You try to notice them as little as possible as they come and go. You read your newspaper or book; you stare down at your feet and hands—anything to avoid eye contact. You know that if you look too closely at someone, he might take offense, or worse, develop a predatory interest in you. If someone looks closely at you, you shrink back and feel afraid. Your whole relationship with fellow passengers is based on the concept that you and they will soon get off the train and go your separate ways, never to meet again. In the meantime, you just want to bother each other as little as possible.

Suddenly, you hear a metallic screeching of brakes as your car veers off into a hidden tunnel. Iron grilles clang down over the windows and doors, trapping you inside. Then a deep voice with an Austrian accent like the proverbial mad scientist or realpolitik Dr. Strangelove comes over the speaker system. "You are being kidnapped!" the voice announces. "Zis is an experiment. It is a qvestion of national security. Zere vill be no recourse, no matter who you are! You vill spend the next year in zis subway car. Food vill be brought to you. You can use ze bathrooms vich are in ze control booths. Your families vill be informed zat you are avay on a purpose of national security and zey vill see you eventually, but zey vill not find you until then. You vill have good food, reading materials, blankets, medicine for illness, and everything else zat you need. But you vill see no one besides ze people who are on zis train viz you right now!"

At first you and the others freak out, shout at the speakers, have panic attacks, yell at each other, weep, and so on. But then eventually it sinks in. You may be stuck in the car for a year, or however long! You are in the hands of a mad scientist! Now how do you look at the people in the subway car with you? They will be your companions for the foreseeable future. You won't be able to avoid them any longer. You suddenly find yourself committed to them in an entirely new way. You need to develop relationships with them. They may become your friends or foes, but either way they are like family because they are all you have for now. You recognize that in this difficult situation your happiness depends on theirs.

When you normally ride on the train, getting on and off at will, it would be rational to be fairly unconcerned with your fellow passengers, unless you happened to recognize someone you know. You'll probably never see them again. Someone you would address might turn out to be a troublemaker. Why bother? You are not connected to them. Best to live and let live. So you bury your face in your reading matter. Or if you've forgotten to bring anything, you read the ads up on the wall. You avoid all contact. A reasonable way to spend your subway ride.

The terminal lifestyle is similar. It is foisted on you by the dominant worldview of our scientific materialist culture. You and others began from nowhere, coming out of nothing, though you have inherited bodies related to your parents, et cetera. You and they will die and go back into nothingness. So why get that involved with any of them? You have connection to relatives and parents. You might feel passion for someone at some time and start a new family. You might feel a continuity through your offspring. You might want fame and want to be remembered by strangers for some outstanding accomplishment or creation. But you are unconsciously aware that you won't be aware after death of however famous you might be, what your descendants are doing, and so forth, so the amount of benefit you can draw from such a limited result—*for you personally*—is so limited it would not be normal for you to make a huge effort to do anything. Better to stay comfortable for the time being, which is all the time you have. If someone talks of *saving the whole world, doing something for eternity,* you dismiss them as having a messiah complex, as being a megalomaniac.

When the extraordinary situation of our analogy occurs, you are jolted by the realization that you have to be involved more deeply with the other passengers on the car. Whether your relations with them are good or bad will now have long-term impact. You now feel compelled to take them seriously, to relate to them passionately. Your happiness depends on them. It becomes instantly clear that the ideal mode of coexistence for all confined together in the car is for each one to feel content and peaceful. No one can be ignored if they freak out. The whole car must take them seriously. So everyone becomes strongly concerned with your state of being, and you become vitally concerned with their state of being. Because you all cannot avoid being interconnected for the foreseeable future.

So now the infinite life perspective makes you see that you have always been sort of stuck in a subway car with every single other person on the face of the Earth. You and they have been born and reborn infinite times in the past, hence have shared relationships in infinite variety with infinite others. Hence, there is no being in the universe who has *not* been your father, your mother, your lover, your brother, your son, your daughter, your friend, your enemy, your protector, your destroyer—and you have been all of those things to them. Now you only know a few of them, because you can't remember the experiences of those infinite past lives. Furthermore, you are contained with them in an infinite future continuity wherein you will once again be all things to them and they will be all things to you. Since every effect has a cause and every cause gives effect, whether you will be good to them and they will be good to you depends on, among other conditions, how you treat each other today. Every thought, word, or deed, every slight interaction—a glance, a facial expression, a casual word, a gesture, however trivial seeming—becomes immense, since it will have *infinite consequence.*

The only commonsense decision you can make in this situation is to take each moment with the utmost concern, become passionately engaged with every being at every moment. Every tiniest thing must be *optimized,* to have *optimal positive effect,* in the moment and in the infinite continuity of consequences of that moment. You have entered the realm of Nietzsche's "eternal recurrence," where you never do anything unless you affirm your willingness to repeat that act again and again, eternally, and enjoy its consequent experience again and again eternally. So just as the only thing you could wish for from all other beings is their total love and compassion, their wish for you never to suffer and always to be happy, so you yourself feel it is altogether natural and fully commonsensical to feel only love and compassion for them, every single one of them, willing them never to suffer and always to be happy.

Thus, once you have adopted such an attitude of infinite interconnectedness, you naturally want to liberate not just yourself but all beings from suffering. The Buddha calls this "the conception of the spirit of enlightenment." It is the soul of the bodhisattva, the person who dedicates him- or herself to helping all beings achieve total happiness. When you open to the inevitability of your infinite interconnection with other sensitive beings, you develop compassion. You learn to feel empathy for them, to love them, to want their happiness. You want to keep them from suffering, and you do so just as if they were a part of you. You don't think your behavior makes you special. You don't congratulate yourself for helping others, just as you wouldn't congratulate yourself for healing your own leg when you hurt it. It is natural for you to love your leg because it is one with you, and so it is natural for you to love others. You would certainly never harm another being. As the great Buddhist adept Shantideva (eighth-century Indian sage) wrote, "How wonderful will it be when all beings experience each other as limbs on the one body of life!"

In a way, this notion of universal responsibility is just as commonsensical as the acceptance of infinite life. We are merely adding the lives of others to our own, recognizing our inevitable interconnection.

But it might not be prudent for all of you to pursue this further implication of the infinite lifestyle right away. It is so important to conceive this spirit of enlightenment, as it results in such a quantum transfiguration of the soul, that you should never dive into it unprepared. You might feel momentarily inspired, but then get discouraged and lose your determination, and the negative evolutionary momentum from such a reversal would be too severe. For example, you might start out wanting to save all beings from suffering but quickly get annoyed with someone just beyond hope. You'd end up feeling alienated and not giving a damn about anyone, abandoning altogether your belief in infinite life and all the positive work you'd accomplished.

Surely many of you have already developed a compassionate spirit, either in previous lives or from following altruistic teachings in this life. So for you it is not such a shock to open to infinite intertwinement with all beings, what the delightful Vietnamese Zen master Thich Nhat Hanh calls your "interbeing" with them. For you, I mention it here at the outset, and for the more cautious, I encourage you just to think of it as an experimental idea for now.

Opening to the Infinite Lifestyle

This book is about the great variety of methods you can use to live a happy, fulfilling, and infinite life of what I like to call "evolutionary sport." You can become a true sportswoman or sportsman in the game of life. You can choose to take up the challenge of competition with yourself, transcending your inherited self-limiting instincts, your conditioned ingrained habits, your carelessly self-destructive addictions to the terminal lifestyle. You can release yourself from the prison of the meaninglessness of consumer culture and from the constraints of absolutist beliefs.

But it is not worth reading another word of this text, for it is not possible to make good use of a single method or art presented here, if you do not dare to experiment with opening up your life to the infinite perspective. If you are looking for a cell in which to lock yourself away from danger, a hole in which to hide, a mechanism in which to entrust your precious self-image, then you should give this book back or throw it away. It will only waste your time.

So I urge you now, once more, to accept the possibility of infinite life, even just as a temporary experiment. Try it on, for size and effect. We all have the potential to travel the path offered to us by the Buddha and presented in this book, as well as in other world religious, humanist, and scientific teachings that flow from the same experience. We all have the ability to walk out of the gloomy prison of self-limiting, uncritical existence into the bright daylight of a boundless, deeply meaningful, and tremendously satisfying existence, with its attendant playful, exuberant, joyous wisdom.

The infinite life is life unbound by time or space. Deaths are only doorways, transitions from one life-form to the next, just as sleep is only a passage from evening to a new day. Your every movement of body, speech, and mind arises from a beginningless past and resonates into an endless future. You are free and boundless in dimension, and also very real and unique. You are lost in oneness with the awesome infinite, yet you have infinite importance due to your total interconnectedness with all other beings. When self-centered and unhappy, you are a big problem for them, often engaged in life-and-death struggles. When enlightened, self-transcendent, boundlessly open, and truly happy, you can be the living solution to all their problems.

Open your eyes and look at yourself carefully. Expand the concept of reality that you live by—your awareness of, and responsibility for, your own personal continuity. Everything you do now, your very breathing, flows from your sense of yourself as a living continuum and your drive to improve your state of being. You are a dynamic evolutionary process. There is no limit to how far you can develop positively into higher states of spirituality, understanding, love, happiness, and creativity.

2

Buddhism: A Joyous Science of the Heart

Speech is a powerful thing. When I speak and you listen, we share our minds with each other. We become one mind, which is bigger than both of our usual minds. I put more thought into what I'm saying because I feel the traction of my words in the terrain of your mind. You let my words flow through you while your own reflections eddy and swirl around my current of thought.

As I engage you in this book, I feel deeply conscious of the responsibility I have when I enter your mind. My words are drawn forth by your interest. I believe there is value in what I say, since the words came to me in turn from other, more enlightened minds. Many of these teachings and methods were first spoken by great philosophers back through time, in this case back all the way to the Buddha. They were a great help to me, so I hope they will help you, too.

I do not try to calculate some sort of effect upon you with my words. Rather, I speak to you from my heart. But my heart is not dumb—it senses your heart. I am moved to speak out about the surges of the heart that can bring relief, movements of the mind that have immediate and noticeable effects, movements of the spirit that call forth feelings of freedom, peace, grace, and love.

I myself do not pretend to be enlightened. But thanks to my practice, I have felt some blessed releasing surges of the heart. I have moved my mind, occasionally, in a positive direction. This has given me the hint that others before me were enlightened. I have been able to verify for myself that these lessons work: they open the heart, they sharpen the intelligence, and they liberate the mind. And so I feel the desire to tell you about them, in the hope that they will help you achieve some degree of happiness and freedom in your own life.

Buddhist Psychology

You can use enlightening Buddhist practices to transform your life. Unfortunately, many people do not know it, but the Buddhist Dharma, or teaching, is actually a scientific system of psychology, developed in India and further refined in Tibet. It is a psychology that works. I call it a "joyous science of the heart" because it is based on the idea that while unenlightened life is full of suffering, you are completely capable of escaping from that suffering. You can get well. In fact, you already *are* well; you just need to awaken to that fact.

And how do you do this? By analyzing your thought patterns. When you do, you realize that you are full of "misknowledge"—misunderstandings of yourself and the world that lead to anger, discontent, and fear. The target of Buddhist practice and the constant theme of this book is the primal misconception that you are the center of the universe, that your "self" is a fixed, constant, and bounded entity. When you meditate on enlightened insights into the true nature of reality and the boundlessness of the self, you develop new habits of thinking. You free yourself from the constraints of your habitual mind. In other words, you teach yourself to think differently. This in turn leads you to act differently. And *voilà!* You are on the path to happiness, fulfillment, and even enlightenment.

The battle for happiness is fought and won or lost primarily within the mind. The mind is the absolute key, both to enlightenment and to life. When your mind is peaceful, aware, and under your command, you will be securely happy. When your mind is unaware of its true nature, constantly in turmoil, and in command of you, you will suffer endlessly. This is the whole secret of the Dharma. If you recognize delusion, greed, anger, envy, and pride as the main enemies of your well-being and learn to focus your mind on overcoming them, you can install wisdom, generosity, tolerance, love, and altruism in their place. This is where enlightened psychology can be most useful.

Psychology and philosophy are really one entity in Buddhism. They are called the *inner science,* the science of the human interior. In the flow of Indian history, it is fair to say that the Buddha was a great explorer of the human interior rather than some sort of religious prophet. He came into the world at a time when people were just beginning to experiment with self-exploration, but mostly in an escapist way, using their focus on the inner world to run away from the sufferings of life by entering a supposed realm of absolute quiet far removed from everyday existence. The Buddha started out exploring that way too, but then realized the futility of escapism and discovered instead a way of being happier here and now. He made interior freedom available to everyone by teaching people to gain insight into reality and then deepen their experience through meditation. Further, he created a *sangha,* a lay and monastic community where people could go to receive teaching and support for their interior explorations.

Before Buddha's time, societies never had much interest in psychology or philosophy. They had religions and rituals, but they just wanted their citizens to work and obey, not to question their existence or the meaning of life. They wanted the warriors to fight battles, the farmers to plant, the merchants to exchange goods, and the priests to neatly explain why things had to be the way they were. That's all the rulers of India wanted then, and the same holds true in almost every other society throughout the history of the world.

In order to create the inner science of psychology, the Buddha had to take extreme steps. He had to leave his beloved, adoring wife and lovely infant son. He had to renounce his position as prince and future ruler. He had to abandon his father, the king, in deep disappointment. After all, his father was about to retire and have his son take over the royal duties. But the would-be Buddha, Prince Siddhartha, said, "I'm going to retire myself. I'm off to the jungle to meditate. Why? Because I don't want to be just a prince, don't want to be a general and fight battles to defend the country. I want to help my people with their deepest problems. I have an interior that I need to explore. I want to find out the meaning of life. I want to discover the nature of my thoughts and my emotions. And I think that's what everyone needs to do. We have enough food around here. We have enough battles. We have enough goods. We have enough childbearing. We have enough everything. What we need to do is find out *why* we are doing all of this. What is the reason for it? Is there a better way?"

So the Buddha took off, leaving his old life behind, and went into the jungle to be by himself so that he could quietly investigate the inner world through meditation. After many years, he gained tremendous insight into the functioning of the human mind and the problems we create for ourselves. He came to understand how negative states develop, how those negative states can be replaced by positive states, and how those positive states can be cultivated without limit. The Buddha realized that the human life-form is the ideal life-form in which to do that cultivation, each person ultimately by themselves but with the help of therapists and teachers and philosophers. And that was the birth of psychology, really:

the beginning of the systematic scientific exploration of the way the mind works.

Buddhist psychology is a do-it-yourself science. As the philosopher Vasubandhu put it, only by discovering for yourself the facts of your own reality, your psyche, your life, your society, the way your mind thinks, the way your body senses, and the way the world works will your neurotic addictions be cured. And without curing your addictions, you are hurled again and again into the ocean of unsatisfactory existences.

But what about Western psychology, you might ask? When I think about that kind of psychology, it reminds me of what Gandhi once said about American civilization. When asked what he thought of it, he replied, "American civilization? Now, that would be a good idea!" So I say, "Western psychology? Now, that would be a good idea!" It would. But it's really still in its infancy. That's because the West as a society has been plagued for thousands of years by poverty, authoritarian social structures and rulers, and militarism. The West has not been, until recently, a rich place. Western societies have not really had time or resources to devote to people's psychological development and well-being. Those people who had problems with their inner lives, with fitting into the machine of the greater social purpose, were mainly cast off into a corner and forgotten. Maybe they played the village idiot role, or, if they were lucky, they wandered off and found a Christian monastery. But no one paid much attention to them. People who were insistent and vocal and therefore attracted many others to developing the interior life tended to get crucified or burned at the stake or locked up, because Western societies viewed them as troublemakers.

Western psychology developed during the era of industrialization. Freud and Jung lived in the wealthier societies of central Europe. Members of the middle class finally had a little time and money to explore their general state of being. When their interiors were maladjusted or abused or neglected, they could find someone to work with them. So these early psychologists began to ask themselves: How does the mind work? What are the problems with the mind? How can these problems be fixed? But their main purpose was only to re-adapt these misfits back into the machinery of industrial society so that their patients could work, function, and "be normal" again. As Freud himself said, his therapy was designed to help people get rid of neurotic suffering so that they could get back to ordinary suffering. There was never any mention of complete freedom from suffering as the definition of health, or even a livable option.

Today in the West, we are trying to further develop this nascent science of psychology. Unfortunately, we don't have a strong base to begin from and we have a big handicap—we are caught up in nihilistic materialism. We are taught to believe that only matter, and not spirit, is real, that the mind is only the brain. So now psychology is pursuing an imprisoning and dangerous path, namely neuroscience, in which the mind is believed to be reducible to chemical and electrical signals in the brain that can be entirely manipulated by drugs. And the primary goal is still to "cure" people, to control their wayward thoughts so that they can fit right back into everyday, eat-work-sleep life, unquestioning and unconcerned about the meaning of it all.

Take the plight of today's schoolchildren in America. Their metabolism is flooded with sugar from infancy. Their minds are deluged with cartoon television, filled with violence and hyperactive drama. Commercials flood them with desires for more sugar, for more hyperactive equipment. When they get to school, they naturally have "attention deficit disorder" (ADD), a supposedly medically diagnosable disease cooked up by our industrial psychology, unwittingly in service to consumer pharmaceuticals. They then are prescribed Ritalin or other amphetamine-type drugs, which supposedly rebalances their "brain chemistry," but actually is addictive and leads to deep internal hyperactivity, ending up with manic depressive states, that are again to be rebalanced by a battery of antidepressants. Buddhist psychology helped us somewhat as parents to avoid the worst of this cycle with our children, and we somewhat moderated the debilitating elements of their growing up in consumerist society. I say "somewhat" because it is very difficult to be totally pure in this world, and perfection is elusive.

What is the solution to this destructive treatment of our children? Do we really need Buddhist psychology to reinforce our common sense? Clearly, we should limit sugar intake drastically, remembering that cereals, breads, and many other supposedly healthy products are laced with sugar by our commercial food industry. Limit the television exposure (eliminating it altogether may end up remanding our children to neighbors' houses) to public broadcasting, nature shows, science shows, perhaps the worlds of Sesame Street–type education shows. Allow absolutely no commercials. Read to your children, teaching them by example to focus their attention quietly on one thing for sustained periods of time. Perhaps include them in periods of quiet meditation, in nature, by streamsides, on mountain slopes watching clouds. In this way, you help them avoid becoming enslaved to consumer culture.

According to the Dharma teaching, psychology is about understanding what human beings are made of, how our world works, how reality is put together, and how our minds function. The purpose of doing this, ultimately, is not to adjust people to go back and live according to how society tells them they should live, so that they can fit into some meaningless, supposedly wealth-producing, militaristic scheme. That's a total waste of human life. If somebody has the good sense to be depressed, malfunctioning, hallucinating, dropping out of society because their mind-body complex is saying "no" to the whole nonsense and looking for some better way of being, a liberating psychology should not try to stuff them back into the box. They should not be just rushed straight ahead, encouraged to wash the dishes, do their jobs, and pounce on the enemy, just because that's what everybody else is doing. People who have the sensitivity and insight to see through the meaninglessness should be able to find someone to help them discover freedom, which is what they are looking for. They should be supported in their endeavors.

That is the big difference between Buddhist and Western psychologies. The original liberating psychology *is,* in fact, the Dharma, and the Dharma is a wonderful thing. These days, some veteran enlightenment practitioners are becoming therapists because they realize it's an effective way in which they can deploy this amazingly practical psychology in the West without stirring up all sorts of religious issues by calling it "Buddhist."

Most Westerners really do need therapy. I certainly do! Fortunately, I'm lucky enough to have a wife who gives me constant instruction and support, as well as wise teachers, including the Dalai Lama, to guide me. In general, we are overstressed, overworked beings who don't even believe in a soul and think that pills should cure all our problems. Many of us have inherited individual traditions of family abuse, suppression, and neglect, as well as societal traditions of racism, prejudice, and religious fanaticism. It's no wonder that modern society is so grisly and gloomy. It's no wonder that when people first encounter the wonderful Buddha Dharma, the joyous science of the heart, they recoil. When someone proclaims, "Come and join us. You can heal your mind and body through enlightening practices. You can be free!" Westerners initially react by saying, "Oh no! The Buddhists are taking over! They want us all to be Buddhists. It's a religious cult. It's weird. Let's run away as fast as we can!"

But most teachers of enlightenment are just out there offering their healing and liberating therapies. It's their profession, as it was the Buddha's. He was the first great therapist. He was the original Freud, the ultimate Jung. Like the Buddha, enlightenment-oriented teachers just want to share their insights with you, as any caring scientist or doctor would. It's just up to you to take the first step by deciding to engage in inner exploration. You can draw your own conclusions and implement your own healing methods. You can keep your own religion, too, though you may soon feel like making changes within it, embracing the more open interpretations available within its doctrines.

Buddhist psychology is a joyous science of the heart. It operates on the assumption that we can use our own sophisticated minds to realize our selfless and thus transformable nature. It teaches us how to take apart our absolutized self-sense in a useful way so that we are no longer in conflict with reality as we normally are, kicking and screaming and miserable but pretending that we've got it all together. It teaches us to free ourselves from our demons by understanding our true place in reality: ultimately selfless while relatively present, aware, and interconnected with all other beings. It teaches us to embrace infinite life. And it teaches us compassion, caring for others rather than obsessing over ourselves.

Transforming Your Life

There are six, or seven, or ten transformations that release the terminal self into infinite life, set forth by the Buddha as the transcendent virtues (*pārāmita* in Sanskrit). During the last two thousand years, by putting these transcending patterns into practice, many millions of individuals in many civilizations have transformed their lives from quiet desperation into happiness.

In each chapter, we'll examine one of the basic Western thought-traps: self-preoccupation, dissatisfaction, depression, pride, envy, and hatred. These habit-patterns ensnare you and prevent you from achieving true happiness. Focusing on the unbounded nature of your existence can change your perspective on your problems and issues, transforming neediness into contentment, resentment into forgiveness, and selfishness into compassion. You can try out a whole new approach to life. Then we'll explore how you can put your new ideas into practice in the world, turning your thoughts into action. We'll examine the repercussions of your personal changes on society and on the fragile, opalescent planet. We'll see how personal transformation *is* social transformation.

Each transformation chapter includes a section called "Practice." These set forth meditation sequences that aim to enable you to understand, experience, and enact the transformations rather than simply reading about them. These sections are the key to your success. Why? Because meditation is the time-tested technique for analyzing old thought-habits and developing new thought-habits and new behaviors. It permits us to gain better control of ourselves. Our bodies and minds are our prime tools for dealing with life. We must develop greater and greater mastery of these tools, as well as improve their quality and capability. Just as we use yoga of the body to enhance its resiliency, strength, and prowess, so we use yoga of the mind for the same reasons.

Meditations are not just one type of practice; there are calming, creative, and critical insight meditations. You should always begin meditation sessions by calming your thoughts and quieting your body. You can easily learn to meditate on letting go of thoughts in order to lessen stress, find pleasure just in being, enjoy calm, peace and quiet, and gain greater detachment from environmental stimuli. Once this is readily achieved, we can focus on creative and critical meditations—meditations on specific topics that will help you to achieve your goals. These are called "practices" because they are not just pursued for their own sake, they are advance rehearsals for your performance of the accomplished abilities, insights, and virtues in your daily life. These meditations will enable you to sustain and intensify your thinking in order to reach insights and conclusions that are transformative. They will serve to make intellectual insights visceral and aspirations practical.

It is not necessary that you accomplish each practice in one sitting or that you finish them all while reading the book for the first time. In one sense, this is a regular book with a message, just waiting to be picked up and read. But in another sense, it is a workbook, in that the practices are there for you to use again and again. As you become more advanced in your practice, you may choose to spend many meditation sessions or a whole retreat on the themes set forth in just a few paragraphs in one chapter.

Physical Preparation

It is considered very important in contemplative traditions that you pay careful attention to the context in which you meditate. The setting and context play an important role in determining the result of the session. So I want to describe the optimal setting for you here.

First, you should try to create a special spot in your house or apartment where you regularly sit down to contemplate. Just as you have a special room to exercise in, and don't usually do push-ups or ride your exercycle in the living room, you need a special space to meditate. My meditation room is a largish closet that I've fixed up. It should be quiet and pleasant, a space where you enjoy being. You might put up a picture of an inspiring person or place on the wall you face. On a small altar or shrine in front of it, place some pleasant offering—a candle to symbolize light or an object of sight, a flower for beauty, a bowl of fresh offerings to please the taste, a beautiful cloth for texture, perhaps an incense burner for pleasant scent, some little cups of water symbolizing sweet sounds and all good things. You'll also need a meditation seat that's comfortable for you. The most comfortable, I find, is the Zen-type rectangular cushion mat with a round sitting pillow in the center. If you have trouble sitting cross-legged, place a comfortable chair there, though then you should start to work on gentle and gradual yoga stretching so you can eventually sit cross-legged after a few weeks or months. Now your room is set up properly.

Once you take your seat, adopt a comfortable cross-legged or sitting posture. Lay your hands flat in a relaxed posture in your lap, with the back of the right one lying flat upon the palm and straightened fingers of the left. Straighten your spine, and drop and relax your shoulders. Now tuck your chin down a bit so that your nose-tip feels in line above your navel. Put your tongue up to touch your palate just behind your teeth, but do not strain. Keep your eyes half-open with a loose focus of your vision a few inches in front of the tip of your nose. Breathe in normally, counting each in-breath up to ten or twenty and then starting again at one. When distracting thoughts start to run away from the counting, let them go on their own, pull your attention back from them, and resume counting or start over again at one. When you master counting, you can develop mindfulness about your breathing process, noticing everything about the act of breathing in and breathing out, without forcing it to be slower or deeper, just observing the inflow and outflow. Spend a little while settling down in this way, sitting peacefully in your pleasant spot, calming and resting, and your energy will build up for your meditation practice.

Mental Preparation

The physical arrangements of the room and your body are important and helpful, but not as important as creating a special space in your mind, an ideal place for transformation and liberation. Before you begin meditating on your chosen theme of the session, it is crucial that you open your mind up to your own vast potential. If you enter the practice leaving your habitual self-image and reality constructs intact and unopened, you are programming yourself to emerge the same as when you begin. "Show me your beginning and I'll show you your end!" is a wise adage. In order to open yourself for new experiences and understandings, you need to imagine yourself in a space where you feel most able to realize your true nature. The preparatory practice below comes from an ancient tradition known for optimizing your opportunity for success in the subsequent practices. I highly recommend that you try it before starting the practices described in each chapter. It is open to modification according to your personal taste and experience, of course.

First, use your inquiring, scientific mind to inventory your reality construct, your sense of your situation in the universe, questioning whatever you take for granted and taking special note of the uncertainties prevailing around you. What do you know really? How do you know it? Where are you really—on a planet spinning a thousand miles per hour, held by gravity above oceans of fire, water, and earth, within an ocean of air, circling a sun ninety-two million miles away, itself orbiting at an even greater speed on the galactic arm? What are you really, how many billions and trillions of subatomic energies or atoms, cells, how many countless neurons? What about your subconscious? Is it a personal store of inchoate memories, or a bundle of instinctual drives imprinted on physical molecules? Continue posing questions to yourself in this manner, melting away your habitual sense of certainty about your nature, structure, location, and presence within an assumed world-picture. Dissolve into "unfindability" and feel yourself rest in the unknown openness.

Now picture the following, or something analogous that you prefer: You arise in a luminous, buoyant body on a grassy bluff at high altitude overlooking a vast, crystalline glacial lake. The sun glints for miles and miles off its aquamarine waters, and majestic Himalayan mountain peaks rise up around it on all sides. Fluffy clouds float in the sunny, deep blue sky. Behind you to the north, the majestic snow-covered dome of Mount Kailash radiates magnificently like a prism, refracting the white sunlight into rainbows of blessing. In front of you, in the lake, is a small island on which minor deities and guardian spirits roam. Dragons sun themselves along the shore. In the center of this island grows a giant tree, reaching almost up into the heavens like the beanstalk Jack climbs in the story. Jewelline flowers and fruits cover its massive branches, making it seem like a huge Christmas tree with glittering ornaments.

At the crown of the tree rests a giant lotus flower, on which stands a lion throne made of many precious gems, on which sits the person who you think is the most enlightened, most all-knowing, most loving and compassionate person in the universe, whether human or divine, the person whom you would choose above all others to be your spiritual, intellectual, and moral mentor. Visualize this person to be large in size, brilliantly radiant, with a body made of light like Obi-Wan Kenobi's after he has died in the later *Star Wars* film. Around her in the tree sit a host of other mentors and benevolent beings. She is looking down upon you with a dazzling smile, and a tube of golden light descends from her heart to reach the crown of your head. Blessings in the form of liquid, jewel, rainbow lights coilingly flow down the golden tube and flood into your body and mind. Their blessings bring your body and mind inexpressible bliss and happiness, driving out the shadows of your confusions, anxieties, doubts, fears, and worries, and bringing you instead confident energy, clarity, joyous enthusiasm for understanding and good feeling.

As you slowly fill up with light and energy, you ready yourself for your meditation practice as a beneficent being with no limit to your potential. You have rid yourself of any preconceived notions about your own inabilities. Now you notice that around you on the grassy bluff, a vast crowd of ordinary sensitive beings has gathered. People and animals (in semi-human form) whom you know personally—those you love, those you hate, those you feel neutrally toward—all stand in the front row. They do not see the island, or the tree filled with mentor persons. But they look toward you and they are aware of how you are filling with light. The blessings begin to overflow from you to them, so that your light washes away their negative thoughts and feelings. Naturally, your loved ones are delighted and your neutral acquaintances are pleased and intrigued. And even your enemies are fascinated and blessed by the light that reflects from you.

Now turn your attention toward the mentor beings that have gathered on your behalf. Celebrate their presence by sending them waves of gratitude for their blessings. If you like, visualize yourself making fantastic offerings to them: commissioning symphonies, creating beautiful works of art and literature, sending clouds of exquisite scents, delicious foods, soft and precious cloths, beautiful lands, jewels, whatever you can imagine. Apologize for your past negative attitudes and deeds, resolve never to engage in them again, and ask your mentors' gracious assistance in helping you maintain your new resolve. Now be sure to rejoice in all the good deeds you and other beings have done, even those of your enemies. Request that the mentor beings turn the wheel of teaching, sending down the rain of Dharma truth and liberating insight. Ask them not to leave you lost in the world of suffering, but to stay with you and all sensitive beings until you are awakened and secure in reliable happiness. Finally, resolve to earnestly pursue the quest for full enlightenment, wisdom, and compassion for the sake of yourself and all other beings.

You are now ready to turn your attention to the meditation practice itself, forgetting about this entire picture, just sensing it's there. Follow the instructions for the practice as described in each chapter. When you conclude your meditation, come back to the image described above. Let your mentors and their magical environment merge completely into your heart and soul. Then melt yourself into pure light and flow into the hearts of those people who stand around you. Dedicate whatever merit or virtue you may have developed during your practice to them, expecting no selfish reward or recognition for your achievements. Once you've emerged from this state of melted oneness into your ordinary existence, you will go about your daily routine with these new insights very much a part of the renewed you.

Don't worry if, especially at first, you find it difficult to imagine all the details of your mentor, the other beings around you, the lake, island, tree, mountains, and clouds. At a minimum, think of yourself in a space filled with light and blessings, and with beings you care for spiritually present to assist you. What's most important is that you visualize yourself on top of the world, empowered, and then just know that you are there. It's like when you enter a room for the first time, how you look around at the floor, walls, and ceiling. You might note some details of the moldings, window frames, drapes, furniture, carpet, and so forth, and then you forget about them and engage in whatever thoughts are occupying you at the time. But the picture of the room remains in your background awareness, as proven by the fact that you might jump up to go out the door without thinking. And the room itself certainly affects your mood, whether it is uplifting in its beauty and elegance or depressing in its ugly mess. The image you create for yourself with the practice described above functions in much the same way as the room.

You should feel free to employ this preparatory practice to whatever degree of elaboration you desire and enjoy each time you work with the meditations presented in the book. However, don't try to visualize too much at one time, which will only leave you feeling frustrated. Remember to open and close with the image of your ideal place and mentor person, but then let that vision go as you engage in your specific practice. The goal of this exercise is to make you feel fully energized and indomitably capable of realizing your aims, as well as to remind you to dedicate your accomplishments to supreme fulfillment for all. Creating for yourself even a minimally appropriate physical and mental setting within which to practice will greatly empower you and accelerate your progress.

If you have trouble meditating, if you are bothered even by the concept of meditation, if it just feels too artificial for you, then simply read the book, returning again and again to passages you find inspiring and illuminating. After all, reading is a form of meditation, as is going to the theater or a movie, or watching television—above all, watching commercials is meditation, though it is intended to be disempowering in that it aims to make you feel you can't do without the product advertised. Even sitting on a bus with random thoughts flickering through your mind, memories of past events, anxious or eager anticipations of future events, tunes, images—even this is meditation. Your sense of self and your sense of your environment and world is not just a fixed thing that sits in you and around you like a skeleton and a tent; it is a constructed picture within and without. Your mind constantly refreshes the picture by scanning over it and ruminating about it, just as the photon gun at the back of a TV set fires light and color so many times a second within a pattern to refresh the picture on the screen. So it is not a question as to whether you should meditate or not. You are meditating all the time. And so the big question is, Are you choosing what you meditate upon, is it what you want to become your ability and reality? Or is it all too often what the powers and principalities around you want you to hold as you and your reality? Your culture, your religion, your society, your government, the commercial industries that need you as participant, believer, member, subject, and consumer?

The bottom line is that you can take responsibility for how you occupy your mind. You can convert negativity into positivity in your life by opening yourself up to the ancient and well-proven philosophies available from the teachers of liberation who have flourished in history. You can study their teachings, not only as a spiritual seeker but also as a scientific investigator, and you can find what makes sense and see if it is verifiable in experience in the world. In so doing, you will transform not just your own individual existence, but also the lives of those around you. Each of us is like a bubble of awareness. When we transform ourselves, free ourselves from inner knots and blemishes and blossom out our inner beauties, our new openness and blissful pleasure resonates instantaneously and reinforces liberation and satisfaction in the other bubbles. Changing ourselves for the better changes the world for the better. Rehearsing positive changes through intelligent meditation practice makes us more capable of performing the more positive world, creating it in our infinite living and sharing it with others.

Part Two

3

Wisdom

Preamble: Selflessness

At one point in the early 1970s, after I'd gotten my Ph.D. and started teaching Buddhism, I went back to visit my old teacher, the Mongolian lama Geshe Wangyal. We were working on a project to translate a Buddhist scientific text from the Tibetan. We were six or seven people gathered around a kitchen table, and Geshe-la began to talk about the inner science of Buddhist psychology, the Abhidharma. He was reading us a few verses about the insight of selflessness, the deep release of becoming unbound, when I began to feel a little dizzy, even nauseous. It was a funny feeling. It felt slightly like a vibration spinning in my head. The vibration came not from Geshe-la, but from this ancient tradition. It was as though my habitual mind couldn't quite find traction. I realized that if I fought it, the sensation would only get more nerve-wracking and I would only feel more nauseous. So I didn't fight it. Instead, I let go and relaxed, and soon I was able to orient myself in another way, away from my "self." I felt like I was slowly but surely loosening my self-centered perspective on life and the world. In a useful way, a strengthening way, I was beginning to experience the great Buddhist mystery that is the selflessness of subjects and objects.

The Buddha based his psychology on his discovery of actual and ultimate reality. This he called "selflessness" and "voidness," or "emptiness." Some people love these words from the moment they hear them, but others are frightened by them. People often ask me, "Why did Buddha have to be such a downer? Obviously nirvana is a happy, cheerful state. So why didn't he just call it 'bliss' or something? Why did he have to label the reality he discovered with negative words such as 'voidness,' 'emptiness,' and 'selflessness'?" When people respond negatively to these terms, it's often because they're worried that the words imply they are going to die, disappear, or go crazy in their attempts to seek enlightenment. And that's exactly why the Buddha called reality by those names. He did it on purpose, to liberate you! Why? Because the only thing that's frightened by the word "selflessness" is the artificially constructed, unreal, and unrealistic self. That self is only a pretend self, it lacks reality, it doesn't really exist. That pseudo-self seems to quiver and quake because the habit that makes it seem real wants to keep its hold on you. So if you're seeking happiness and freedom, then you should want to scare the heck out of your "self"—you want to scare it right out of your head!

Actually, *it* is constantly scaring the heck out of *you.* Your "self" is always busy terrorizing you. You have a terrorist in your own brain, coming out of your own instincts and culture, who is pestering you all the time. "Don't relax too much," it is saying, "you'll get stepped on. A bug will bite you. Someone will be nasty to you. You'll get passed by, abused, sick. Don't be honest. Pretend. Because if you're honest, they'll hurt you." And it's ordering you, "Be my slave. Do what I tell you to do. Keep me installed up here at this very superficial level of the brain where I sit in my weird Woody Allen–type cockpit. Because I'm in control." Your falsely perceived, fixated, domineering self is precisely what's getting between you and a fulfilling life.

Early on, some of the Western psychologists who were beginning to learn from the Buddhist tradition—members of the transpersonal and other movements—came up with the idea that the relationship between Buddhist and Western psychology is this: "Western psychology helps somebody who feels they are nobody become somebody, and Buddhist psychology helps somebody who feels they are somebody become nobody." When I first heard this, I was at an Inner Science conference with the Dalai Lama. Everybody laughed, applauded, and thought it was a great insight. The Dalai Lama just looked at me and kind of winked and was too polite to say anything. I started to jump up to make a comment, but he stopped me. He told me to be quiet and let all of them ponder it for a few years until they realized the flaw in their thinking. Because of course that idea is not even remotely correct.

The purpose of realizing your own selflessness is not to feel like you are nobody. After he became enlightened, the Buddha did not sit under a tree drooling, and saying "Oh, wow! I'm nobody!" Think about it: If he just "became nobody," if he escaped from the world through self-obliteration, then he wouldn't have been able to share so many teachings here on earth, to work for the good of all beings for years and years, long after he achieved nirvana. He would've just stayed in his "nobody" state and forgotten about all of us poor humans busy suffering through our miserable lives.

The reason why we sometimes think that the goal of Buddhism is just "to become nobody" is that we don't understand the concept of selflessness. "Selflessness" does not mean that we are nobody. It does not mean that we cease to exist. Not at all. There is no way you can ever "not exist," just as you cannot become "nothing." Even if you go through deep meditation into what is called "the realm of absolute nothingness," you will still exist. Even if you are so freaked out by a tragedy, such as losing your only child, that you try to end your existence completely, you will still exist. I have a healthy respect for tragedy. We do have terrible tragedies. Personally, I don't bear misfortune well; it knocks me out. But there is no way to become nobody. Even if you were to succeed in killing yourself, you will be shocked when you awaken to disembodied awareness, out-of-body but still a somebody, a ghostly wraith who wishes he hadn't just done that. And a terribly unfortunate living person who has been so brutalized that he blanks out who he was in a seemingly impenetrable psychosis is still somebody, as everybody else around him knows.

Our mind is so powerful that it can create a state of absolute nothingness that seems totally concrete. Thousands of yogis in the history of India and a few mystics in the West have entered such a state of nothingness. But no one can stay there forever, and it is not where you want to be.

Have you ever had a minor experience of nothingness? I've had it in the dentist's chair with sodium pentothal, because I used to eat a lot of sweets and not brush my teeth as a youngster so I had to have teeth pulled. They give you this knockout anesthetic, and if you are a hard-working intellectual, you are tired of your mind, so you think, "Oh great, I'm going to be obliterated for a little while." You're really pleased, and you feel this little buzz, and you're just about to get there. You're going to experience nothingness, a little foretaste of the nihilistic notion of nirvana! But suddenly the nurse is shaking you awake saying, "You've been slobbering in that chair long enough. Get out of here." It's over. You started to pass out, wanting to be gone, but now you're suddenly back with no sense of having been gone at all! And that's what it is like in the state of absolute nothingness. It's like being passed out in the dentist's chair. There's no sense of duration of time. But eventually you wake up, totally disoriented with a nasty headache, and you never even got to enjoy the oblivion.

So we can never become nothing, as appealing as that may sound to those who are addicted to the idea of nothingness after death. We are always somebody, even though we are selfless in reality. We are just different sorts of "somebodies" than we used to be. "Realizing your selflessness" does not mean that you become a nobody, it means that you become the type of somebody who is a viable, useful somebody, not a rigid, fixated, I'm-the-center-of-the-universe, isolated-from-others somebody. You become the type of somebody who is over the idea of a conceptually fixated and self-created "self," a pseudo-self that would actually be absolutely weak, because of being unrelated to the reality of your constantly changing nature. You become the type of somebody who is content never to be quite that sure of who you are—always free to be someone new, somebody more.

That's the whole point of selflessness. If you don't know exactly who you are all the time, you're not sick, you're actually in luck, because you're more realistic, more free, and more awake! You're being too intelligent to be stuck inside one frozen mask of personality! You've opened up your wisdom, and you've realized that "knowing who you are" is the trap—an impossible self-objectification. None of us knows who we really are. Facing that and then becoming all that we can be—astonishing, surprising, amazing—always fresh and new, always free to be more, brave enough to become a work in progress, choosing happiness, open-mindedness, and love over certitude, rigidity, and fear—this is realizing selflessness!

I never met the late, great comedian Peter Sellers, except splitting my sides in laughter while watching some of his movies, especially the *Pink Panther* series. I know he had his ups and downs in his personal life, though you can't believe all the things you hear from the tabloids. But I did read a quote from him, or maybe from his psychiatrist, that he was deeply troubled and distressed because he suffered from "not knowing who he really was." He would get into his roles as an actor so totally, he would think he was the person he was playing, and he couldn't find himself easily as his "own" person. So he suffered, feeling himself "out of control" in his life. When I read this, my heart went out to him. I imagined his psychiatrist sternly telling him he had better calm down and track himself down, and put a lid on his ebullient sense of life, leading him on and on in self-absorption in therapy under the guise that he was going to "find himself" once and for all. I, feeling a bit more freed by having awakened to even the tiniest taste of selflessness, wanted to cry out to Peter Sellers, "Stop suffering by thinking your insight is confusion! Don't listen to the misknowing and even fear your freedom! Learn to surf the energy of life that surges through your openness! You have discovered your real self already, your great self of selflessness, and that openness is what enables you to manifest the heart that shines through your work and opens the hearts of your audiences. Your gift is to release them into laughter, itself a taste of freedom! Why be confused and feel your great gift is something wrong?" But I didn't know him so I could not tell him what I'm telling you. But our lives are infinite and I will be telling his ongoing life-form one of these days, whether I recognize him or not!

The Buddha was happy about not knowing who he was in the usual rigid, fixed sense. He called the failure to know who he was "enlightenment." Why? Because he realized that selflessness kindles the sacred fire of compassion. When you become aware of your selflessness, you realize that any way you feel yourself to be at any time is just a relational, changing construction. When that happens, you have a huge inner release of compassion. Your inner creativity about your living self is energized, and your infinite life becomes your ongoing work of art.

You see others caught in the suffering of the terminal self-habit and you feel real compassion. You feel so much better, so highly relieved, that your only concern is helping those constricted other people. You are free to worry about them because, of course, they are having a horrible time trying to know who they are and trying to be who they think they should be! They are busy being ripped apart by the great streams of ignorance, illness, death, and other people's irritating habits. So they suffer. And you, in your boundless, infinitely interconnected, compassionate state, can help them.

This is the other crucial point about selflessness: It does not mean that you are disconnected. Even nirvana is not a state of disconnection from the world. There is no way to become removed from yourself or from other beings. We are ultimately boundless—that is to say, our relative boundaries are permeable. But we are still totally interconnected no matter what we do. You cannot disappear into your own blissful void, because you are part of everyone and they are part of you. If you have no ultimate self, that makes you free to be your relative self, along with other beings. It's as if your hand represents the universe and your fingers represent all beings. Each of your fingers can wiggle on its own, each can operate independently, just as each being has its own identity. And yet your fingers are part of your hand. If your hand did not exist, your fingers would not exist. You are one of many, many fingers on the hand that is all life.

To my surprise and delight, I learned recently that even some Western psychologists are now beginning to study and understand the harm done by self-centered thinking. The psychologist Dr. Larry Scherwitz conducted a study about type A people—the aggressive, loud, annoying types, like me. Scientists used to think that type As died younger because of their fast-paced, stressful lives. But this new study reveals that, in fact, some of us type A people are not going to die of a heart attack that soon after all. The type Bs out there, the mild-mannered, quiet, inward-focused types, might find this worrisome! We may stay around for years bothering them, because it turns out that the type A personality is not a risk factor for coronary heart disease or other stress-related health problems. It turns out that some people, like me, though we freak out all the time, are not always that stressed. Some of us actually enjoy being this way.

What is the real risk factor, then? Scherwitz and his colleagues reanalyzed the data and conducted some new studies. They discovered, by analyzing the speech patterns of type As and type Bs, that the high risk of heart disease and stress-related illness is correlated with *the amount of self-reference* in people's speech—the amount of self-preoccupation, self-centeredness, and narcissism. "Me, me, I, I, my, my, mine, mine. My golf course, my country club, my job, my salary, my way, my family, my religion, my shrine, my guru, my, my, mine." The more "I, me, my, and mine" there is in their speech—"mine" most of all—the more likely they are to succumb to stress, to keel over because their bodies revolt against that pressure of self-involvement. Whereas even though some people can be aggressive, annoying, loud, and seemingly "stressed," if their overall motivation is altruistic and they don't pay too much attention to themselves, they live longer. And the quiet type Bs who are also more concerned about others, not necessarily out of any altruistic religious inklings, but just naturally not paying much attention to themselves, tend to live longer, too.

I find this study amazing. I was with the Dalai Lama when he heard about the results. He was intrigued and very pleased. "Oh, really?" he said. "Let me see that paper. In Buddhist psychology, we also have this idea that obsessive self-preoccupation—possessiveness and selfishness and self-centeredness—is life's chief demon!"

Let us explore the problems created by this demon of self-preoccupation, the ways in which it causes us suffering. We will then practice a fundamental meditation in which we look for the fixated self and find that it does not, after all, exist. Once we have freed ourselves from the constricting habit of always thinking that we are the center of the universe, we will experience our first taste of the boundless joy and compassion that is infinite life.

Problem: Misknowledge and Self-Preoccupation

One of the hardest things we have to do on a regular basis is to admit that we are wrong. We stubbornly insist that we're right in situations where we're not quite sure if we are, and even when we sense that we've slipped. How much more indignant do we become when we feel certain that we're right and someone has the gall or the stupidity to challenge us? In this case, we feel an absolute imperative to jump up and trumpet our rightness. If we still cannot get others to agree with us, we soon become self-righteous and then outraged.

Believe it or not, the fact that we struggle so much with being wrong is of tremendous importance to our task of awakening to the reality of selflessness. We should examine our habit of needing to be right carefully to see why it feels so good.

Being right means that the world affirms us in what we think we know. "Knowing" something is a way of controlling it, being able to put it in its proper place in relation to us so that we can use it effectively. As Dharmakirti, the seventh century Indian philosopher, said, "All successful action is preceded by accurate knowledge." So knowledge is power, in the sense that it empowers us to act successfully. Misknowledge, misunderstanding a situation, is weakness, in the sense that our actions may fail in their aim, backfire, or have unintended consequences. Knowledge is security, in that we know our vulnerabilities and can avoid harm. Misknowledge is danger, in that we don't know what others might do to us or what traps may await us. We therefore feel powerful and secure when we're right, weak and vulnerable when we're wrong.

Viewed in this context, being right seems like a struggle for survival, a drive to win. It's natural for us to cling to that feeling, even when we have not investigated the reality around us because we don't really want to know if we are wrong. We think that finding ourselves in the wrong means a loss of power and safety, forgetting that actually *it is the only way* for us to discover what is truly right and truly wrong, thereby gaining real power and real safety. When we pretend, we focus our attention on appearing to be right no matter what the reality, we distract ourselves from being awake to what really is going on, and so place ourselves at a disempowering disadvantage.

In light of this simple analysis, what lies at the center of our constant need to assure our rightness and, therefore, our power and security? Is it not the certainty that "I am"? Does not the strong sense of "I am" seem absolutely right, unquestionable, in fact? Every self-identification, judgment, and impulse beginning with "I am"—"I am me," "I am American," "I am human," "I am male," "I am right," "I am sure," "I am angry"—seems natural, undeniable, imperative. As such, we are habitually driven to obey in feelings, thoughts, words, and deeds whatever comes from within the inexhaustible fountain of I am's, I think's, I want's, I love's, I hate's, and I do's. "I" is the absolute captain of our ship, the agent of our fate, the master of our lives.

When apes or bulls or mountain goats snort and paw the ground and then charge head first at one another, we interpret their behavior as an "I" versus "I" contest, sometimes to the death. Similarly, the imperative issuing from our "I" can be so adamant, so unchallengeable, that we human beings, too, will sacrifice our lives. Just think of the nature of such statements as follows, when the "I" is aligned with country, church, God, family, race, gender, or species: "I am a patriot!" "I am a Protestant!" "I am a Catholic!" "I am a Christian!" "I am a Muslim!" "I am a believer!" "I am an atheist!" "I am white!" "I am a male!" "I am human!" In these situations, the "I" exercises tremendous power over us, and can often lead us to our death.

The "I," the ego-self seemingly absolutely resident in the heart of our being, is the one thing of which we each are absolutely certain, which we will die for, which we will kill for, which we will obey slavishly and unquestioningly throughout our lives. We are so accustomed to our habitual sense of self that we consider even the slightest absence of it—a moment of derangement, a loss of consciousness in fainting or deep sleep, a disorienting distraction of passion or terror, a dizzying state of drunkenness or drug-intoxication, a psychological or neurological disorder—absolutely terrifying. We can't imagine our lives without our "I" as a constant, demanding presence.

What is shocking and difficult for most Westerners to accept is that the Buddha discovered that this most certain knowledge of the "self" is actually "misknowledge"—a fundamental misunderstanding, a delusion. And what's more, he realized that this discovery was the key to liberation, the gateway to enlightenment. When he saw the false nature of the "I," he emitted his "lion's roar," pronouncing the reality of selflessness, identitylessness, voidness. This was his *Eureka!* moment, his scientific breakthrough, his insight into reality, from whence has flowed for thousands of years the whole philosophical, scientific, and religious educational movement that is Buddhism. Identifying this habitual, certain self-knowledge as the core misknowledge allowed the Buddha to give birth to wisdom, truth, and liberating enlightenment.

But the Buddha knew perfectly well that it would do no good to simply order people to accept his declaration of selflessness as dogma and cling to it as a slogan or creed. The instinctual entanglement of human beings within the knot of self-certainty is much too powerful to be dislodged in this way, selflessness at first too counterintuitive to be acknowledged as truth. No, the Buddha realized, people must discover their real nature for themselves. So he made his declaration of selflessness not a statement of fact but rather a challenge to inquiry.

"I have discovered selflessness!" the Buddha announced. "I have seen through the reality of the seemingly solid self that lay at the core of my being. This insight did not destroy me—it only destroyed my suffering. It was my liberation! But you need not believe me. Discover the truth for yourself. Try with all your might to verify this 'self' you feel is in there, to pin it down. If you can do that, fine, tell me I'm wrong and ignore whatever else I may have to say. But if you fail to find it, if each thing you come up with dissolves under further analysis, if you discover, as I did, that there is no atomic, indivisible, durable core 'self,' then do not be afraid. Do not recoil or turn away. Rather, confront that emptiness and recognize it as the doorway to the supreme freedom! See through the 'self' and it will release you. You will discover that you are a part of the infinite web of interconnectedness with all other beings. You will live in bliss from now on as the relative self you always were; free at long last from the struggle of absolute alienation, free to help others find their own blessed freedom and happiness!"

Though in this paraphrase of his core teaching the Buddha offers us much encouragement, the challenge remains its central thrust. "You think you're really you? Don't just accept that blindly! Verify whether or not your 'self' is actually present within you. Turn your focused attention to it and explore it. If it's as solid as it seems, then it should be solidly encounterable. If you can't encounter it, then you must confront your error."

The great philosopher Descartes made a grave error when he thought he discovered in his fixed subjective self the one certain thing about existence. After demolishing the entire universe of observable things with hammer blows of systematic doubt, he was unable to give even a tiny tap to collapse this sense of self. And so he set down as the basis for his entire philosophy the famous proposition, "I think, therefore I am!"

Believe it or not, in his deep exploration for the "self," Descartes almost took another path that would have led him to enlightenment. He got very close to discovering that he could not find the "self" he felt to be so absolutely present. After intensively dissecting appearances, drilling through layer upon layer of seeming certainties, he came out with nothing that he could hold onto as the "self." But then he made the tragic mistake. Instead of accepting his selflessness, he instead said to himself, "Ah! Well, of course I cannot find the self. It is the self that is doing the looking! The 'I' is the subject and so it cannot be an object. Though I cannot find it, still my knowledge that it is the absolute subject cannot be doubted. It confirms its existence by doubting its existence. *Cogito ergo sum!* Of this I can remain absolutely certain."

Why was this mistaken? His logic sounds plausible enough at first. It is, after all, a clever way out of the dilemma of looking for something you are sure is there but cannot find. But what's wrong with it? Let's say that I am looking for a cup. I find it, so I can be certain that the cup exists. I look for my friend and find her, so I can be certain she's there. I look for my glasses, I do not find them—so I proclaim certainty that they are there? No—I go get another pair because I acknowledge I've lost them. I look for my oh-so-familiar "I," and I cannot find it! Why would I think it's there, then? Because I've arbitrarily put it in the category of "things that are there only when I can't find them"? No, when I can't find it, it's rather more sensible that I must give up the sense of certainty that it's there. I feel it's there when I don't look for it, but as soon as I look for it with real effort, it instantly eludes discovery. It seems always to be just around the next corner in my mind, yet each time I turn around to seize it, it disappears. And so I must slowly come to accept the fact that it may not be there after all.

Put another way, imagine that you are walking through the desert when, far off on the horizon, you see an oasis. Yet when you get closer, it disappears. "Aha!" you think to yourself. "A mirage." You walk away. Miles later, you turn around and look back. There's the oasis again! Do you feel certain that the water is there now? No, on the contrary you feel certain that it is only a mirage of water. In the same way, when you look for the "self" and don't find it, you must accept that it is merely a mirage. Your solid self-sense is only an illusion.

Had Descartes persisted and found the door to freedom in his selflessness, as the Buddha did, then instead of proclaiming, "I think, therefore I am," he might have said. "Even though I can find no concrete, fixated 'self,' I still can think. I still seem to be. Therefore I can continue to be myself, selflessly, as a relative, conventional, but ultimately unfindable being."

Whenever you decide to try a particular yoga recommended in this book, the crucial first step is always deciding to make the change. You must begin by accepting the fact that your habitual conceptions could be wrong. If, for example, you live with the delusion that it is just fine to remain addicted to nicotine, that three packs of cigarettes a day puts you in optimal operating condition, then there is no way you will successfully complete a yoga to quit smoking. Likewise, in this crucial quest of the self, the presumed core of your self-addiction, you must first convince yourself through empirical observation that the way you hold your self-identity—the constricted feeling of being wrapped around a solid, independent core—is uncomfortable and disabling.

Why should you even care if the rigid "self" that you believe in so strongly really exists or not? Our self feels most real when we are right and righteous, when we are wrongly or unfairly challenged. And it also seems unique, completely separate from everyone and everything else in the universe. This separateness can feel like freedom and independence when we are in a good mood. But when we are in trouble, lonely or angry, under pressure or dissatisfied, this separateness feels like isolation, alienation, unfair treatment, or deprivation. When we are wholly gripped by fury, the searing energy that wants to attack a target picks our "I" up like a mindless tool and flings us at the other person. It is so disconnected that it even disregards our sense of self-protection, making us take actions that injure us, ignore injuries undergone, and even harm others with no regard for the consequences. There is no more powerful demonstration of our strong sense of being an independent entity than when we give ourselves over completely to anger.

When we look around at others, we see that they are just as alienated from us as we are alienated from them. As we want things from them, they want things from us. As we reject them, they seem to reject us. We don't love them, so how can we expect them to love us? And yet they are endless, while "I" am just one. So I am badly outnumbered. I feel threatened. I can never get enough, have enough, or be enough. I will inevitably lose the me-versus-all-of-them struggle in the long run.

We can, of course, experience moments of unity with other beings, through falling in love, or having a child, for example. When we do, we experience tremendous relief—for a moment, there are two of us teamed up against all the others together. We have an ally. But unfortunately those moments are too rare, and they do not last long before the old self-isolation reemerges. Even lovers can turn into adversaries, couples often seek divorce, and children recoil from their parents, who in turn reject them.

This alienation caused by the presumed independent, absolute self was why the Buddha saw its illusion as the source of human suffering. The situation of feeling that it's always "the self versus the world," with the self as the long-term loser, is unsatisfactory and untenable. When we recognize the inevitable nonviability of our self-centered reality, it motivates us to engage in the quest for the true nature of the self. It makes it existentially essential for us to pause in our headlong rush through life and turn within, to verify whether the "self" really exists as we feel it does.

We can take great encouragement from the fact that the Buddha told us we could escape from our suffering. Still, we cannot merely accept someone else's report. No one else can do the job of replacing misunderstanding with understanding for us. We must look at reality and verify for ourselves whether our habitual sense of having a fixed self or the Buddha's discovery of selflessness is ultimately true. In this way, we can begin to transform the self-preoccupation that causes chronic suffering into the insightful, gradual opening and letting go of the self that is, paradoxically, so self-fulfilling. We want to be happy, but ironically we can only become happier to the extent that we can develop an unconcern for our "self." This process is long and gradual, though you will experience frequent breakthrough moments that will thrill you and motivate you to continue.

Before we actually engage in the meditation practice used to discover the true nature of the self, we must set up our parameters in practical, clear terms. When we look through a darkened house for a misplaced key, we first remember what the key looks like, and then we search for it carefully, room by room, turning lights on as we go. We use a flashlight to look under beds and in hidden corners. When we have looked everywhere exhaustively and not found it, we decide we've missed it somehow, so we go back and repeat the process. However, after one or two searches of this kind, we come to a decisive conclusion that the key is not in the house. We know we could continue looking endlessly, but that would be impractical. So we decide to proceed accordingly with our lives.

In the case of the quest for the self, we will look through all the processes of our body and mind that we can find and investigate them thoroughly. Our physical systems, sensational feelings, conceptual image bank, emotional energies, and consciousness itself constitute the house through which we will search. There are also various vaguely defined areas such as "spirit" and "soul" that, like a dusty attic or dank cellar, we may feel the need to explore. It is easy to get lost in these murky, dank, and oft-forgotten quarters of the mind. So we must get a clear picture of what we want to find ahead of time. And most important, we must set some limits to the exercise, since practically speaking we cannot continue to search indefinitely.

At this point you should search through the house of your body-mind-spirit a few times with great concentration and systematic thoroughness, with my help and the help of many experts who have guided me through this practice. If, during this process, you find a "self," then enjoy it to the full. If, however, as I suspect will be the case, you do not find what stands up solidly as your "real self" by the end of the process, then you will have to live with the fact that there is no such thing. You will need to make the practical decision to turn from seeking the "self" to explore instead the ramifications of being a relative self without any absolute underpinning.

This commitment to practicality in your quest for the self is of great importance at the outset and will have a significant impact on the success of the endeavor. Once you have made the commitment in your own mind, you may begin.

Practice: Trying to Find Your "I"

You are now prepared to deepen your understanding of your selflessness. You will be looking at yourself introspectively, trying to grasp exactly what your essence is. When you do this practice well, you will begin to feel yourself dissolving, just as I did at my mentor Geshe-la's house many years ago. You will start realizing—gradually and also suddenly, in spurts—that you can't find this mysterious "self." Your strong feeling of having an absolute "I" is maddeningly elusive when you try to pin it down precisely.

As with all meditations, start by performing the visualization I outlined in Chapter 2 to create an appropriate mental setting. Once you have done this and are comfortable in your physical or mental shrine space, you can begin your first meditation. In looking for your "self," start with your body. Ask yourself, "Am I my body?" In order to answer this question, you must define your body. It is composed at least of your five sense organs, right? Your skin and sensitive inner surfaces constitute the touch organ, then you have your eyes for sight, your nose for smell, your ears for hearing, and your tongue for taste. So first let's explore all of your senses together, your sensory system.

Identify the sound sense. What do you hear—a dog barking, a phone ringing, music playing, or perhaps just the sound of your own breathing? Now notice the visual field. You are reading words on the page. What else do you see? What are the images on the edge of your peripheral vision? How about smell? Perhaps you smell the scent of incense burning, or of musty wood. Do you taste anything: something you ate a while ago, tea you drank, or just the taste of your own mouth? The tactile field is everything touching your skin, including other parts of your skin touching your skin. Your hand may be resting on your knee, for example. Your bottom is touching a pillow. Just identify all the sensations, the textures, smells, tastes, sounds, and sights.

Now notice your internal sensations, like the breakfast in your stomach. You might have a slight pain in your back or your knee. Maybe your foot is falling asleep, and you're annoyed because there's a slightly painful sensation there. You might have a pleasurable sensation in some part of you that is feeling good if, for example, you worked out yesterday or had a massage.

Recognize that for each of these sensations you are experiencing, you are receiving data from the outside world. The sensations are not all coming from your own body. So your body is not just inside your skin; your body is both your organs and the field of all incoming sense objects. It's everything you are seeing and hearing and smelling and tasting and touching. It's the chair or pillow you're sitting on. The words you are reading on this page. The incense drifting into your nostrils. If you look at one sensation, you realize that you are sharing your material body with the outside world. Say, for example, you are looking at light bouncing off a table. That light is a part of your shared sensory system, and therefore part of your body, too.

So already you have begun to expand your self-definition, just by looking at your five senses. Suddenly you are not just something that sits there inside your skin. You are your environment as well. Your body interfuses with the outside world that you perceive with your senses. All of our bodies are totally overlapping, all the time. Do you see? And when you think, "this is 'me' over here inside this skin," you are unrealistically thinking that "I" am not connected to others through the sense perceptions that we have in common. But you are connected, even before you talk to them or think anything about them, through your shared environment.

Now you can move to the next level of analysis of the self, which exists at the level of your mind. First is the sensational system, the feelings of pleasure, pain, and numbness associated with sense perceptions of sights, sounds, smells, tastes, textures, and mental sense inner objects. When you experience these six kinds of objects, you react as pleased, irritated, or indifferent. Mentally inventory your sensations at the moment, and notice how you react at this basic feeling level. Notice that this heap of sense-reactions has no self-core within it.

Next is your conceptual system, your ideas, mental maps, and internal images. You have a picture of yourself as you exist in the world. You have a concept of yourself as human, not animal. You have a picture of yourself as male or female. You have a body image, and an image of each part of your body. You have a concept of your identity as a teacher, a manager, a doctor, or whatever. You have a concept of yourself as successful or as a failure. Inventory this mass of ideas and images and notice that you have whole clouds of pictures and concepts. But is this incredibly chaotic mass of images and words and diagrams and maps and so forth that is your conceptual system the real "you"? Your perception of yourself changes all the time, depending on your mood, whom you're with, or what you're doing. Sometimes you think, "I'm a high-powered executive," whereas other times you think, "I'm just a tiny speck on a tiny planet of six billion people." So surely your conceptual system cannot be your "self." The "you" self is not any of these ideas, since it seems to be the entity that is noticing all of them.

At the fourth level of analysis, find your emotional system. You are constantly reacting to all of these images and notions. Right now, you're probably feeling a bit irritated with me. You're thinking to yourself, "Why is he making me do this? Why doesn't he just crack a joke? Let's have some fun. What is this terrible business of exploring the self, 'discovering selflessness'? How is this helping me?" And so on and so forth. You're feeling annoyed and anxious and confused. Or maybe you're just feeling bored. Anyway, your emotions are there in your mind, always functioning, but always changing. You can take a peek at them now, as they swirl around in your heart and head, and you can see that they are not fixed. You are not defined by your emotions. They are not the elusive "self" you're seeking.

Lastly, turn your attention to your consciousness system. It is the most important system of all. You see at once how it is a buzzing, blooming, swirling mass of subtle energies. Nothing is fixed, nothing stable within it. With your mental consciousness, you hop from one sense to another. You analyze your ideas, you focus internally on your emotions and thoughts, and you can even focus on being thought free. Your consciousness aims itself at being free of thought by the thought of being free of thought. How strange! As you inventory your consciousness, don't allow yourself to rest with a bare awareness, but go a bit deeper—explore further with your analytic attention. Ask yourself, "Who is this supposedly rigid 'self'? Is it the same self right now as the one who woke up grumbling this morning, preparing that cup of coffee, rushing to get ready, quickly brushing its teeth? Is it the same self who was born a tiny, unaware, helpless infant years ago? Who is the 'me' who knows my name, who knows what I want, where I am, and what I'm doing? Who is the 'me' who knows I'm an American, who knows I'm a—whatever: a Buddhist or a Christian or an atheist? Where is that person now? Where is that absolute, unchanging structure?" You can see how your self-consciousness is a buzzing, blooming, swirling mass of confusion—nothing is fixed, nothing stable within it. You can barely remember what you did yesterday morning—I can't remember at all at my age! So how can you possibly have a rigid self? See how releasing these sorts of thoughts can be!

Now think about this: How is nirvana going to have any meaning to you if you didn't first isolate all these systems analytically and release yourself from your normal sense of yourself as some sort of integrated package? How are you going to experience bliss and voidness, wisdom and compassion, if you are a rigid, independent self? You can't enter into the ideal universe, the "buddhaverse" as I like to call it, of enjoyment, wisdom, and compassion, until you first detach from this world of suffering, this prison that is the fixed and absolute self-image. How do you release yourself? Through the analytic knowledge of facts. How can you stay angry if you are aware of yourself as a constantly changing process? The continuity of your anger gets broken. How can you stay depressed? The continuity of your sadness gets broken. It transforms. You associate with the not-mad and the not-sad. You take responsibility for your mad and sad. You stop being stuck in those same old thought patterns. You stop thinking over and over again, "Well, I reacted once with anger, and now I'm stuck here. There's nothing I can do about it." Because you absolutely can do something about it. The fact that you are selfless means that you are not a fixed entity; you are changeable. You can transform your thoughts in order to transform your life.

Let's say, for example, that you have a fight with your partner. You get upset. You start thinking to yourself, "I hate it when he does that. He's always saying nasty things to me." You stew around in your anger, blaming him or her for making you suffer, for creating your problems. But then you take a step back. You disengage yourself with a short meditation on selflessness. And you remember that the real reason you are angry is because you chose to interpret what happened to you in that way. You created your own reality. And if you are selfless, then your suffering is your partner's suffering, and her suffering is yours. Don't you want to make the suffering stop? Take responsibility for yourself: your emotions, actions, and evaluations. It's so simple, although of course that does not mean it is always easy. Just go up to your loved one and apologize. Tell him you're sorry. Explain why you got upset and ask him, compassionately, to try to work out another solution with you in the future. You'll instantly feel less angry, your partner will feel better, and you will be in a much happier place.

The fact that you are selfless means that you are not a fixed entity. You are changeable. You can transform your thoughts to transform your life. You do that when you learn to maneuver your mental elements by learning to observe them in meditation. When you scan, observe, and analytically penetrate your body-mind components in an intense and sustained way, you will gradually develop your stability of attention, your contemplative focus and durability. Your awareness moves from being a scanner to being a drill. Everything that comes up in awareness is scanned and noted, but then your awareness goes beneath its surface, looking for its essence, its full reality. When it does, the object dissolves under that analytic gaze. It's as if you experience X-ray vision, an increasingly effortless movement into ever finer awareness of ever finer dimensions of the object. Your point-of-vision type of reflective awareness intensifies through mobilizing imagination of other perspectives on the object, its parts, its micro components, its causal temporality, including its moment-to-moment subtle process of disintegration. Your scanning awareness remembers its pictures of the parts of the objects, the inside of it, its parts and processes—and you continue down to the level of its molecules and atoms and subatomic particles and energy waves and presumed empty spaces between those particles and waves. Any mental or physical object thus examined dissolves under the examination.

The deepest stage of awareness comes when your consciousness begins to turn inward to gaze upon itself. At first it thinks, "I now know that these sensory, mental, and emotional systems looming before me are not the 'self,' they are not 'me.' But the awareness that looks at them, that contemplates and investigates them, that is my 'self.'" And yet you soon discover that you are mistaken even in this conclusion. The moment you begin to examine your own conscious mind, you engage in a whirling, internal dervish-dance where your awareness spins round and round upon itself. This contemplation can be dizzying, nauseating, painful, and even a bit frightening, as the felt "self" disappears and evades its own attention. You can never catch it, even as you become more experienced at this meditation and come back to this place again and again. Time and again you will feel frustrated by your continued failure to come up with a result. Yet you must not lose heart. You must remember that looking for your "self" is the most important thing you can ever do in your evolutionary development. You must keep faith that you are on the brink of a quantum leap; you are so close to awakening.

As you enter into this confusing realm of spinning self-seeking, be careful not to make the mistake Descartes made by withdrawing from it all with some sort of decision about "you" being the subject and therefore not any sort of findable object. Also, be careful not to fall into the nihilistic trap of withdrawing from the spinning by deciding that all is nothing after all and so naturally the self-sense is an illusion. Keep whirling upon your "self" as long as you feel absolutely there is a self to whirl upon, to look at, to catch. Put your full truth-seeking, analytic energy into the drive to find it.

Eventually, you will experience a gradual melting process. The whirling will slowly dissolve without fear: you won't shrink back in terror of falling into an abyss-like void because you are already overcoming your self-addiction. You control the tendency to shrink back in terror of falling into a looming void by your drilling, whirling energy of awareness itself. You dissolve your fearing subject, the object for which you are feeling fear, and the imagined nothingness that only the pseudo–self-addiction wants you to fear. However fully you feel such processes at first, what happens to you is that, as you begin to melt, your drive intensity lessens, you feel buoyed by a floating sensation coming from within your nerves and cells, from within your subjectivity as well as your object-field. At some point, you lose your sense of self entirely, as if you were a field of open space. Like Neo and his colleagues in the movie *The Matrix* when they entered one of the computer-generated training fields, you will find yourself standing in a blank white space—except in your case, in this transcending moment, you break free from your "digital residual self-image." You will be only the blank white space, a bare awareness of yourself as a boundless entity. Dissolving into this space, you'll feel intense bliss, a sense of extreme relief.

When you first melt into the spacious experience of freedom, it is enthralling, like emerging from a dark cave into infinite light. You feel magnificent, vast, and unbound. If you inadvertently fall into this state unprepared by arriving there too quickly, you may be tempted to think that you have arrived at the absolute reality, and this is a bit of a danger. You might think, feeling it nonverbally at this stage, that you've conquered the differentiated universe and realized its true "nothingness," experiencing it as such a profound and liberating release that you never again want any contact with the real world. Remember, however, that nothingness is not your ultimate goal—you are not trying to escape reality, but to embrace it. If you reach this space of release gradually through the repeated whirling of your self turning upon itself, then you'll be able to enjoy the vastness and magnificence without losing awareness that it is only another relational condition. You'll realize that the great emptiness is ultimately empty of itself; it is not reality, either.

Since you *are* the void, you do not need to remain in the void, and your original self-sense slowly reemerges within the universe of persons and things. But you are aware that it is not the same "self" you had before—it is forever different, now become infinite and unbound. You have changed. You now perceive your "self" consciously, living with it yet maintaining an educated distance from it. You are like one of the characters in *The Matrix,* present and active as real being, yet at the same time realizing that the apparent reality that surrounds you is only illusory. All that was apparent becomes transparent.

One of the most significant changes you will notice upon discovering your selflessness is that your sense of being separate from everyone else has now eroded. Your new awareness enables you to perceive others as equal to yourself, a part of you, even. You can see yourself as they see you, and experience empathically how they perceive themselves as locked within themselves. You have arrived at the doorway to universal compassion, and it frees you from being locked away behind a fixed point-of-awareness and opens you to a sort of field awareness wherein others are really just the same as you while simultaneously relationally different.

Through the sense of sameness, you feel their pains as if they were your own: when they hurt, you hurt. Yet through the sense of relational difference and balanced responsibility, you naturally feel moved to free them from their pains, just as you move automatically to eliminate your own pains. When your hand is burned by a hot pothandle, you react at once to pull away from the heat, you plunge it into cold water, you rush to find ice. You respond instinctively to remove the pain. You don't consider it a selfless act of compassion for your hand. You just do it through your neural connection to your hand. Your new open awareness feels others' hands through a similar sense of natural connection.

Luckily, you experience this expanded field awareness with its empathetic connectedness to others at a slight remove, as if you were in a dream. You might reasonably worry that the attainment of such openness of spacelike consciousness would lead you to an agonizing state of empathizing with all the pain in the world. You overcome this fear by remembering how blissful is your sense of release when you melt into your spacelike, infinitely open, balanced concentration. In the aftermath of your release, when your own sense of individuation returns, it feels dreamlike, with an illusory quality, somehow both there and not there at the same time. Can you remember how you felt when you burned your hand on a hot pothandle in a dream? Can you imagine it? Though it hurts, when you awaken there is no burn on your hand. If you were capable of lucid (self-aware) dreaming, you could control the pain by reminding yourself, "I am in a dream—my hand and body here are nothing but digital residual self-image in the virtual, dream reality—they cannot be injured by heat." So you know the pain of that experience, you feel something, yet you can remove it simply by an act of awareness.

This is a good analogy for your empathic awareness of the pains of others when you awaken to enlightenment through melting into the spacelike selflessness-awareness. You can feel them as the others do, and you automatically react to soothe them or remove them. Yet you are not torn away from your blissful energy; it keeps on going at the same time. It is not possessed as a separable thing so it cannot be lost. Without numbing yourself to their pains, you can still act with joy and confidence to soothe them, and so you are optimally effective in your healing actions.

These are the steps of the investigative and contemplative quest for the "self." I like to do this meditation often as a reminder of my open selflessness. It gives me tremendous comfort to remember (since one of the things about living overstressed is that I forget everything all the time) that I am free. I enjoy experiencing a taste of the feeling that I am infinite. But you have to risk going into a sphere where you can't quite remember exactly who you are. You have to negate it anytime you feel the "I" emerging as a fixed, independent, absolute thing, and then negate it again. It's not that nonexistence is your final goal, but that you want to rid yourself of your habitual sense that you exist in a static way. This practice has its thrilling moments of revelation, its unsettling moments of doubt, its quiet moments of mindfulness—all of which add up to a continuous, ever-deepening, evolving flow of liberation.

Your infinite life thus becomes grounded in the greatest virtue of all—wisdom. Your wisdom deepens constantly as you gain a deeper and deeper understanding of your own selflessness and your resulting interconnectedness with all other beings. You engage other people with generosity, sensitive and empathetic justice, and invincible tolerance, forbearance, and forgiveness. With practice, you gradually erase the division between meditation and action until you are filled with endless joy and bliss. Your newfound freedom energizes your actions in daily life, and you become an inexhaustible source of the infinite life force. Your embrace of beings who feel lost and frightened and abandoned does not ruffle the surface of the great ocean of your happy, loving presence, as you unleash waves of dynamic effort to help them.

There is a fantastic passage that encapsulates our wisdom practice most readily, channeled by the great Lama Tsong Khapa (1357–1419) from the archangelic bodhisattva, Manjushri, the eternally youthful prince of transcendent wisdom.

Though you have experienced renunciation,
And conceived the spirit of enlightenment,
Without the wisdom realizing voidness,
You cannot cut the root of cyclic life—
So you must strive to realize relativity.

If you see the inexorability of the causality
Of all things of cyclic life and liberation,
Your insight dissolves all objectivity-habits
And you find the path that pleases buddhas.

Appearance inevitably relative
And voidness free from all assertion—
As long as you understand these two apart,
The Buddha-intent is not yet known.

But when they coincide, not alternating,
Your mere sight of inevitable relativity
Secures your knowledge beyond objectivism,
And your investigation of the view is perfect.

This beautifully outlines the critical meditation we just tasted that discovers selfless voidness as revealed by the total interconnectedness of relative and absolute things, the absoluteness of relativity. You do not rest content with transcendent detachment, your vision of the ephemerality and insubstantiality of mundane things that frees you to drop out totally from any lesser concerns than total evolutionary fulfillment and enlightened happiness. You do not become complacent with your cultivated spirit of enlightenment of love and compassion for all sensitive beings. You want freedom, so you turn your attention around toward the reality of all inner and outer things, determined to discover their true nature, no matter what the cost, since that is the only way to fully awaken.

You then bear down on the individual pieces of that relativity in quest of verifying what you acknowledge to be your habitual sense of their seemingly absolute thing-in-itself nature, you drill through their objectivity-halo and ultimately dissolve your own subjectivity-assertion, and thus you enter into the spacelike balanced concentration, released into pure sky awareness free from perplexity. You do not fall for the seeming absoluteness of that magnificent sky experience, you re-enter the dreamlike aftermath reality, and you hold the two in a balanced unity-and-diversity experience of the inconceivable, nondual, perfectly liberated and fully engaged, open-field infinity-awareness.

There have been millions of persons who have awakened to their true reality, who have been called "enlightened" in many civilizations. They have not seen the universe in the way only we moderns are taught to see it—as a vast, dark, freezing void through which galaxies are scattered, where very few stars have planets that are bathed in a green-blue film of oxygen and carbon, and perhaps just one planet supports sentient life as we know it. Ours is an impossibly paranoid, lonely, isolated vision. No wonder we feel weird. We conceive our living awareness to be such a rare exception, so fragile, so random and meaningless.

As you become more truly alive, you see an infinitude of universes, a beginningless, boundless sea of life, energy, and delight, full of goodness, aware of itself in its absolute ultimate peace and security, freedom and happiness. You see yourself and all of us, even as we struggle to stay separate, so totally incorporated within that sea of joy, nothing neglected, no one excluded. You feel one with us completely, just as we are, and you experience our individual feelings of confusion, loneliness, and terror. You see precisely how we have closed off from our own deeper sense of union with the sea of all goodness, bound by our habitual misperception, our ignorance, our misknowledge.

People today have looked through the Hubble telescope, they have walked in space, they think they know it's dark and cold out there. Some figure statistically that there must be life on other planets, but still they have not yet found another planet that can support life. They may think that "enlightened" people have fallen into a psychotic delusion, hallucinating lights in the darkness, warmth in the cold, life in dead stone. Perhaps they're right. But when you put on the U.S. Army's latest night-vision infrared combat glasses, you can see things in what looks to your naked eye to be pitch darkness. Solar panels extract heat from light rays in freezing space. Radio signals activate receivers in silent space. Space and atoms are filled with unseen energies, the four theorized physical forces—gravitational, electromagnetic, weak, and strong. What if enlightened people see on the more subtle levels of quantum forces? What if they experience the strong force directly as the energy of life? Or of consciousness? What if they naturally identify with limitless space as a live body? Our dark space may look to them like a sea of light. Our solid bodies may seem diaphanous, holographic arrangements of infinite space to them. How can we insist, after learning that the atoms making up our bodies are mostly space—each a Yankee Stadium whose "matter" is a nucleus the size of a golf ball on home plate, its electrons circling like flies buzzing in the bleachers, and even that nucleus and those electrons dissolving under finer analysis into emptiness—that our habitual sense perception of outer space as cold, dark, and dead is a revelation of the one and only reality of space?

Religious people, West and East, have always tended to feel that there is a mysterious power of life in everything. In most forms of religions, the appearance of darkness and pain and death is overcome by the glorious light of goodness you have tasted in the wisdom meditation that discovers the open space–like freedom concentration. What Jews, Christians, Muslims, and Hindus call "God," or sometimes "Godhead," is a force of reality much like the infinite ocean-body of living joy that the great enlightened meditators experience. When a believer asserts unshakable faith in the face of the worst experience or apparent reality, she or he is reaching for connection to the deepest awareness of infinite living energy. Enlightened people do not see this boundlessness as something other than themselves. They experience themselves as one with all gods and all other beings, and they consider us all capable of becoming fully aware of our own freedom and happiness. Faith in such a possibility is a good place to begin this journey to liberation; it encourages us to set forth. But we all can move beyond faith to direct experience and full knowledge of our true state.

Performance in Daily Life

Lama Tsong Khapa continues with one more verse that I have always found to be utterly extraordinary. It reminds me of a woven Chinese finger-trap, or a particular hand gesture where you interlock your fingers as if to do "all the people" inside the church and steeple, then twist your hands around back-to-back with fingers still locked, extending your arms forward so that the pressure pulling your fingers apart locks them ever more tightly together. It is a kind of creative double-bind awareness, an illustration of the ever-expanding, infinitely free awareness as the ultimate mode of the enlightenment called "the tolerance of cognitive dissonance."

Furthermore, as experience dispels absolutism
And voidness clears away nihilism,

You know how voidness dawns as cause and effect—
And you never will be deprived by extremist views.

Your transcending inquiry cuts through the false sense of independent self by sustaining the focus on the pure negation of failing to find any nondissolving objectified self anywhere with the body-mind processes or anywhere else outside yet still related to them. You then have moments of breaking free from the enclosure within a sensed self inside the sense-consciousness and thought-consciousness. You feel open and spacious and can even experience the exhilarating freedom of gently melting into vastness. Luckily, your penetrating inquiry awareness—without requiring any further discursive thought—does not allow you to reify even such magnificent experiences into any absolute. Even the vastness disappears, and your relational self, the body-mind complex, other persons, and other objects reappear, seemingly really "there" as before as things-in-themselves, yet now immediately, intuitively known as dreamlike and illusory, like reflections in a mirror, reflections in the mirror of voidness. As the liberating experience of dissolving dims in your memory, things seem more and more real again; you relate to them with compassion, but they begin to hem in your awareness, until you return to your critical meditation and refresh yourself in ever-more-powerful moments of breaking free. This oscillation continues for months and years, and the two states gradually come closer and closer together. Eventually, you reach your goal of complete nondual freedom, the simultaneous nondual experience of supremely liberated cognitive dissonance, wherein you joyfully live the moment-to-moment reconciliation of all dichotomies.

This is how your practice deepens into performance. In this, voidness dissolves your absolutizing of persons and things and moves your awareness toward the spacelike image of voidness, and appearance dissolves your absolutizing of any state of emptiness into real nothingness and moves your awareness back into the dreamlike engagement with differentiated beings and things.

Performance itself comes when you focus on encompassing the duality of meditating and not meditating. It is when you reverse the beginner's modality of voidness dissolving things and vision returning you from voidness. You deepen the nondual awareness all the time in all your doings, staying in the inconceivable surface of the voidness-mirror of wisdom while compassionately engaging with beings and things. Just seeing things, you intensify your sense of being present in voidness, of their suchness as absolute elusiveness, their thatness in absolute thereness. Why? Because in seeing them you relate to them, which you can do only because you, your organs of perception and mental patterns of conception, are devoid of intrinsic reality—so the mere seeing dispels absolutism, without a second thought about their voidness. At the same time, seamlessly, your experiential sense of floating free in voidness keeps you engaged in the differentiations and beings and things, deepening your insight of the utter impossibility of nothingness. So you are beyond any oscillation; your daily life is inconceivably joyfully engaged with relative others while ever-deepening your meditation on the absolute. There is no limit to the expansion of your awareness of this in all situations. Your bliss becomes more and more unshakeable, and your compassion more and more effective as it develops consummate skill in the art of lifting others into freeing their own understanding and enjoying their own growth of inner bliss.

When someone hurts you and you feel anger and annoyance, you think about how you got in their way, how they feel about you. You relativize your wish to retaliate, you disidentify with your drive to hurt back, and you let the heated energy surge out into the air without mobilizing your punching arm or lashing tongue or kicking leg. You let it dissipate, and revel in your freedom from its compulsion.

And you then go further than detachment and tolerance, and you begin to make an art of your interactions. You start to give things you like, part with things you're attached to, but not for your sake, only if they could be helpful to others. Of course the will and ability to give is the key, not the actual gift—unless it is just what the other needs. You start to make use of injury and hurt, embracing them as opportunities to deepen tolerance, let the hurter have the victory—but again not just for your own sake, only if that helps them. You might well evade the hurt or defend against it if the hurting of you would be bad for the adversary, would deepen their negative ways, deepen their own addiction to anger and violence.

Your infinite life thus becomes a moment-to-moment performance of all the transcendent virtues, all grounded in the greatest of these, transcendent wisdom. Your wisdom deepens constantly throughout, with seeing eroding absolutism, and freedom eroding nihilism. You perform your infinite living engaged with others through generosity, sensitive and empathetic justice, and invincible tolerance, forbearance, and forgiveness. You perform in engagement with yourself in intensifying your serenity, your contemplative concentration, your one-pointed control of your mental focus, which intensifies your wisdom transcendence, gradually erases the division between meditation and action, and fills you and your expanding field of infinite living with joy and bliss. Your creativity energizes both your altruistic and your self-evolving performances, and you become an inexhaustible node of the infinite life-force, feeling more and more saturated with the sense of indivisible union with all enlightened beings. There is evolution without anxiety or stress, energy without restlessness, relentless progress without greed or feelings of deprivation.

Once you have begun to see the truth of your self-addiction and gain some measure of release from it, then you can begin to have a positive influence on other beings and effect change in your society. There is no need for you to formally promote certain doctrines: your very presence becomes a teaching example to others, a liberating art that opens their imaginations to the potential freedom they also can experience.

Our first crucial step as a society must be to help all of our citizens become aware of their deluded worldview and the harm that it causes. Once they have realized that their self-centered attitude lies at the heart of their discontentment, they, too, will want to make a change. We must make it our chief priority to assist every individual in his or her quest for personal release and evolutionary improvement.

Seeing the limitations of the solid self-sense helps us, as individuals and as a society, to understand our infinite interconnectedness to all life. We realize that no matter what we may have been taught, no matter what we initially thought, we are one with all beings. If one person suffers, we all suffer. As a result, we act more responsibly. No longer obsessed with our own needs and concerns, we make a commitment to helping others achieve happiness and fulfillment.

If we want to move our entire society from cynicism to social commitment by moving each person from delusion to wisdom, we must begin with education. Buddhists believe that the primary purpose of any society is to educate its individuals. And the goal of education is not to prepare people for some other task or life purpose, but rather to enlighten. As the fundamental tool for ridding ourselves of delusions and finding the truth, education is the highest purpose of human life. Our society should offer every citizen ample opportunity for individual growth. Only through education can people achieve personal development. Only through personal development will society evolve.

Sadly, America is falling very badly behind in the educational endeavor. Television is the main educator of Americans. Children spend about 25 percent of their time watching TV, which is almost as much as they spend in the classroom. Only 2 to 3 percent of programming is educational, only a slightly higher percentage is informative in even a rudimentary sense, and almost none of it is educational in the fullest sense of being elucidative, liberating, and empowering. Our educational system should focus primarily on promoting enlightenment thinking, on teaching people how to see clearly the true nature of their selves and their world. We should also provide training in ethical thinking. We should not present our children merely with a set of commandments ordering them to behave a certain way. Rather, we should teach them to thoughtfully consider the full impact of their actions on other people and on their own well-being. We should encourage them to think of others as assets in their quest for happiness, not as obstacles. If we are truly interconnected, we must acknowledge that other people figure very centrally in our achievement of happiness. We need to overcome the dualistic thinking that makes our happiness seem attainable only through others' misery.

If we are concerned about the ability of our society to implement such grand and noble educational programs, consider Tibet as an illustration of what is possible. Tibet offers us the best example we've ever had of a human society that made a multigenerational, multicentury attempt to create a culture and civilization that reflected the commitment and values of enlightenment. If, as the Buddha said, the best-of-all-possible-worlds reality that is our destiny and our human birthright can indeed be created on this earth, then Tibet is our toehold.

This does not mean that Tibet is or ever was perfect. Tibet is imperfect, like every other human society. Due to the Chinese invasion, occupation, and temporary annexation, it has been largely physically destroyed. When it regains its independence, it will have to completely rebuild, which will surely result in Tibet itself becoming something quite new and different. But intact, as it was for centuries until just forty years ago, Tibet was unique. We have much to learn from it.

The Tibetans succeeded in keeping alive and further developing for our study the spark of a great philosophy, Buddhism. And the current leader of Tibet, His Holiness the Fourteenth Dalai Lama, has become a Nobel Peace Prize laureate, a world leader of the spiritual movement insisting on and working for a sane and humane global civilization. The teachings that he has shared with us are a product of Tibet's education systems.

The Tibetans were totally committed to education, setting it as their society's highest priority. Just before Chinese occupation, approximately 20 percent of Tibet's population were monks and nuns living in monasteries. Buddhist monasteries are, fundamentally, educational institutions. This means that many Tibetan individuals were able to devote all of their time to educating, and therefore evolving, themselves on an ongoing basis, with no other task in life. Each person was given ample opportunity for spiritual development. As a result, Tibetan society attained a remarkable degree of nonviolence, optimism, and unconditional compassion, unmatched by any other culture in the world.

Do not allow your old selfish cynicism, then, to encroach. Remember the example set by Tibet and realize that there are other possibilities for our children. Don't be afraid to use your newfound wisdom to help create a better world.

Through our meditation on the boundless nature of the self, we have begun to cure ourselves of the most fundamental and damaging delusion—that we are separate and alone, isolated by an independent "I." The inevitable conclusion we have reached together is that we are infinitely alive, intricately connected with everything around us. We therefore have a responsibility to evolve our selfless self, and to make a passionate commitment to helping all other beings do the same.

This evolutionary process, with its final result of buddhahood, has profound effects on us as individuals, on the society we are members of, and, by morphic resonance, on the whole planet. The effects are incalculable by our usual yardsticks of self and social improvement, being a transformation of the very ground of the social contract. A society of enlightened beings is bound to be an enlightened society.

4

Generosity

Preamble: Boundless Giving

The great thing about the infinite lifestyle is that you discover you have endless resources for sharing. You might still like some things you possess, some of the time. But finally, over the course of a life and certainly at death, your world, your environment, your country, your gender, your race, your nation, your town, your ball club, your house and garden, your apartment, your furniture, your jewels, your money, your clothes, your shoes, your books, your name, your friends, your relations, your family, your body, your speech, your mind—memory, identity, command of thought—all are gone. You know that not a single one of these things *is* you. The sum total of all of them together even *is not* you. They are conventionally "yours" for a time, and then they are no longer yours. Everything changes. Anything acquired is eventually lost. All that is lost is eventually regained. Everything and everyone also come back.

The terminal lifestyle is constantly plagued by the fear of death, since you fear that when you die and lose everything, it is forever gone, though your regret might be muted temporarily by the assumption that you will not be there to miss it. The infinite lifestyle lets you hold on to things more lightly, to people, even your body and mind. Your soul—your relative, changing, conventional subtle mind—is more important, since it goes with you from life to life. It changes for good or ill according to your acts and thoughts. During the between-state after your death, the soul gravitates to your next life-form driven by the instincts you have cultivated. Your instincts are themselves shaped by your positive or negative acts of body, speech, and mind. The "soul" is sometimes called the "spiritual gene" (*gotra*), since its encoded patterns guide your mental and physical processes as they elaborate new living forms.

If you are strongly deluded about your independent, separate selfhood, and therefore strongly attached to what is "you" and "yours," opposed to what is other, your spiritually and materially genetic soul-coding predisposes you to fortresslike embodiments, embodiments that have a highly hardened boundary between inside and outside. A turtle with its hard shell, a rhino with hard hide, reptiles with brittle scales, insects with exoskeletons, mollusks such as oysters, snails, and the like—these physical embodiments may be attractive to the instincts of a living continuum habituated to a hardened boundary between self and other. Diminished sensory awarenesses become desirable for a person who doesn't want to be invaded by too many stimuli, flees loud sounds, bright lights, strong tastes, odors, and textures. How much better to have eyes with less rotation, ears with less sonic range, and so on, as long as you have just enough sense exposure to find food in that embodiment!

In this spiritual vision of karmic evolution, life forms are expressions of habitual mental attitudes crystallized into instincts, brought along from previous life experiences as codes of attraction, selection, and construction. The patterns are very simple to understand and visualize. Strong grasping leads you to be attracted to forms with big claws, prehensile appendages, lobster pincers. More and more insensate grasping leads to insect forms with many hands and feet. More and more hatred becomes embodiments with fangs, stingers, and powerful poisonous venom. Once your instinctual attraction impels your loss of human vulnerability and adoption of one of the more instinctually hard-wired and physically limited life-forms, it is too late to attempt to reverse course easily. Choices have become severely restricted, memory is unavailable, learning from others is limited by the lack of language, and it might be eons of lifetimes before the strange, ungainly, ambiguous, multioptional human embodiment is regained.

The human form is mammalian, permeable in boundaries, the female bearing the young within the core of her own body, the male and female interpenetrating to reproduce. The human form must seem weird to lower, more highly programmed animals, who are used to reacting with little thought to standard stimuli and are streamlined to pursue survival in routine ways. What healthy animal, well-suited to its struggle for life and not often troubled by anticipation of death, would consider the human form attractive? How easily could it gradually evolve an instinctive attraction to the human predicament? Very, very hard to imagine.

Humans can share minds through speech, possess huge memory and anticipatory capacities, can imagine and empathize. Humans are relatively soft-wired, capable of deprogramming all instincts, reprogramming new instincts. They are nearly unlimited in their options regarding how to behave, what to do, say, and think. They can evolve toward whatever they can imagine. Their very vulnerability is an advantage in that it causes them to think creatively, not accept routine without questioning and inquiry.

Thus, the human life-form has immense evolutionary advantages and can become the platform for the final mastery of evolutionary processes that is called buddhahood, awakening and blossoming. Buddhahood represents the achievement of conscious control of impulses of lust, hate, fear, and delusion. It has the ability to soar free from all forms and to respond to other beings by shaping images in matter enfolded by spiritual energy, in order to adopt whatever embodiment the environment and other beings may require. At the same time, because of the power of the mind and the imagination, the experience of the ephemerality and transformability of all forms, the human courts the great evolutionary danger of projecting a powerful retrogressive impulse toward lower life-forms, fancying herself a beautiful antelope, a powerful tiger, a magnificent elephant. Such projection in the precise moment during the death-rebirth between moments could result in a precipitous evolutionary fall, likened in societies with a buddhistic scientific and literary culture to a fall from a high precipice into a deep abyss.

The key to avoiding this kind of danger is sheer openness of awareness, transcendent wisdom, the critical insight into the freedom of all persons and things from any intrinsically objective reality. As you have experienced, through the wisdom exercises, this wisdom continuously sweeps your inner and outer consciousnesses and cuts through your entanglements with outer forms and inner impulses, de-absolutizing and dissolving rigidities, keeping the reality of freedom present. This ensures against any hardening of the imagination, any irresistible instinctual projection of lust or hate that would cause your subtle soul-process to get trapped in a more limited life-form, derived from a more limited, terminal worldview.

Wisdom is the first virtue you just began to adopt in your journey toward enlightenment. The other five transcendent virtues, which you will seek to develop in the next five chapters, will transform wisdom's freedom into true happiness. They will deepen and expand immeasurably your infinite lifestyle, since your happiness depends not on you alone, but is intricately merged with the happiness of others. Transcendent generosity, justice, patience, creativity, and contemplative serenity—acts, words, and thoughts that express these transcendences shape your spiritual gene in ways that secure and empower your positive evolution, creating ever-increasing stores of wisdom and merit.

- *Generosity* keeps you open through deeds, making you aware of other's needs. It seals your insight into selflessness by allowing you to let go of all possessions—including your body, your mind, and even your good deeds—in order to find true contentment in helping other beings.
- *Justice* encourages you to make your relationships with others as fruitfully harmonious as they can be. Its positive resonance with others reinforces within you a personal ethical system that leads you away from conflict and anxiety and toward peace and happiness.
- *Patience* armors you against any negativity that might be caused by others purposefully or inadvertently inflicting injuries upon you. Wearing your shield of patience, whatever harm you may experience, you will never lose your freedom through explosions of anger.
- *Creativity* empowers you with limitless, joyful energy that frees you from the bonds of self-loathing and despair. It enables you to progress energetically toward buddhahood and toward turning this world into a buddhaverse for all beings.
- *Contemplation* provides the central strength that empowers you to achieve a new level of focus and serenity. With it, you gain the full benefit of your wondrous mind, your compassionate spirit, which encodes your subtlemost soul, the core nexus of your infinite relationships with all sensitive beings and the creator of your developing buddhaverse.

All of these virtues are transcendent because they are indivisible from the understanding of the true, selfless nature of reality that is wisdom. Once we have begun to enjoy freedom from being driven around by our rigid self-sense, we can start to dismantle our enslavement to the dictates of our formerly domineering "I." We already know that we will continue to suffer as long as we remain trapped by self-preoccupation. Of all the negativities that arise out of our traditional, self-centered view of the world, selfishness is one of the most difficult and critical for us to overcome.

Our consumer culture teaches us to look for satisfaction in material things. Over and over again we are given the message that if we want to be happy, all we need to do is spend money. A new car, a new pair of shoes, a big meal, the latest gizmos . . . we always want more stuff. We are a nation and, more and more often in this day and age, a world, of consumers. Despite the fact that we're able to surround ourselves with many of the material goods we are so firmly convinced we need to be happy, we are still dissatisfied. We feel restless, always driven to want to consume more, yet never content. Furthermore, we are haunted by low-grade anxiety as we sense the harm that our selfish habits are causing other living beings and our planet every day.

The wonderful news is that you can free yourself from selfishness quite easily. If you are not single-mindedly, self-centeredly focused on what you have, then you can discover boundless resources for generosity. In fact, the truly generous do not even perceive their giving as a virtue. They don't think to themselves, "I'm such a selfless giver!" The transcendence of generosity comes from not regretting, missing, or even noticing the thing given, and from not expecting any gratitude or even acknowledgment from the receiver. When you give something away, you experience great karmic gain, since you have thereby not only helped another person, but also freed yourself from attachment to that object. But you engage in your act of generosity only with the other person's well-being in mind.

In Buddhist countries, monks and nuns often beg for their noonday meals. The civilian donors who rush to fill their bowls with food would be offended if the monks thanked them. Not receiving thanks helps the donors make the gift selflessly, without any sense of self-congratulation. They don't sit back for a moment and feel proud that they have given, calculating how much merit they have gathered. This makes the gift far greater in merit. In fact, the less you consider the value of your good deeds, the greater their inherent merit becomes. This allows your generosity to become truly boundless, rather than simply serving as a means to earn you karmic bonus points for future lives. The thought is always more important than the act in Buddhism: You must not simply perform good deeds, but you must perform them for the right reasons.

Generosity is the form of action that expresses the pattern of wisdom, the seeing through of all things that opens the way for the vow of the spirit of enlightenment: love and compassion for all sensitive beings. When you give something away, *you* have the greater gain, since you thereby free yourself of attachment. The receiver may experience temporary satisfaction, receiving something they like or need, but they also become ensnared by another object of attachment. Their new possession at once becomes something to take care of, worry about, and finally lose. If they are lucky, they will eventually give it away to someone else, and thus make it a source of tasting freedom for themselves.

One of the Buddha's former-life stories (*jātaka*) illustrates just how far enlightened beings will go in their definition and practice of the transcendent virtue of generosity. In his last lifetime before attaining enlightenment, the Buddha was an Indian prince named Vessantara (so called because of his fondness for the merchant classes). His main purpose in that life was to give away anything and everything that he had to anyone and everyone.

When Vessantara was born, a royal white elephant was born in the king's stables at the same time. This elephant was pure white and as huge as a mountain. When he trumpeted, all other elephants were terrified. So as soon as his presence became known, all neighboring kings gave up any thought of attacking Vessantara's father's kingdom.

As Vessantara grew up, he displayed legendary generosity. Petitioners would come from all over the country and the world to request gifts from the prince. He set up large gift-houses at each of the four gates of the capital city, and devoted all his time to going around to them one by one, giving and giving. He gave away equipment, carriages, lands, homes, money, jewels—whatever people asked. Strangely, the more he gave, the more the kingdom prospered. People brought with them fabulous goods to trade. All of nature joined in the symphony of generosity, rains were abundant and the harvests were continuously overflowing. Peace reigned throughout the land.

When he was of the proper age, Vessantara met the noble and beautiful Madri and fell in love. But he would not ask her to marry him at first. When she asked why, since she knew that he loved her, Vessantara said that he could not ask anyone to marry him, since his lifetime vow was to give away whatever was asked of him. That meant that if anyone asked for her, he would have to give her away; he could not ask anyone to suffer such a fate. (These were ancient times when wife and children were considered the property of a man!) But Madri argued that she didn't care, that she would gladly join him in his lifetime of giving under whatever conditions. So they married and in due course had two lovely children.

One day, an aggressive and conspiring neighbor king hired two Brahmins to visit Vessantara and ask the prince for the gift of his magical white elephant. Vessantara was delighted to give the elephant away, as he was truly attached to the magnificent creature and so the giving was difficult. He experienced an unfamiliar twinge of possessiveness, and thought,

"This is exactly the sort of challenge I needed." The two Brahmins quickly rode off with their prize.

When the citizens of Vessantara's kingdom heard that he'd given away their prized elephant, they were dismayed. They promptly forgot how much they loved their generous prince. Instead, they could only focus on the fact that their national defense had been compromised. Without the elephant to protect them, the long peace and prosperity they had been enjoying would be threatened, and Vessantara was to blame. They wanted his head.

The king was torn. He was angry at Vessantara's reckless giving and loath to go against the will of his people. However, he loved his son with all his heart. So as punishment for betraying the country, he banished Vessantara far into the wilderness. The prince tried to stop Madri and the children from going with him, but they insisted. They began their journey with princely equipment: a four-horse chariot, household goods, supplies and money for building a home in the forest, and so on. But of course they didn't get far before people began asking for things, and Vessantara gave it all away. Soon they were walking, carrying only a few supplies on their backs.

When they got to the forest, they built themselves a humble hut of reeds and began the happiest period of their lives yet. They were not troubled by anyone with requests. They lived by gathering fruits and nuts for food. They were, in fact, perfectly blissful.

But then everything changed. One day, while Madri was out gathering food, an old Brahmin named Jujaka came seeking gifts from Vessantara. Jujaka had been driven mad by the incessant demands of a young wife who made them live beyond their means. He asked the prince to give up his two children so that Jujaka could offer them to his wife as servants. The children ran away when they heard this request, which the prince granted only with extreme emotional difficulty. Vessantara eventually found the children hiding underwater in a stream, breathing through hollow reed snorkels. He presented them to the old Brahmin, who dragged them off by the hair. "No, Daddy! Don't do this!" they hollered piteously. "This man isn't human! He's a cannibal demon! He's going to eat us! Please save us!"

When he heard his children's cries, the bodhisattva prince felt intensely agitated despite his vow to give away everything, even life and limb. He reached for his bow and arrows, then put them down, then reached for them, then put them down again. Although he shook violently and wept for the first time at this unhappy giving, Vessantara let Jujaka leave with his beloved children. When Madri returned later and heard the news, she suffered a complete nervous breakdown.

Shortly thereafter, the king of the gods, Indra, manifested himself as another Brahmin and asked Vessantara for the gift of Madri herself. Vessantara was further shattered by this challenge, but he did not hesitate to hand over his beloved wife. By that time, Madri was so dazed that she was barely aware of what was happening to her.

This was Vessantara's ultimate gift—the gift of family, more dear to him than his own life. People never hate an enemy so much as when that enemy kills their spouse or child. Revenge is never so righteous as when one avenges the death of one's kin, and people will easily sacrifice themselves for such a cause. Therefore, generosity in its most transcendent, supreme form manifests itself as the ability to give away even your dearest child. Of course, in reality, no being, even a child, belongs to any other, even a parent, for the giving.

The story ends happily, thank heavens. The god Indra, after testing the bodhisattva by asking him to give up his wife, reveals his true identity. He returns Madri to Vessantara, and arranges things so that Jujaka passes through the prince's home kingdom on his way back home to his wife.

The people recognize the king's grandchildren and buy them back from the evil Brahmin. Jujaka then takes the large sum of money and gorges himself so greedily that he dies of indigestion. The people and the king repent of their mistreatment of Vessantara, acknowledging that his generosity is their greatest wealth and supreme defense, and bring him back to the kingdom to reunite him with his father and his children.

This fable has some similarities to the Biblical story of Abraham being called upon by God to sacrifice his beloved son, Isaac. Yet there are also key differences. Abraham is willing to give up his son only because an omnipotent Being whom he fears, God, commands him to do so. Vessantara, on the other hand, gives away his beloved wife and children not because someone orders him to but because he believes it is the evolutionarily right thing to do. His generosity grows from his wisdom of selflessness, and his resultant vision of the interconnectedness of and compassion for all beings. He recognizes the equality between Jujaka and his own sweet children. He can see that the horrid Brahmin was his beloved child in many previous lives, only now fallen into selfishness and confusion.

If you have mixed reactions to this story despite its happy ending, you are not alone. When the fable is performed as a passion play at festivals in Buddhist countries, people often find it highly controversial. They hate Jujaka of course, and they're thrilled when things turn out right in the end. But they find the idea that Vessantara should give away his children too much to take. They view it as monastic propaganda, inhuman, unrealistic, and just plain wrong. You yourself might be thinking right now, "How ridiculous! I would never give up my family, nor should I be expected to do so! If that's what it takes to be generous, who needs enlightenment?"

Don't worry. Personally, I deeply share these sentiments. I have a beloved family, too, after all! Yet intellectually, logically, I can't help but recognize the underlying value of and need for boundless generosity. We will not have peace on Earth, nor will we be able to build a buddhaverse, until we are capable of forgiving people even for harming our nearest and dearest. Ultimately, of course, no one living in a true buddhaverse would ever ask us for our children or spouse. But we must be willing to give them away in principle. Why? Because only when we are generous to the fullest, most selfless degree can we be completely free and happy. Then we won't need to ask for anything, because we will all effortlessly, thoughtlessly share. Wouldn't that be a wonderful way to live? Isn't that a goal worth setting for our community of living beings?

Problem: Dissatisfaction

Our selfishness expresses itself as stinginess, greed, and, above all, dissatisfaction. We live with a constant sense of somehow being deprived, no matter how much we have. When Mick Jagger sings that he "can't get no satisfaction," we all understand what he means. Habitual selfishness makes us think that we will be satisfied if we can hoard everything we have and watch it grow. But then we are surprised when we do not feel content. As soon as we feel temporarily secure about our possessions, we worry about losing them. And we begin to think about how nice it would be to have more—something else or someone else's. When we cannot have "more" right away, we become dissatisfied with what we do have. We become obsessed with the next acquisition, the next target. Therefore, as we accumulate things, experiences, relationships, and attainments, we only get more desperate. Having more only causes us to want more. We can never have enough to feel truly satisfied. Each rise we top reveals a further succession of mountain peaks we have yet to scale.

It seems that everyone wants to win the lottery. We are conditioned to view it as the ultimate solution to all of our problems. "If only I had one million, two million . . . okay, maybe twenty million dollars, then I could be truly happy," we say to ourselves. And yet there is absolutely no validity to this belief. Psychologists have conducted extensive research demonstrating that after people win the lottery, they are actually *less* happy than they were before. The winners, after a year or so, realize that money does not, in fact, solve their problems. In fact, it creates them. They buy a new home, a new car, they pay off their credit card debt, and they think life will be beautiful. But they're stuck with the same old insecurities they had before, as well as some new ones. They suddenly find themselves surrounded by people claiming to be their friends who are really just looking for ways to get a piece of the pie. Winning tons of money, it turns out, is an incredibly frustrating and disillusioning experience for all but the most balanced individuals. It proves the extent to which we are forever dissatisfied.

The infinite life insight enables your awareness of your interconnection with other beings, since they and you have been intertwined in interaction in various life-forms for an infinite amount of time. You took rebirth in this human lifetime by taking advantage of the presence of your father's seed in the womb of your mother, when you merged with them, all three of you transcending boundaries in the intensity of passion. You grew bigger and defined your human form by absorbing energy and nutrients from her body and building your cells of bone and flesh and nerves and sense organs. Once born outside, others held you, fed you, cleaned you, protected you day by day, year by year. Your sense of well-being came from your deep knowledge of your interconnection with the beings who cared for you. You only learned to perceive yourself as a being apart by learning from others the terms of perception and thought.

Selfishness stems from our habit of perceiving ourselves as separate, unique beings. Because we see our fixed selves as independent, we often feel alone, sad, and insecure, dwarfed by the vast world out there. How can we possibly stand on our own against the immense universe? We try to reconnect with others, but do so without questioning our intrinsic separateness. So we end up trying to absorb as much as we can of the world around us, imagining that by attaining things and people we can make ourselves feel bigger and more secure, better able to stand up to the universe. If we can devour enough of the universe, then we will have nothing to fear, and we will therefore know contentment and happiness. Or so we think.

But this is senseless. How could finite things added up together ever possibly come to equal or match infinity? You can easily recognize the futility of this approach. The more you get, the stronger you temporarily feel, but also the better able you are to perceive the vastness of the universe and the fact that you'll never catch up. It's as if you have an insatiable appetite: the more you eat,. the bigger your appetite gets, and the more you need to eat. It's a never-ending process. That is why there is no safety, no satisfaction to be found.

Fortunately, there comes a moment when we finally realize that we'll never have enough. At that time, we begin to search for another way to satisfy our appetites. We understand intuitively that there must be another route to the island of contentment, another art of happiness. And there is. The key to it is recognizing that true satisfaction lies within us and not in the exterior world, the possession of things, or even relationships with other people.

The moment you begin to let go of your attachment to things, you feel a sense of freedom, like you've emerged into the air after a long tumble under a wave and can finally breathe again. Isn't it a joy to know that you don't need to buy that shirt you saw in the store window yesterday? Isn't it a relief to know that moving into a bigger house won't make you happier? You don't need to earn more money or go deeper into debt. Instead of allowing yourself to be consumed by thoughts of what you don't have, you can actually sit back and appreciate what you do have. Spend a few minutes counting your blessings: Family, friends, freedom, health, interests, time to contemplate your life and question the choices you're making. What do human beings really need, after all? Basic shelter, sustenance, safety, and freedom. You have all those things. You are so fortunate! You have every reason to be content.

We have all known people in our time who seem untouched by the events taking place around them, unmoved by society's expectations of them, and not needing to acquire wealth, power, or fame. Such people are generally content, are they not? Look at His Holiness the Dalai Lama, for example. When the Chinese invaded Tibet decades ago, his peaceful country and its magnificent culture were all but destroyed, and many of his dearest friends and family were tortured and killed. He has lived in exile ever since. And yet still he finds it in his heart to love all humanity. He teaches tolerance and forgiveness. And he exudes inner peace. He does not need fancy clothes or homes to be happy. He gets his satisfaction not from material goods but from his insight, his faith, and his deep and powerful compassion, which he devotes to sharing with others.

We can learn from these sorts of people, these buddhas and bodhisattvas. And what's more, we ourselves can become living examples to others. We can look to ourselves as the true source of our happiness or unhappiness. Many events in life may be beyond our control, but our approach and attitude are totally up to us. We can choose to be dissatisfied, always wanting more, or we can choose to be generous, appreciating what we do have and sharing as much as possible with others. This turn from outward to inward sources of contentment is an essential step on our path to infinite life.

Practice: Reaching Out

In the previous chapter, "Wisdom," you learned to develop a critical reversal of your habitual awareness, looking carefully at your sense of having a fixed, identifiable "self" and getting used to the idea of your intrinsic freedom in selflessness. As this awareness becomes more natural, the relativity of your sense of self becomes more apparent, and you begin to feel deeply your total interconnectedness with other beings. The more you become aware of this intimate bond with all life, the happier you feel.

At the same time, your sense of interconnection brings with it deep compassion for others' pain. If they are suffering, then you suffer, too. So you want to alleviate their suffering. You want to give them any material goods that they might need, offer them reassurance, and free them from their own misplaced anxieties. Most of all, you want to give them happiness. When you reflect that your own newfound happiness comes from understanding the nature of selflessness, you want to give them the Dharma. You realize that teaching others the liberating Dharma is the supreme form of giving.

Each time you increase your attitude of generosity, you must break through the entrenched habits of selfishness, greed, and dissatisfaction. You have to overcome the feeling that you still need this thing, that you just don't know if the other person deserves your gift, or that you at least should get something in return. The best way to deal with these entrenched habits is to proceed step by step, gradually developing better habits. It is useless to pump yourself up on the greatness of generosity in theory, but then actually give away something precious and spend the rest of your day regretting it. Your regret will only set your attempts to develop the transcendent virtue of generosity back more than your initial gift set it forward.

This meditation provides an excellent and proven method for unleashing your innate, bodhisattva-like generosity. Open your mind, and your generous words and acts naturally will follow. The great eighth-century Buddhist teacher Shantideva offers us an outstanding example of what we are trying to attain with this practice when he says, "Transcendent generosity is a state of mind. If I wanted to walk around the world, I could not possibly find enough leather to cover the surface of the earth. But just covering the soles of my shoes with leather works even better. Likewise, I could not possibly transform all bad things outside in the world. But if I can transform this mind of mine, what need do I have to transform everything else?"

There are three main types of generosity: the generosity of giving material goods, the generosity of giving protection to the defenseless, and the generosity of giving the Dharma, teachings that enable beings to realize freedom on their own. Some people add a fourth type: the generosity of love. But in truth all kinds of giving, in order to be transcendent and meritorious, must be motivated by love. So most teachers view love as an intrinsic part of generosity. We will work on developing all three types of generosity in this practice.

Begin by setting yourself up in your meditation shrine. Reflect on what you have mastered of the selflessness practice from the last chapter. Deepen your sense of your own and all things' lack of intrinsic reality. Remember the feeling of melting into spacelike voidness, and of then reemerging into the dreamlike aftermath. Taste the bliss of knowing the magical, illusory nature of all apparently solid objects and beings. Then focus your compassion on others who are suffering due to their lack of knowledge of reality.

Let your joy well up in your heart like a diamond light. Visualize it radiating outward in all directions, refracting through the prism of the diversity of the world into rainbow light rays. These beams of happiness and true knowledge—laser-like yet almost liquid, flowing gently and brilliantly—permeate the environment and penetrate the minds of all sensitive beings.

Notice that most beings remain unaware of the blessings they are receiving from these powerful light rays. They are too wrapped up in their misguided vision of reality. Take note of their actual circumstances. Many live in extremely difficult situations of poverty, war, or addiction. Even those people who, at first glance, seem to be well off physically experience inside their minds bitterly anxious fantasies. Worrying about the terrible things that could befall them or their loved ones, they experience either constant inner agitation or deep depression.

Now you are going to visualize bringing the three types of generosity to bear for all these people. As you do so, remember to take your time and keep reflecting back on your well of bliss energy. Then slowly return to the suffering beings, imagining what you can do to help them one situation at a time. Do not feel that you need to implement the entire meditation described below in a single sitting. You may well choose to spend an entire practice session applying your generosity to the situation of a single person. You can always expand your vision to other beings in other sessions. Remember, this and all practices in the book are the work of your infinite life. Eventually, even if not until your future lives, you will have time to actually embrace all beings with your boundless generosity.

First, practice the generosity of material comfort. Imagine helping those afflicted by poverty by giving them what they need. You are able to emanate real, effective, short-term and long-term helpers of all kinds. Imagine convoys of pilots, truck drivers, and powerful guards who successfully deliver tons of delicious food from places where there is abundance to places where there is not enough. Picture corps of engineers with heavy equipment who dig wells and excavate irrigation ditches, plant forests, and construct shelters. Envision agricultural experts who bring seeds, organic fertilizer, and recovered topsoil to farmers, then help them plant and cultivate their land. Use whatever knowledge you have of modern technologies such as solar cells for powering ovens, heating houses and water to picture saving forests and regenerating local climates. Emanate investigative reporters, aid officials, and honest government leaders who discover the truth about how the poor and weak are being exploited, and rectify the situation. Imagine even corrupt officials, who have diverted previous aid into their own pockets, helping out because you have offered them special sensitivity training so that they can understand the pain they have inflicted and vow to change their ways. In this way, visualize slowly transforming even the seemingly most hopeless slum or destitute area into a garden of abundance and self-sufficiency, a beacon of prosperity.

I recently saw on WorldLink TV, an excellent satellite station, a model for this generosity meditation. They were broadcasting a documentary about a charity based in Belfast, Northern Ireland. The charity heard about an orphanage for disabled girls in Moldova, a small country located between Romania and Russia. In the orphanage, two hundred girls and their caretakers lived in the most appalling conditions of gut-wrenching squalor and disease, bitter cold, and food deprivation approaching starvation. The girls were skeletal, their eyes hopeless, like concentration camp inmates. On average, one of them was dying every week.

The charity corresponded with the management of the orphanage, offering their assistance. They put together a convoy of trucks with food and supplies, and sent it over with a team of plumbers, electricians, carpenters, nurses, and aid veterans. Sadly, when they arrived at the orphanage after driving across Europe, the charity team discovered that the orphanage management was corrupt. The people in charge immediately locked up the food and supplies, and then stalled bureaucratically. They hoped to wait until the aid team went home, then sell the charity items on the black market, leaving the girls as destitute as ever and pocketing the money for themselves.

But the charity team was not so easily deceived. They found out from the kind caretakers, who'd been terrorized into submission, that the management had stolen the supplies of previous aid missions. And they wouldn't give up their efforts to help the girls. The aid team stayed in Moldova far longer than they'd planned, keeping up pressure on the corrupted management and eventually getting government officials involved. They went to work without waiting for permits, installing a heating system and washing machines. They renovated the playroom and replaced the horrendous, urine-soaked, crumbling mattresses. In a brave maneuver, they even burned the children's old clothes, forcing the management to release the new clothes that had been locked away.

In spite of all they did, the aid workers couldn't force the replacement of the corrupt director and top staff members. Still they persisted, approaching the government again and again. Finally, they succeeded in getting a meeting with the president of the country! When he saw the horrifying pictures of the girls living in such desperate conditions, he promised swift action and he delivered. He fired the director and his cronies, putting in people who really cared about doing their job. The charity's hard work was finally rewarded. The disabled girls finally had a prospect for a decent life. A horrible situation had been alleviated.

I describe this documentary at length because it serves as an illustration of just how detailed and complex your meditation can be, relating to real situations across the globe. I also like it because it destroys several of our stereotypes about the world around us. Our media usually depict Northern Ireland as a hopelessly violent place where people constantly kill each other due to religious differences. It also tends to depict places such as Moldova as black holes of despair and inhumanity created by decades of communist dictatorship and corrupt government. In this story, however, the Northern Irish were the living bodhisattvas of generosity, and the people of Moldova were greatly enriched by their assistance. Finally, this example teaches us not to shy away from even the most complicated and difficult circumstances in our quest to alleviate suffering.

Do not accept any situation as hopeless. You can imagine a solution to every problem. Visualize yourself helping beings even as they die. Emanate nurses, doctors, psychologists, and monks to found hospices that provide palliative care for those who cannot be saved and need instruction about how to die well. Imagine yourself as a spiritual guide who finds the subtle body-minds of the departed souls and ushers them through the between-state, helping them reach a positive rebirth. Imagine sending out instructors to teach even the most miserly how to develop a generous heart of giving. Be as skillful as you can in your meditation on the giving of material goods and assistance.

Next, use your increasing skills in visualization to work on the second type of generosity: the practice of giving protection, security, and freedom from fear to beings who are oppressed, tortured, and terrorized. First picture the world's 137 currently active war zones, where people are committing atrocities against one another daily as we sit here calmly meditating. See into homes across the globe where women, children, and also men are suffering from domestic violence and abuse. Imagine all those people slaving in labor camps, living under dictatorships, and unjustly incarcerated due to race, economic class, beliefs, unjust laws, or unfortunate circumstances.

You can also focus your attention on beings in the animal kingdom who need your protection. Picture endangered species on the verge of extinction as a result of environmental degradation, drought, habitat loss, or human predation. Visualize domesticated animals being treated inhumanely when raised for food production, overburdened in work situations, or abused as pets.

Imagining these violent scenes will open you up to the terror carried within the minds of so many beings, human and animal. Now let your heart's freedom-bliss shine forth, bringing peace to the frightened. Visualize yourself creating fierce guardians who shield the weaker from the stronger. Your powerful legions offer protection and diminish fear, calming troubled homes, neighborhoods, regions, and entire countries. Picture the entire planet encased within a grid of protective energy created by the compassion of infinite enlightened beings. This grid detects the presence of fear and rage, manifests barriers between the violent and their prey, and encases the vulnerable within impenetrable force fields that ward off blows, projectiles, blades, and even harsh threats. It brings empathy to the consciences of the aggressors, making them self-aware, causing them to relent, repent, and seek to heal. As you do this, feel the relief radiating from the hearts of the almost incredulous beings you have saved, who are experiencing safety, peace, and calm for the first time in many years.

A final meditation on the generosity of giving material things and of giving protection is the ancient rite of "giving away the cosmos" ("offering the cosmic mandala," as it is called). Visualize yourself as a bodhisattva in the inconceivable liberation—like a comic book hero, Superwoman or Captain Marvel—gigantic in dimensions, so huge that you can see the entire planet Earth like a little ball, the size of a softball, the opalescent green and blue and iridescent cloud-white globe seen in pictures from space. Cast your imagination's eyes upward to the enlightened blessing and protecting beings above you in your shrine-sky, and imagine yourself picking up the cosmic globe within your two hands and offering it aloft. Recite quietly, "O enlightened beings, teachers, mentors, buddhas and bodhisattvas, gods and goddesses, here is this beautiful planet Earth turning on its great axis, with all its oceans, lands, mountains, plains, forests, deserts, valleys, lakes and rivers, cities and villages, farms and gardens, environments of creatures great and small, with all its beauties, beautiful vistas, heavenly music, delicious foods, sweet scents, smooth textures—I take it up in mind, let go of all sense of ownership, and offer it all to you! Please accept and care for it and all of us, the beings on it, in your wisdom and compassion!" You can recite the ancient mantra that millions of practitioners have used with this visualization, *Idam guru ratna mandalakam niryatayami,* roughly, "I hereby release this jewel cosmos into your care, o enlightened teachers!" Use the Sanskrit syllables as much as you can, as it resonates magnificently with countless millions before you who have entered the infinite lifestyle and countless millions who will come after.

Finally, meditate on the third and most noble type of generosity—the intention to make the gift of the Dharma, the liberating truth that gives all beings access to the nurturing reality of freedom. It is wonderful that you can help so many suffering beings by imaginatively giving them an abundance of material goods and protection from harm. But now visualize people who already have wealth and security. Notice how they are still not satisfied, how they still suffer, if perhaps more subtly, with addictions that only increase when their basic needs are met and with anxieties that survive despite the fact that their basic external security is assured. When you do, you realize that those poor, terrorized beings that you have been helping are not the only ones who need your help. All people, regardless of circumstances, are capable of immense suffering.

What is it that people need in order to overcome their suffering? Think of your own experience. Recognize that knowledge and awareness make the biggest difference—the knowledge of the true freedom that is selflessness, the awareness that inner happiness comes from understanding your interconnectedness to all life. How can you help people get this knowledge, which you and I have been so fortunate to discover? It won't help just to preach at them, because they cannot get it merely from believing what you tell them. They must understand it for themselves. So you must truly educate them. Education in this sense means not lecturing, forcing, or dictating, but rather *drawing out* their wisdom from within themselves. You should seek to evoke their own innate intelligence, the inner compassion of their own hearts, the concentrated awareness of their own minds, so that they can by themselves and for themselves understand the reality of their world.

Belief alone cannot transform a person for long—in fact, too often it leads to fanaticism and greater insecurity. Conditioned habits alone cannot change the inner quality of a person's experience, since the egocentric person will cling to good habits as doggedly as to bad ones, and will still be cut off from free reality, still be seething underneath with unsatisfied longings and nameless fears. So beings can only be saved from their core suffering of self-enclosure by a new understanding of reality. They must themselves experience the broadening awareness and increasing happiness that arise from liberated understanding, and the natural goodness, ease and friendliness, love and compassion that effortlessly arise from them.

Reflecting in this way, visualize educating the great masses of egocentric, deluded beings, confused about self and other, rushing headlong after happiness while unknowingly using means that instead condemn them to even greater suffering. Visualize your heart's blissful diamond light rays shining toward them all and let their inclinations refract them into rainbow energy that forms itself into every kind of teacher—spiritual leader, schoolteacher, professional instructor, coach, therapist, whatever each particular individual most needs. Teach people in the manner most appropriate to their level of ability and insight by enrolling them in institutions, classes, programs, meditation retreats, or one-on-one sessions. Visualize this teaching activity in a leisurely fashion and in great detail, with a powerful sense of reasoned faith, as you did with your previous two generosity meditations.

Don't worry that you don't yet understand the enlightenment principles well enough to teach them to others: what you don't know, the virtues you don't fully command, the buddhas and bodhisattvas of the infinite universe do know and command. Their vast insight and highly developed art suffuse and energize your words, thoughts, and deeds, making your teachings extremely helpful in guiding others to higher awareness.

As you practice the three types of generosity, you may at times feel bogged down, too exhausted to continue focusing on all the details of your visualizations. This is a perfectly natural response. When it happens, take a break and rest in the immense compassion of the angelic buddhas and bodhisattvas, such as the angelic, compassionate bodhisattvas Avalokitesvara, Tara, and Manjushri, the prince of wisdom. Imagine these enlightened beings using their fully evolved, infinite energies to accomplish the generous acts you've been picturing. Relax in your awareness of their blessings and constant miraculous activity. If you prefer to think of Jesus, the Virgin Mary, Muhammad, Khizr, Krishna, Lao-tzu, or any other beneficent being from whatever your religion or belief system, that's perfectly fine, too. In fact, making your vision personally meaningful allows your rest to be even more effective. All these beings are really emanations of the same divine force of love and compassion that suffuses every atom of the universe, anyway. The point is simply for you to recharge yourself so that you can return to your generosity practice.

Personal Performance: Sharing Yourself

It's important to realize that performing generous acts does not mean giving mindlessly, indulging everyone with everything they want whether it is good for them or not. In your practice of this virtue, you should strive to behave like a loving parent who cherishes yet carefully avoids spoiling his or her children. You know that if you give in to their every whim, you will only weaken them by making them selfish and unable to cope with a harsh "real world" that will not be so indulgent. So always think skillfully about what people really want, helping them avoid trivial and unsatisfying preoccupations. Make an effort to give them objects and opportunities that will prove truly beneficial in the long term.

Our wise mentor Shantideva says, "Whatever I do, always and anywhere, for myself and for the sake of others, I must strive to implement the teachings." We have already taken an essential step toward establishing the transcendent virtue of generosity in our lives by visualizing all that we may do for the poor, the oppressed, and the misguided. However, if we want to achieve a truly radical transformation, it is not enough for us just to meditate. We must put our practice into action, performing generous deeds in our day-to-day interactions with others.

In order to be generous with others, you must first learn to be generous with yourself. How can you develop the automatic habit of giving if you are unforthcoming with your own needs? This doesn't mean that you should indulge yourself in addictive ways, but only that you should be sure to treat yourself well. For example, are you always running around frantically doing things for your job and your family, feeding yourself nothing but hasty bites of sandwiches made with dubious meats and chemically grown vegetables, munching chips and sweets on the side, and washing it all down with gulps of coffee and soda, or forgetting to eat at all? Do you work incessantly, only stopping when you're exhausted? Is the sole form of relaxation you afford yourself the mental relief of mindless channel-surfing, allowing random suggestions, feelings, and ideas to implant themselves in your head when you are at your most vulnerable? Do you live unquestioningly in the vise grip of an inner monologue of self-preoccupation, letting nagging images of the past and anxious concerns about the future dominate your life, preventing you from becoming aware of this precious, present moment? How can you expect to treat other people, animals, and the earth well if you are letting your own body and mind be abused in such ways?

Being generous with yourself means maintaining a certain quality of diet, recognizing that your body needs balanced, poison-free, and pleasant nutrition to flourish. Being generous with yourself means exercising in a steady and zestful, but not frantic, style. Being generous with yourself means taking time off from your work, no matter how important it is, to contemplate your existence. Being generous with yourself means regularly engaging in activities to lower your stress level, such as meditation, yoga, massage, hot baths, or reading. Being generous with yourself means taking your attention and energy away from unrealistic inner monologues and directing it toward your own best interests, which often means being more concerned with the interests of others.

All in all, being generous with yourself means securing a perimeter of physical, mental, and emotional comfort within which you feel healthier and more relaxed, and are less self-preoccupied than you were before. When you do this, you can feel the energy of hope arising within you. You believe truly that things can change for the better, that the world can be transformed, and that you can play a critical role in making this happen through your own actions.

Now that you have successfully nurtured yourself, you can practice generosity with others. Think about what your friends and family might want and need, and try to give it to them skillfully, especially if it is helpful to them. Use various excuses to offer them assistance in unobtrusive ways. Surprise them with little gifts here and there. During the holiday season, which provides such an excellent opportunity for giving in our culture (despite the fact that it has been irritatingly commercialized), choose presents thoughtfully. Reflect carefully about what each person would truly find most interesting and useful. As you get older and, hopefully, wiser, you can plan ahead better. Long before the holiday shopping madness starts, have your secret closet ready with the appropriate gifts already purchased or made. Every year at Christmastime, I end up wishing

I'd taken more time to think about what my loved ones really wanted so that I wouldn't have to run around at the last minute grabbing a bunch of things that might or might not satisfy them. Also, remember that some of the best gifts are things you make yourself, made precious by your investment of time and creative energy.

It's equally important to be generous in your relationship with your life partner, if you have one. You have to be able not only to give yourself to your beloved, but also to allow your beloved to give him- or herself away. In other words, you must recognize and rejoice in the ultimate freedom of your beloved. If you cannot, it means that your love, your wish for the happiness of the other, is constricted by an element of possessiveness. "I love you and I really want you to be happy," you say to your beloved, "as long as you are mine!" Oops! Where did that last statement come from? Clearly not from a place of true generosity!

This reminds me of the famous test devised by the wise King Solomon to discover who was the true mother of a child that two women were both claiming as their own. He offered to cut the child in half to satisfy both. Thus, he determined that the real mother was not the one who accepted his offer; it was the one who let the boy go. The false mother would have killed the child in her attempt to possess him. The real mother, on the other hand, only wanted her boy to remain unharmed, no matter what the cost to her. This is the profound paradox of generosity—the paradox of love. "If you love someone, set them free," sings Sting in his famous ballad. The more you care, the more you need to give what you care about away.

In addition to performing kind acts that influence those who are close to you, you can practice generosity in a mass context, as well. You can influence more than just the people who form your immediate social circle. An easy and effective way to begin is this: when a beggar comes toward you with a hand or cup outstretched, overcome your impulse to avoid the person or recoil. Instead, give some money, no matter how little. Offer a quarter, a nickel, or even a penny. If you honestly have no money on you, share a smile or a pleasant word, even if the beggar acts annoyed with you. Do this with an easy attitude—don't think of your giving as a big deal. Over time, you may even come to consider it a privilege.

Similarly, when you get appeals in the mail from legitimate groups making an effort to improve the state of the world, such as charities collecting money for children in the U.S. or abroad, environmental organizations, or political accountability movements, you should welcome the opportunity to give. If these organizations and their efforts check out, send them even a small donation, again without thinking it a big deal. If you absolutely cannot afford to help many causes, send positive thoughts and wish their efforts well.

Next, you can make a commitment to giving back to your society by resolving to participate in politics. This doesn't mean that you need to run for office; you can start simply by voting. In Europe today, more than 90 percent of the population participates in every election. But sadly, in America, the supposed worldwide bastion of democracy, less than half of all eligible voters actually make the effort to vote. Often it is the most idealistic among us who get disgusted with the system and drop out first, leaving the most selfish, unrealistic people to determine how we spend our resources.

Give yourself time to study the issues, the candidates and their networks of supporters, their honesty and likely effectiveness in implementing beneficial policies. Then vote as best you can. You must participate in the process because you are inevitably a part of your larger society and therefore responsible, to a certain extent, for what it does. If you feel torn over whom or what to vote for, remember that the lesser of two evils is just that, a lesser evil. A bit less evil is a good thing, there's no denying it. Offer the generous gift of your enlightened understanding to prevent your government from implementing greedy, ignorant, and violent policies.

Stay engaged all the time in your government, informing yourself about what your leaders are doing. Support them when you think they are right and criticize them appropriately when you think they are wrong. Political participation offers an invaluable opportunity to share material goods, protection of those in need, and enlightenment teachings. If 100 percent of Americans fully involved themselves in this way, I have no doubt that our nation would become an immense force for good in the world, rather than a problem in many respects.

There is the opportunity for heroism in your performance of generosity. A Buddhist tale tells of a bodhisattva who feeds a starving mother tigress and her four cubs by jumping off a cliff into her lair, sacrificing his own body as food. Contrary to what modern skeptics believe, such heroism is not uncommon in this day and age. Many people successfully deprogram their selfishness and reprogram themselves in altruistic and heroic ways. Look at the way emergency workers regularly sacrifice their lives for others, like the brave members of the New York City Fire Department who died to save the innocent victims of the September 11 terrorist attacks. Everyone, even children, can be educated to break out of the prison of self-concern and live at a heroic level of altruistic generosity and self-transcendence.

However, you should not push your heroism too far, especially if you are just learning to put generosity into practice in your own life. Let's say that you have been on a meditation retreat contemplating the story of the bodhisattva who gave his life to the tigress and her cubs. If you encountered a similar situation at that precise moment, you might transcend your normal reactions and fling your life away in a passionate, heroic gesture to save them. *This would be foolish—not generous.* Certainly your intentions would have been generous, in that you were fully aiming for heroic compassion in your mind. But your act would be ungenerous to yourself and to other beings because you would have not yet become fully enlightened. As a perfect buddha, you could become a being capable of feeding millions of tigresses. Even with a little deeper practice, you could found a Tiger Society to feed the animals across the globe. You must give yourself time in this life with your newfound wisdom to develop justice, patience, creativity, and serenity. Don't cut short the excellent opportunity for practice and accelerated evolution that you have right now by leaping too readily to the ultimate generosity, which is self-sacrifice.

Shantideva says that there will come a time when you have deepened your wisdom and expanded your compassion to such a transcendent degree that sacrificing your life for the sake of others will be pure joy. You will be so completely assured of the fact that dying is merely a means of traversing from this existence to the next that you won't mind giving away your body. You will see the process simply as changing costumes in a play, then emerging onstage as a new character. When you have reached this point, you will have come very close to fulfilling the supreme evolutionary purpose of living, to achieving the blissful, altruistic state of buddhahood. Then, your every breath will be filled with generosity, your every cell will be a gift to all sensitive beings, and your compassion will enfold the world in a perfect environment of happiness and peace. Until then, small steps such as the ones suggested above—being thoughtful in your attitude and approach to loved ones, giving donations to people and organizations in need, participating in government—will help you genuinely share yourself in ways that will spread the light and love of the infinite life all around you.

Societal Performance: Transforming Consumerism

Bodhisattvas often want to be reborn as kings and queens or merchants who spend their lifetimes accumulating vast fortunes so that they can practice generosity on a broad social scale. Capitalism, viewed from their compassionate perspective, does not signify the greedy consumption of resources. It doesn't necessarily mean depriving others by hoarding wealth for your own good. In fact, the capitalist system was started by selfless monks who made objects of worship, beauty, and utility out of love and sold them to earn money for projects benefiting the entire community, keeping very little of what they earned for themselves. Since they produced much more than they consumed, they generated wealth that spread throughout their society and on to future generations.

When viewed in the best possible light, the capitalist practices of merchants imitate those of the monks. Merchants who produce more than they consume accumulate wealth that can be saved and invested, producing yet more wealth. This money spreads throughout society as the merchants hire people to work in their shops, build them homes and offices, and sell them luxury items. If motivated by generosity, the merchants have the ultimate goal of creating fortunes for their posterity so that their children can enjoy better lives. They operate with self-restraint, resisting the urge for immediate consumption.

Of course, this rosy picture does not always correspond with the reality of the situation. Capitalistic wealth can be self-indulgently squandered. It also creates power, which can be used for totally selfish purposes. All too many unwise, confused people think that wealth should be hoarded and used to spoil oneself by overconsuming to the maximum degree. Even when they have more money than they could possibly spend, they never believe they have enough.

Unfortunately, our consumer culture teaches us to use and abuse our wealth in this negative fashion. And as the wealthiest nation on Earth, our bad habits are destroying our planet. Those of us in the "first world" live off of the misfortunes of those in the "third world"—our corporations take advantage of low-cost labor and we reap the benefits in nice, inexpensive goods. We purchase food and clothing derived from products that are mass-produced and chemically treated. We are wasteful in our consumption of natural resources. Even though we have found totally acceptable and reliable alternative sources of energy such as solar and wind power, we don't take advantage of them. We eat too much meat, the production of which abuses animals and overuses land and food that could be put to better use. Our overconsumption is ruining our environment, changing weather patterns, and burning holes in the very atmosphere that has enabled life to flourish on our planet.

We are hurting ourselves on a financial level, as well. Despite the fact that America enjoys the highest mean income level of any nation, we also have one of the lowest savings rates. We constantly spend beyond our means, building up credit card debt instead of wisely setting aside some of our vast stores of wealth for our children and giving the rest away to those in need. In the end, we find ourselves even more dissatisfied because of our poor financial habits.

Of course, these statements are not true of everyone. Some people are careful to reduce their use of nonrenewable energy sources, eat vegetarian and organic foods, recycle, and live modestly, even boycotting multinational corporations that have poor track records in other countries. But not enough of us act generously. In general, our society is perfectly willing to consume away.

It is not my goal to simply lay down a huge guilt trip about our standard and style of living. That would be ineffective and incorrect. But by the same token, we in the first world cannot tell those in the third world who are striving to elevate themselves materially, to earn some money so that they can buy a few possessions and feel some financial security, that they are wrong to do so. We love to lecture newly industrializing nations about how they are choking us with their pollution, destroying their rainforests, and ruining their natural beauty, when we have already done these things ourselves. There has to be a better way.

We, as a society, should make a move from consumerism to spirituality. However enlightened, however generous we may be, however much good we do in our immediate circle, we must wake up to the essence of our societal consumption neurosis. Unless we take action now, we will have to pay for what we are doing, which will make life harder for us and most especially for our children.

We should try to instill the value of "quality over quantity": we can compensate for the diminishing quantity of our consumption in every sense by enhancing the quality of our experiences. We can cultivate ways of enjoying fewer things more intensely, while at the same time continuing to practice our meditation from earlier in the book on developing the mind of generosity. This will increase our sense of freedom and detachment, leading to inner contentment. This cultivation of a sense of satisfaction with what you are and what you have is the key to overcoming selfishness and consumerism on the societal level.

You can have an immediate impact on your society by trying to reduce your own selfish consumption of material goods. The next time you want to buy a new item, think carefully about it first. Consider whether or not you really need it. If you decide to make the purchase, do so consciously, with not just your own wants and needs but the welfare of the entire society and even world in mind. Meditate for even a short while on how fortunate you are to be able to afford something new. You can do this practice in relation to any consumer item: a piece of fashionable clothing, a car, or a fancy vacation. It is also good to remember that inevitably, you will offer this object to others, in one way or another. So mentally offer it right away—and if it's not worth offering to another, it's not worth offering to yourself.

When you are mindful of your purchasing habits in this way, they will automatically tend to decrease. You'll discover that you can separate the contentment you'd previously associated with the desired object from the object itself, and you'll begin to find contentment within yourself. In so doing, you'll help your entire society become a little less constrained by its rabid, thoughtless, and ultimately unsatisfactory addiction to consuming.

Wouldn't it be great if, instead of obsessing over the consumption of goods, our culture focused instead on generosity? What if we thought as much about our contribution to our own development and the well-being of others as we did about the latest dress design or car model? What if, instead of plastering pictures of semi-clad women on billboards everywhere to sell moisturizing lotion, advertisers suddenly posted commercials showing the peace that you can find from helping others? What if television commercials asked us to question our self-centered beliefs and donate to worthy causes rather than mindlessly commanding us to buy? It could happen, you know. Businesses would discover that it was more profitable to share their money than to pocket it. Everyone's top priority would be to educate others about their freedom and potential for inner happiness.

A simplicity movement has begun to take hold in the U.S. in recent years. More and more people are rejecting traditional consumerism. Fed up with the pressure and widespread discontent of modern life, they're looking to yoga and meditation, simple communal living, alternative medicine, and spirituality rather than commercial products for the answers to their problems. They're saying, "No, thank you" to the entire concept of "keeping up with the Joneses." This is a positive sign. A spiritual revolution is beginning. By practicing generosity, we can contribute to it. We can share more of ourselves, lessen our own addiction to consumerism, and help our society evolve.

5

Justice

Preamble

We have begun to expand our awareness by deepening our wisdom. We open things up bit by bit by looking critically at the confines of our habitual worldview and the lonely world of isolation it maintains around us. We are energized to do this in a long-term, sustainable way by having entered into the personally revolutionary context of our infinite life. We feel an urgent need to expand our horizons and experience the wider world beyond our habitual expectations. It has dawned on us that if we keep on unconsciously creating a confining world, there will be no limit to our imprisonment within it. It can become more and more unpleasant without end—even death will not release us from our fabrications. So we must work with the utmost care to open our world and free ourselves. We must improve our situation bit by bit in every tiny but massively significant way.

A wonderful verse in the *Royal Meditation Sutra* describes this process:

Things made from cause and conditions are ultimately not made—
Examining causality, you know things' freedom from intrinsic reality,
Understanding freedom, the more you are mindful of every little thing.

What I love about this verse—and the process it describes—is that it does not indulge our unconscious tendency to escapism. It discourages our wish to look for a big escape from all problems in some la-la land of heavenly bliss or at least in a securely anesthetic, negative nirvana, imagined as nothingness. It is tempting to imagine the experience of freedom to be a sort of flying away into the infinite sky of sublime aloofness, like a giant goofy dissolving bird. Unfortunately, many "spiritual" sayings can be interpreted as indicating this. Maybe that is what will happen to some, for a while—who knows for sure. However, it is simply logical that relational things are doomed to remain relational. A person, an experience, a state—all these are relational; and their natures or aspects that can be felt as freedoms are also relational—they must be relational in order to be experienced. When we embrace our infinite life, obviously its infinity is not that which we can embrace. We embrace its relational reality, moment by moment. Simultaneously staying both aware of its infinity and engaged with its changing continuum, we embrace these moments more lightly.

We enhance such lightness of embrace by developing detachment, contentment, and generosity. Our awareness of impermanence, change, and freedom intensifies with each experience of separation—instead of waiting to separate from things by losing them, we develop our freedom by letting go of them voluntarily, enjoying the pleasure of giving them away. The more we give, the more others open up to their connection to us, seeing us less as a danger, an obstacle, and more as a benefit, a resource. This brings back to us more than we can give in the long run, and this process intensifies the less we think about it or expect it and the more natural and free our attitude is toward possessions and relations.

Expanding awareness of momentary causal processes and things critically sees through fixation on any one of them being ultimately there in itself and by itself. It experiences its freedom from any fixity. This awareness of freedom does not distract us from the moment. It makes its relative feel and weight and consequence all the more significant, since its inevitable changing is driven in quality by its relative nature and structure. The concern of mindfulness is thus not only to stay aware of the ultimate freedom of infinity in each thing, but also to focus on its relative positivity or negativity. What is positive is what avoids harm and brings happiness to sensitive beings. What is negative harms and brings suffering. This brings us to the sublime virtue of justice, with its related codes of ethics and morality, and perhaps even etiquette.

The ancient enlightenment understanding of justice may bring out a new dimension in the English word, from the Latin *iustitia.* All too often nowadays, we let "justice" degrade into the meaning of "punishment." People say "I want justice!" when they merely want retaliation for injury perceived. Wisdom societies tended to recognize that justice is something far more grand, and there is also a common wisdom. I heard a West Virginia coal miner, disillusioned with the government's favoring the mine owners over the workers by sending police to break up strikes and workers' protests, say with passion in an interview, "Around here, we got plenty o' law—but we got no justice!" There is always the need for discernment and judgment, discrimination between good and evil, help and harm, benefit and detriment—but ultimately there is human sensitivity, mutual grace. The Sanskrit term Buddha used for justice in its highest sense was *sheela,* which relates to the word for "cool," and to verb roots for calming and pacifying. The word "just" in English also means "right" in the sense of "fitting." "Just right!" we say when something takes place, holds its place, in a way that is exactly harmonious with what is around it, causing minimal disturbance, positive consequence, reinforcement, lessening of stress and tension, perhaps even pleasure through its beneficence and beauty. "Just" can mean "mere" or "only," as in "just so!"—indicating a thing's aptness and sufficiency in its impact or role. This connects with the enlightened vision of things' ultimacy in their unique particularity, as in the term "thatness" (*tattvam*), or the more elusive "suchness," or "thusness" (*tathata*). So "justness" can have a metaphysical feel if we use the abstract suffix "-ness," as if its rightness, propriety, and correctness was positively "gracious," in the sense of imparting peace, calm, happiness, and well-being to all sensitive beings around it.

In this sense of its guiding beings' actions to remain graciously attuned to the nature of reality, we find in justice the effective source of ethics and morality. It is effective in guiding them because it is based on a reality that can be discovered and verified. So people can reasonably internalize such justice as a code of ethics or morality and enact it in their thoughts, words, and deeds. It thus energizes the grand system of ethics or morality that transformed enlightenment societies throughout history, bringing individuals and nations abundant blessings.

What is "ethical" is what is purposefully done, said, or thought (or *not* done, said, or thought) that fits gracefully within such justness (as attunement to reality), what is beneficent to sensitive beings, what increases the harmony of the relative world by enhancing our sensitive adaptation to it. What is "moral" is the same, though "moral" connects perhaps more to the following of rules, at best also an internalized sense of the rightness, propriety, and justness of such rules. Thus the superior ethical and moral life is not just that which follows a rigid set of rules set down by arbitrary authority and hallowed in particular traditions. These can tend to ossify as conditions change and end up sometimes accomplishing the opposite of what they originally intended. Nor is this ethical and moral life merely what seems most useful for each situation, what can be calculated from a certain perspective as accomplishing the greatest good for the greatest number. There *are* sets of rules. There *are* calculations of positive consequences. These *are* important. But ultimately it is justice, as "justness," that is the ultimate warrant and the ultimate goal of all ethics and morality. It is the sheer graciousness of justice, its conducivity to the happiness of sensitive beings that grounds the rules and guides the calculations.

For example, when Moses set forth his rule of "an eye for an eye," he was *reducing* violence in his time, since otherwise people would kill to avenge the loss of an eye, and then the other side would commit genocide on another tribe to avenge the killing, and so on. By Buddha's time in India and Jesus' time in Palestine, people were capable of greater self-control, it was too dangerous in a more urbanized setting for people to take the law into their own hands and seek their own revenge for harm, so "an eye for an eye" had become an example of something harmful, of what not to do, and both teachers taught people to respond to violence with nonviolence. The point is that a rule can be good in one setting and harmful in another, so moralities and ethics, as the internalized following of rules, have to be regrounded in justness as societies evolve.

The discovery of enlightenment is that justness can be known by wisdom. Reasonable rule-following can be recommended before such wisdom is attained, but there is no need to demand blind obedience ultimately, since wisdom can be developed by most people without too much difficulty, eventually by everyone. In the beginning it makes sense to follow the rules for body, speech, and mind set forth by the Buddha, the Jewel Teacher, and the wise leaders of the Jewel Community. The foundational set of these rules stipulates, for example, that one should minimize physically the taking of life, the taking of others' property, harmful sexual conduct, verbally lying, speaking divisively, speaking harshly, speaking meaninglessly, mentally nurturing greed, harboring malice, and entertaining unrealistic worldviews.

The opposites of these physical, verbal, and mental things not to do are the ten things to do, namely, saving lives, giving gifts, beneficial sexual behavior, telling truth, reconciling conflict, speaking sweetly, speaking meaningfully, being detached and generous, being forgiving and loving, and holding realistic views. These ten negative paths of evolution and their ten opposite positive paths are virtually the same as the basic rules of all successful religions and legal systems. For example, the Mosaic "Thou shalt not kill, steal, commit adultery" are almost the same as the three physical rules. "Thou shalt not lie, bear false witness, and blaspheme" are almost the same as three of the four verbal rules. "Thou shalt not covet, bear malice, or be idolatrous" are the almost the same as the three mental rules, though of course belief in one God is the Abrahamic form of a "realistic worldview," which is quite the opposite of the enlightenment tradition. The Hindu *Laws of Manu* and the Confucian ethical rules also contain most of these rules, each with its own slight differences.

There is another ancient logical arrangement of three kinds of justice: justice that prevents harm, justice that does good, and justice that accomplishes the aims of beings. The first two help others by not hurting them and by benefiting them in positive ways. The third helps the justly acting persons themselves by increasing their aptitude for justice, their evolutionary merit. It is important to recognize the evolutionary element here, since Western notions of justice, even modern ones, stem from a monotheistic tradition in which rules are set forth by a Creator and people are bound to obedience rewarded by that all-powerful Being from outside the world, with disobedience also punishable by Him. Modern secular ethics has dispensed with the Creator, but reward and punishment have been taken over by the state, which itself tends to assume omnipotent status if not constantly resisted.

The enlightenment understanding of nature and the biology of lifeforms is that they are not created by anyone other than themselves in interaction with others, which they have been doing since beginningless time by means of their good and bad actions of body, speech, and mind. A good action causes the being to evolve in a positive way, a bad action causes the opposite, a negative devolution. A good work-out regime increases strength and health, and prolonged inactivity causes weakness and health problems. You lift a weight and your muscle increases. You do good deeds, speak good words, think good thoughts, and your acting, speaking, and thinking muscles become stronger and healthier. In your new infinite life context, this kind of evolving change progresses limitlessly, so that incremental changes in the quality and structure of a particular life-form can lead to radical, species-changing transformations through the death and rebirth cycle. Just as exercise causes wear and tear in muscles, with certain cells dying from the exertion to be replaced by newer, stronger cells in a growing structure, so does ethical exercise lead to evolutionary change with the death of old structures to be replaced by new structures. It is important to understand that this kind of evolution can be in a negative direction as well as in a positive one. This intensifies a reasonable prudence.

In fact, in karmic biology, the human life-form emerges from experiences and actions done in previous lives when the being is embodied as various subhuman animal life-forms. The karmic evolutionary biology of the Buddha is very close to the modern Darwinian vision, except that the individual is engaged throughout as a conscious subject. While the way its details are explained may seem strange to us at first, it is necessary at least to know how the Buddha viewed them, to understand how he saw justice working as an evolutionary system.

The types of actions that result in embodiment in the human form are precisely those that are *just;* that is to say, that minimize killing, stealing, and so forth, up to hating and being unrealistic. The general characterization of the tendency of goodness is that it leads to a greater attunement with reality by becoming more and more connected to other beings and things. Thus, the lower the life-form, the more isolated it is in its individual state—the worst example being an inhabitant in one of the various hells, who feels utterly isolated and totally terrified of all contact, as all contact is experienced as painful. What Easterners call a *pretan* and Westerners a "hungry ghost" is also totally isolated in its extreme, starving sense of deprivation of food and drink, perceiving others only as potential food or as competitors for the extremely scarce nourishment available in that realm.

In the animal realm, the lower forms are less capable of connection, exhibiting defensive exterior skeletons as most insects do, reproducing by egg or by moisture, minimizing contact with others except as required for reproduction or consumption. The higher forms, the mammals, have much more contact, reproduce by a more unifying sexuality, have therefore more elaborate systems of communication, developing greater empathy with each other, the maternal and paternal altruism, and even community brother or sister bonds.

This awareness of connection reaches an apex in humans, who reproduce through relative lengthy sexual interpenetration, bear their young within their bodies for a relatively long time, and then have to nurture them in a helpless state for quite a while. They can identify with each other almost completely, feel overwhelming empathy, and communicate through complex language systems. As they move up toward enlightened states, they show that they can identify with an infinite network of life, and can move their minds even outside their bodies via vivid imagination, conscious or lucid dreaming, and nowadays also via technologies.

Sensitive beings expand their interconnectedness through attuning to one another more and more widely and sensitively. Such attunement in evolutionary action is the essence of acting justly. That is how enlightenment biology can make the claim that humanity is primarily the evolutionary result of justice. A person who has the huge good fortune of being reborn as a human being, when evolving from below, performed numerous acts of justice, exercised an ethical mind, connected more and more widely with beings around her, and developed the imagination of the others' perspectives. It was the biological momentum of those positive habits and accomplishments that propelled her to assume the human form. The same holds for one who devolves down from the angelic and divine embodiments above the human embodiment. The evolutionary momentum of justice brought them to those higher embodiments originally, overshooting the human form, so to speak, only later to settle down into the human by the gravity of divine complacency and lethargy.

This principle is widely illustrated in ancient stories, especially in the "former-life stories" (*jātaka*), in which the Buddha uses his ability to remember former lives of himself and others to tell his listeners how they got to be the way they are. For example, once he was a magnificent king of deer, living with his herd in the environs of Varanasi, a deer so highly evolved that he had the gift of human speech, unlike most deer. He was unhappy about deer hunters, naturally, and so he negotiated a deal with the king of Varanasi. Each day, a deer would come to the royal kitchen voluntarily to be slaughtered for the royal table, and the hunters would not come into the forest to kill large numbers of animals, way beyond the need. The deer king instituted a lottery among the deer, and the system saved lives and worked well for some time. Then one day a pregnant doe, soon to deliver herself of her fawn, was chosen in the lottery. She was upset, not so much for herself as for her fawn, who was so close to being born. She went around the herd begging other deer to take her place, pledging to offer herself the very next day when their turn came, so she could deliver the fawn. No one would give up another day of life to help her. Finally, the deer king came to know of her plight. He put her mind at ease, told her she could give birth to her fawn at the due time, and even live longer in order to bring it up as a mother doe does. He then went himself to the royal palace and delivered himself to the royal cook. When the cook saw such a magnificent deer, with great antlers and gold and silver spots, a deer who could speak in human language, he was afraid to slaughter him and went to get instructions from the king. Upon hearing that the deer king himself had come to give his life for food, the human king came down to the kitchen to ask why. The deer king told the story of the mother doe. The human king was so moved by this tale of two altruisms—first, that of the doe trying to save the life of her fawn; and second, that of the deer king saving the two lives by giving his own—he was ashamed of his arrangement made to secure venison for his table. Henceforth, he proclaimed, none shall kill the deer of Varanasi, who have shown such great virtue, enough to set an example for us humans.

In this story we see justice at work, springing from empathy for others. The doe felt empathy for her fawn and saw no reason why it should die along with her, just because of the timing of her duty, itself part of an agreement that regularly one deer should sacrifice itself for the many. The deer king had made the original deal because he felt empathy for the members of his herd, and saw how an altruistic deed on the part of one could save many lives. He then identified with the mother and the fawn, and so easily chose to give his life for theirs. This act on his part, which had not been part of the agreement, as kings normally do not give their lives for their country, so moved the human king of Varanasi, that all the deer lives were saved. The Varanasi citizens were introduced to an element of nonviolence in their lives that certainly improved their evolutionary positions, even though it might have frustrated their taste for venison. The impact of such stories is certainly not unrelated to the fact that India even today has by far the highest percentage of vegetarians in the world.

There are thousands of these stories that convey the vision of positive evolution as a progression toward greater empathy, unity, and happiness on the part of ever greater numbers of beings. They became foundational in Indian civilizations. The stories migrated into numerous story collections that spread throughout the subcontinent, and their migration into world literature has been clearly traced by scholars. I like to refer to them as the first "Walt Disney" animal stories in history, portraying the morally uplifting deeds of the ancestors of Lassie, Old Yeller, and so on.

Problem: Injustice

Now, as we decide to change our lives and move in the direction of real happiness, we must begin by recognizing that to a large extent, how we feel is determined by how we relate to the larger nexus of beings around us. We must look around us, especially in America today. We immediately become mindful of the great fortune we have in being here at all, especially in the middle and upper classes. Our national military and economic power, our relative comfort, our unusual physical resources and spiritual ideals, all combine to enable us to accomplish unprecedented good things in this world. At the same time, we must also recognize that in actual day-to-day fact, we are drowning ourselves and others in a toxic flood of injustice.

Take killing, the taking of life, which causes us to lose our lives over and over again in a difficult future. We are consuming too many animals, breaking the evolutionary code and preparing our own future downfall, killing far too many beings, destroying the environment of those we don't kill directly. Of course, it's hard to avoid killing beings in daily life—indeed, beings are killed by our ordinary metabolism, in the sense that a single human being is a colony of countless micro-beings, and our personal digestive and respiratory processes involve the living and dying of numerous beings. Our food comes from the death of many beings, even producing vegetables involves killing masses of insects. All the products we use involve killing creatures, polluting the environment. We drive huge cars over roads paved on the bodies of small creatures, the survivors often piling up on our windshields. The Buddha was moderate even about this, acknowledging that some killing is unavoidable until we become buddhas, and that our human lives are still specially precious because we are near to becoming buddhas. In contrast, some other Indian teachers of the time despaired of purifying the sins of any aggregated life-form.

On the collective level, we have unwittingly shifted from being a nation of liberators, defenders of freedom, into becoming a nation of arms dealers and mercenaries, fabricating our own weapons of mass destruction and arming tyrants with the tools to oppress their own people. Within our own society, we jail more prisoners than any other country in the world, 85 percent of them people of the nonwhite races—red, black, brown, and yellow. We are one of the few nations that still indulge in the death penalty for increasing numbers of these prisoners. We must become mindful of these negative things, since we need not support these actions of our nation to be affected negatively by their evolutionary impact, unless we mentally, verbally, and ultimately physically, disassociate ourselves from them.

Consider stealing, defined as "the taking of what is not given," the negative evolutionary action of depriving others of their property. As scrupulously honest as we may be personally, we are still individually entwined in our collective taking of others' property. Our nation was founded upon imperialism. Our ancestors took this land of the Turtle Island continent away from the native peoples without giving anything in fair exchange. They killed most of the original inhabitants and enslaved the rest, and then brought more slaves from other colonies. On the good side, some of our founding fathers then identified with the imperialized, made an earth-shaking revolution, and created a theory and system of equality, freedom, and justice. We then sided against imperialism for some time, rid ourselves of slavery, and got involved in the great wars among the imperialists themselves, still fighting for freedom and democracy. The creativity and energy released even by our imperfect practice of freedom made us ultimately invincible in these struggles.

But now we have unleashed our multinational corporations to enfold all world cultures into our commercial culture of consumption, even though most other peoples will never have the means to consume the majority of goods we parade before their spellbound eyes. We are letting these corporations alter the genes of every plant on Earth, patent them, and thus try to sell everyone their own water, food, fuel, and even air. We are standing by while they destroy the environments of weaker nations in extracting resources, making their people sick in the process, then selling a few of them the technological medicines they desire to replace the healthy diet, lifestyle, and natural medicines their civilizations have long enjoyed. Within our own society, we have a huge disparity between rich and poor, even though all are supposed to be equal. In the area of sexual harming, the rich citizens of all the industrial nations support a booming slave trade that exploits tens of millions of young girls and boys in brothels. We promote a culture of sexual promiscuity that exploits young women and men in many ways, while our ever more powerful religious fundamentalists block their access to sex education, contraception, and other basic health measures.

So much for the tip of the iceberg of the physical level of injustice. On the verbal level, as for lying, we lie to our children in the educational arena, giving them a sanitized, whitewashed version of American history, suppressing the true horrors of conquest, native genocide, agricultural slavery, industrial exploitation of immigrants, and the continuing horrors of racism, sexism, religious bigotry, and classism. We lie about our role in the world, pretending to defend freedom everywhere, when we in fact support the tyrants, export violence and sell weapons, and subvert freedom whenever it rears its supposedly unprofitable head. Our leaders lie all the time, promising one thing and doing the opposite, and then denying it. Our media distorts its coverage of the facts, since it has become monopolized by corporations that manipulate us all to extract more profits.

As for speaking divisively, we pretend to be peacemakers, but in fact we don't subscribe to international law or justice, we deny power to the U.N. community when it goes against our commercial interests, and, though we send out diplomats to defuse dangerous situations, our military-industrial merchants vie with each other to sell weapons to both sides of every conflict. In order to disunite the popular will and vote, our politicians lie to poor whites that poor blacks on welfare are making their lives miserable, when in fact our corporations are exporting the jobs of both to even poorer people under dictatorships we support abroad.

Speaking harshly is endemic in the media, which keeps up a drumbeat of focus on violence and oppression and danger and terror, subliminally frightening people into submission to the dictates of our self-serving leaders.

Speaking meaninglessly is often thought of as entertainment, used to distract people from what is really happening, reinforcing the epidemic depression of "the mass of men today" who "lead lives of quiet desperation," as Thoreau once said so eloquently.

Coming to the negative evolutionary paths of thought, nurturing greed is widespread, since hours of TV commercials, billboards, and print advertisements feed us daily a concentrated diet of discontent, making us feel we have to buy numerous unnecessary things.

Harboring malice is also hard to avoid, since others are portrayed in our mythology and media culture as harsh, violent, dangerous, hateful, and inhuman. We could never accept such a poor quality of politician if we were not indoctrinated to feel divided against one another so that each thinks the leadership will protect them against the other they so fear and hate.

Finally, the unrealistic worldviews we are taught to hold by our confused philosophers and scientists have reached a new height of senselessness. Either we are material quanta with brains but no minds, emerging randomly and purposelessly from a cosmic chemical soup only to disappear meaninglessly back into the physical elements, worth less than a penny on the commodities market; or we are immortal souls temporarily confined in filthy bodies on a filthy planet, all of which is also worthless, but our souls will be yanked back into peaceful oblivion or antiseptic angelic boring existence in heaven as long as we maintain blind faith in the right prophet and God. These unrealistic worldviews or ideologies come from gross misinterpretations of religious and scientific teachings. They reinforce our sense of disconnection from everyone and everything around us. They encourage us to be irresponsible to other beings and confuse us about the great purpose of our human embodiment. They line us up to be the mindless minions of the industrial-corporate machinery that is beyond control, even by its owners.

When we face it squarely and stereoscopically in this way, we can see that there is a great problem of injustice permeating our lives. Its toxic effects seep into our unconsciousness and enter our consciousness in the form of a nagging conscience that leads us to despair, depression, numbness, and cynicism.

Some writers in the spiritual development movements tend to lump all this injustice under the rug of, "It's just the hopelessness of the material world—the unenlightened life! Better withdraw from it all and get enlightened!" or ". . . holy!" or ". . . spiritual!" Some psychologists react to the plague of depression that afflicts our citizens—there are staggering statistics of the near-clinically depressed—by conceding to the drug companies' marketing efforts and prescribing tranquilizers, mood-lifters, and antidepressants.

Both these efforts have good points, appropriate in some ways. But all time-tested spiritual traditions of conscious evolving prescribe, first, developing recognition of the full weight of the negative conditions around us; then cultivating insight into how they cause our depression; then making serious lifestyle changes, practicing mind-transformation, and, finally, attaining realization. Real cure is the total understanding by wisdom of the reality of things, which again reinforces the lifestyle changes and the mind-transformations. So we should turn to the proven methods. Now, how can we address effectively the problem of massive injustice binding us into sadness and negative evolution? How can we lift our moods of depression by ameliorating the injustice swirling within and around our lives?

Practice: Meditation as Mental Evolutionary Action

Even if you're not usually depressed, if you tend to be a cheery and upbeat person, when you look around you at your world, your life, your interconnection with others globally today, you tend to feel quite down. You are clearly blessed in your personal situation, or you wouldn't be free to read these words and to meditate in this way. But look at most of the people in our world, not to mention all the animals. Register the killing, deprivation, violation, deception, betrayal, distraction, abuse, envy, hatred, and confusion that swirl around every being on this planet. Now begin to meditate upon all this.

As usual, first visualize yourself in your seat of good fortune on the top of the world, calm, comfortable, with your mentor heroes above and all around you in the sky, blessing you from on high. Sit yourself down on your meditation seat, your lion throne, if you wish, with its lotus, sun, and moon cushions, and then become aware of all beings in a vast field around you. In this meditative shrine-space, perform all the preliminary visualizations. Absorb blessings in the form of light, radiate light rays out to all the sensitive beings in the host around you, and equalize your attitude to all of them. Salute and praise the luminous mentor beings, and take refuge with them. Make offerings, confess your sins, rejoice in your virtues and those of others, request liberating teachings and the ongoing presence of the enlightened mentors, and dedicate all your merit to your own full enlightenment for the sake of all.

Now, transform your meditation room into the cosmic newsroom, or a situation room, like the ones in the Pentagon or at the NORAD base in Colorado—you've seen enough of them in *War Games* or other military action movies. Imagine the dozens of TV monitors surrounding you in diaphanous walls, with a huge map of the Earth superimposed and traced in light on the ceiling. Keep the sense of the mentor heroes and heroines in the luminous space above this, but focus on the Earth and the beings on the Earth. Imagine that the monitors are bringing you graphic, in-depth news reports of what is going on with every being imaginable on the planet at that very moment. Not only people being blown up by suicide bombers, as in Israel; civilians caught in cross fire by revolutionary soldiers, as in strife-torn Liberia; search and destroy governmental actions, drug wars, police suppressions, border conflicts, criminal activities, as in Colombia or Sudan; but also children starving in situations of famine and drought, in the Sahel, Bangladesh, India, China, among tribal people everywhere.

See animals dying due to deprivation of habitat, as rainforests are clear-cut; fish and coral reefs dying from pollution, global warming. Scan the people right in your home cities who are homeless, in prison for petty crimes, starving, elders eating cat food, children malnourished in urban ghettoes and rural backwaters. Even well-fed people, note how they are eating unhealthy diets, vegetables grown with chemicals or genetic manipulation, animals fed with steroids and antibiotics and female hormones, living in misery, filled with endocrine substances generated by fear, frustration, pain, and despair. Animals have emotions and therefore negative neurotransmitters permeate their flesh.

Note how prosperous people overeat, overindulge in drink and drugs, live under self-imposed high stress, get into conflicts with their loved ones by having affairs, desiring more and more pleasure and excitement, get into car wrecks, get mugged and killed by desperate criminals, attract assassination by mental cases. Look at all those with birth defects, insane, retarded, deficient in sense organs or limbs. Look at the people in the countries under various forms of overt tyranny—such as the 1.3 billion Chinese people ground under the heel of the Communist Party bureaucrats, living very sparsely while the party members and their families whiz by in sleek Mercedes limos; sent to labor camps for protesting, beaten, arrested, and tortured for seeking to practice spiritual disciplines such as qigong, trying to be a Buddhist or a Christian without following the state institutions; seeing their sons and daughters killed in infancy or forcibly aborted due to population control policies. See the members of the 55 million non-Chinese "minorities" who are basically colonialized, enslaved people who have lost their lands, their relatives, their culture and way of life and belief. Think of those many people who belong to a minority race or religion in whatever country and how they are persecuted. Visualize sniper alley in Sarajevo, Beirut, Jerusalem, and so forth. Go back in history if you want, to the Hitler Holocaust, the world wars—the many wars of the twentieth century—Stalin's gulag archipelago, Mao's prison provinces filled with dying people trapped in famines, slavery in Africa and America, and serfdom in Russia, the innumerable conquests and wars, the genocide of the native Americans and Africans, and Australian aborigines, the genocide of Asians under imperialism. Let what you can visualize of these horrors flood over your imagination as they pour forth from the monitors.

Look unflinchingly at all the dreadful things that are happening to all these people, and note carefully how these things connect back to you in your situation. Don't think right away about what to do—just observe everything carefully, excruciatingly if necessary. Don't recoil, don't let your mind veer away in any partial explanations, whether confused or insightful. Just take it in. If you were feeling a little down when you started, you will go through a phase of feeling really down, perhaps angry, then maybe despairing. Try not to shut it off or go into denial. "Why should I pay attention to this? What can I do about it? I am just getting myself dragged into it and adding to the chaos!" Realize that just by attending to it, just by overcoming areas of denial and neglect in your mind, you are taking powerful action. You are remembering the horrors of the past. You are attending to the horrors of the present. You are anticipating the horrors of the future. Just by doing that, you are honoring those who suffer. You are laying the foundation of things that could help them. You are sending out a resonance that will subliminally nudge others to remember, attend, anticipate. You are making mental baby steps that are part of true caring.

People trying to be spiritual sometimes don't like cultivating this kind of awareness. They think it's useless, can't help, just depresses people. Such an attitude is not only part of the problem, it leads to methods of spiritual development that don't really work, just cover things up temporarily. They may palliate your symptoms for a while, but won't heal your spiritual malaise. We humans are totally interconnected, intersensitive, naturally empathetic beings. The condition of those around you totally affects your state of experience. If all around are in agony, you will suffer. If you wall yourself off, live in denial, you will be depressed with a nagging, sinking mood. You won't know why and will seek distractions.

But the dominant mood will keep rolling over you. So the first step to overcoming your own depression is to turn away from your self-preoccupation, open the doors and windows of your life, and take a wide look around at the reality of others all around you. This is the first step in truly satisfying spiritual growth.

After an intense period of exposure to these realities, we can start to cultivate good reactions. Analyze the situation and take actions in your mind. The first good reaction is to count your blessings. This is like the classic meditation of developing awareness of the "preciousness of the human life privileged with liberty and opportunity." You, after all, are not immediately caught in the horrors you are witnessing on your cosmic monitor array. Those so caught are there because of their evolutionary momentum; you don't have to feel existentially guilty about it, though you should also not make this an excuse to forget about them.

I remember once a dying horse we found collapsed in the road in Almora, an Indian Himalayan town in the Uttar Pradesh state. It was a little packhorse, employed in those hills to carry heavy slate panels used for roofing houses. It had been worked to death, was lying on its side breathing heavily, oozing pus from eyes, nostrils, and mouth, with bad sores on its back and sides. A few crows were hanging around, but no vultures yet. It was in a rocky dirt path right in front of a farmhouse rented by a group of spiritual seekers, what tourists in 1971 would call a "hippy house." We were driving on a barely better dirt road, nearby across a field, and for some reason we got out and discovered this soon-to-be horse carcass. My wife and I and our two children thought this was a cruel way to die, so we decided to take the horse in our VW bus to the garage of our rented home and call a vet. We got some villagers to help carry it across the field and load it in exchange for piling in and getting a ride up the mountain. They were laughing and making jokes about us, but willingly helped. Once we had lifted it, the horse took steps, and, propped up, staggered across the field. Once we started in, throughout the whole process, a couple of the "seekers" in the house came out and were very upset with our humanitarian efforts. "It's just the karma of the horse, man! What are you doing! You can't do anything about it! It's just the custom around here! Shouldn't interfere with karma!" And so on. They were a bit irate. I just said, "Well, it's our karma to try to help in some way, and so it's its karma to get helped!"

We got the horse home, put an old blanket over it, our three-year-old brought it water, and we went to get the vet. He came, had already heard about the situation, and after looking over the horse, told me it was too far gone. He then, to avoid problems for us, took me down to a tea shop where he found the horse's owner. After glasses of tea all around, he scolded him, in a firm but friendly way, about how he had warned him some time back to let the horse rest and get a foreleg problem worked on before it was too late. Then he explained how I had been unhappy to find the horse in the road waiting for the leopards and vultures, and had taken it to shelter and offered to pay for a humane death injection, provided the owner would give permission, and come and get the carcass. The villagers were bemused by my involvement, but not angry. They agreed to the doctor's conditions, we paid fifteen rupees for the shot, and they came and took the carcass away.

This all happened during the summer when the atrocities committed by the Pakistani army against Bengali civilians were at their worst; the Nixon–Kissinger–controlled U.S. was supporting Pakistan against India; China and Russia were in conflict on the Manchurian border; Kissinger was preparing to join up with China against Russia. The Indian press was full of horrendous news. I remember having a dream around that time, in which I saw my original teacher, a wise old lama from Mongolia, who sat silently looking at me while I protested strongly—"Look at these babies being impaled on bayonets! Look at these suffering beings! Where are the buddhas and bodhisattvas and fierce protectors? How can we talk of the all-pervasive Truth Body of the buddhas, their Emanation Body manifestations, as many as beings need to help them?" He said nothing, but then his body began to grow and grow, and soon it was much larger than the high Himalayan peaks that ringed our horizon at five miles' height, reducing my sputtering self to less than flea size, impressed with an immeasurable magnitude, my railing away trailing off into inaudibility.

Years later, I remembered this dream when I heard Ram Dass tell how, that very same summer, at an ashram near the Himalayan town Nainital not very far away, he asked his guru, "What about the horrors in Bengal?" The guru smiled and said to him, "Don't you see it's all perfect!" Ram Dass then said, "Yeah! It's perfect—but it stinks!" I was so delighted at that, as I thought, "There he touches nonduality!" This seeming paradox preserves how it can be seen as perfect from an enlightenment evolutionary wisdom point of view, while simultaneously being unbearable from the sufferer's point of view, which that same wisdom never allows compassion to ignore.

We might think, "What's the point of insisting 'But it stinks!' when there's nothing we can do about it?" The point is that by not letting go of our empathy for the victims, by our refusal to accept that such things should happen to any being, *we are doing something of critical importance!* Our mind is performing an evolutionary deed, it is acting powerfully, sending out tendrils of connectedness, setting up a morphic resonance with other minds and hearts that this must not stand. This must not be. We must intervene. We must help. This morphic resonance reinforces compassion and mercy in other hearts, and a wave goes round the world. Eventually, people with power do change their policies. Perpetrators feel tired, feel disheartened about their horrific acts, begin to pull back, try to restrain the truly insensate ones, ultimately rebel against them, and these things end. It is the callousness itself, the ideologically forced, behaviorally conditioned hardening, the ignoring of the pain, the shutting off of our natural, innate human fellow-feeling, that sets up its own vicious morphic resonance and unleashes waves of violence and causes these horrors. So our not surrendering to the slightest temptation to shut off in our depths of heart, far away and seemingly totally unconnected, except by the wrenching and numbing news, is a powerful act. It is resistance. It is mental evolutionary action. It stirs other minds invisibly, and it will spur our own and others' speech, and our own and others' physical acts, inevitably.

After counting your blessings, your second positive reaction is to recognize the impermanence of all these conditions, remind yourself of your special new—perhaps still experimental—infinite life context and vow to stay with anyone who suffers, whether they die or not. If they do die, then stay with them in the between and in all their future lives. If they survive, then wish them well and help them in whatever way possible later in this present life.

In your daily meditations, you should always take a moment to reflect on the beings who have died that day, who are dying that minute, of natural causes or caught in wars, street conflicts, starvation, disasters. You should reach out to their souls that have just broken free from embodiment, wandering in confusion in a dreamlike state while thinking they should be normal, present in their bodies, perceiving their bodies as alien things, or familiar but wondering what happened. Think of them and use the *Tibetan Book of the Dead* type of address to them. Send them calming lights, sweet soothing sounds, beautiful sights, encouraging words. Urge them to recognize where they are, what a fantastic opportunity to drop the hankering, fearing, worrying, and wondering, realize they're evolutionary beings, think of the ultimate nature of the light, its wisdom, lovingness, their unity with it; merge with it, seek its advice on how to proceed evolutionarily, how to serve self and others according to its all-permeating loving wisdom. Visualize and project for them portraits of desirable life-forms in useful life circumstances, and impel them to seek such rebirth, in attunement with the great wisdom of the light. In meditating like this, you become liberated from just focusing on the tragedy of the departed one losing her body, you accept the inevitable about it and turn to the positive opportunity of better rebirth. This resonates helpfully to the departed in fact, and she is encouraged to make the best of their dreamlike between-state situation, instead of being caught in the poisonous disappointment and anger and frustration about not being able to cling to her discarded form—emotions that can lead to a painful ghost existence, causing much harm to self and others.

Your third meditation is to investigate the causality of it all, resolve to avoid the causes of such suffering, and not try to solve the situations by adding more to negative karmic patterns. Try to see how the ten paths of evolution operate in specific ways, how someone suffers like this because of having thought or spoken or acted like that. Think of the positive turns people can and do take, how they restrain this or that reactive behavior, how they succeed in acting transcendently here and there.

Fourth, realize that there are no egocentric states you can move these people into that won't get messed up and that there is no alternative to helping each individual wake up totally. It is very important not just to get caught in utilitarian calculation and lost in schemes about improving the world as if it were merely a linear project. Such thinking will ultimately prove exhausting and unworkable.

Fifth, analyze your personal involvement in changing anything from negative to positive. Are you invested in any companies that cause any of this? Do you buy products from any of them? Does your government, whether North American, South American, African, Australian, Asian, or European, have anything to do with these activities? If not, have you tried to get that government involved in a positive way? If so, have you tried to influence that government's activities, changing them from negative to positive? Do you find in yourself any attitudes about how, "it's not my business, it's all too much, it's just dragging myself into misery, I have the good karma not to have this happening to me right now." It is not necessary that you run out in the street to protest, though that is not at all out of the question to an aware person. It is necessary that you meditate clearly on how you should protest, become clear how what is being done by the powerful is mostly destructive, and become clear about the alternatives.

Clarity and confidence about the heart of justice is what is necessary here. This is action of the heart. Public actions of body and speech will come later. They will be effective when they come from this wise and compassionate heart of clarity. Here, the practice of confession and repentance is extremely important. Once you face your involvements, personal and collective, you must decide forcefully that you don't want any longer to do such things or be collectively involved in them. You feel great regret that you have thought, spoken, or done such things on the individual level, or overtly or secretly agreed in your heart when others did them. Thus, repent when you did something violent to another, slammed the door on them, shouted at them, cursed them or made an ugly gesture, hated them for something, coveted their things. When the U.S. president bombed some country or did something aggressive or threatened someone, did you approve it and enjoy it? You must confess and repent and resolve no more to do such things in your mind. When someone is executed, confess and repent if you thought, "Good riddance!" as if that solved any of your problems.

Performance: Living Justly

To live justly is to begin our quest for enlightenment by coming into our true humanity. The human animal is the most other-regarding, empathetic, and imaginatively sensitive in interaction with others. Of course, humans can be just as egocentric as any other animal, and their selfish actions can be far more destructive, precisely because they have greater knowledge of and power over relationality. Living justly requires the three kinds of just activities. First, you restrain the negative actions—of your own body and speech primarily, and ultimately of your mind—focusing on not doing anything harmful or evil. Then you perform positive actions, focusing on doing good for self and others. Finally, you perform liberating actions, those that ultimately fulfill the aims of other beings by leading them toward their own freedom and enlightenment.

Negative evolutionary actions are divided along a scale from gross to subtle, moving from the three physical (from killing onward), through four verbal (from lying onward), to the three mental ones (from coveting up to misknowing or misbelieving). Refraining from such actions is harder than it seems. If not from before, through practicing your meditations above, you have already become more highly attuned to the processes of violence in life. You know how your sheer existence as a separate entity—mere breathing, heart beating, digesting, metabolic functioning—all wreak havoc upon countless beings at the micro level. You are more aware, too, how as an American your historic, economic, and social interconnections with sensitive beings all over the world have numerous destructive aspects. Due to such attunement, people throughout the history of the awakening movement on the planet have renounced home life and entered monastic orders, taking vows of nonviolence, poverty, chastity, and spiritual honesty, as well as numerous smaller commitments to self-restraint, some of them verging on behavioral reconditioning and a heightened level of etiquette in interpersonal interactions. This is too often thought of as a negative, self-flagellating, morbid thing to do, as if these people were denying life and trying to hide away from it. For many, there is no doubt an escapist element. However, transcendent renunciation of the egocentric, misknowledge-driven life of inexorable suffering is the result not just of a wish to escape, but rather of a wish to be generous, just, and compassionate to oneself, for starters. When you renounce the terminal lifestyle, with all its depressed sense of self-worthlessness, self-deprivation, loneliness, anxiety, purposelessness, and inadequately compensating self-indulgence in fruitless materialistic goals, you are not punishing yourself—you are doing yourself a favor.

Why feel lousy all the time when you could be feeling great? Why struggle and stress over beauty, youth, property, wealth, fame, and status, when none of these things will fill up the empty hole in yourself coming from thinking you are a cosmic freak, a random accident, a purposeless, disconnected, isolated piece of ultimately meaningless trivia? Why agonize over relationships with others who, like you, are hypnotized by their self-obsessions, their inner reveries of regrets and future dreads, and hardly know you are there, just as you most usually think of them as a pawn on your own mental chessboard? Why invest your life's energy in everything that will be cancelled in a second by the inevitable advent of death? Why suffer the terminal lifestyle if there is a more logical alternative, an infinite lifestyle?

Renouncing all that entraps you in the terminal lifestyle is thus a huge release, a taste of tremendous freedom, that brings immediate ease and long-term room to evolve. The more you control your physical actions to minimize violence, possessiveness, and sexual obsession, the more alive you feel, the more free you feel, the more peaceful your inner feeling. With violent interactions with others lessened, the more you can open up your sense of interconnection with others, from which your life energy draws immense sustenance. With possessive bonds with other persons and things lessened, the more free you are to appreciate persons and things perceived as owning themselves. With your erotic feelings of love and connection made less dependent on external persons and objects, they are free to well up within you in sublimated—that is, more sublime—forms of creativity, or even simple well-being. The language of renunciation in the East is much less focused on isolation and self-deprivation than in the West. Instead of "ordination," membership in renunciate communities is called "release," "fulfillment," and "graduation." Full behavioral entry into the infinite lifestyle means dropping everything that reinforces habits of the terminal lifestyle, to free yourself for enjoyment of your expanded evolutionary path. The main lesson here is that lessening your entanglement in superficial concerns and interactions is caring for yourself, being loving toward yourself, and establishes the basis of justice and love toward others.

I am not suggesting that performance here means becoming a nun or a monk in any sort of religious group. Such a course may be appropriate for some, at some times in their lives. The point is to establish the principle that here in the performance of justice, less is more in a very direct way. It is like going on a vacation. When you go on a vacation, you drop your daily preoccupations, your obligations, your habitual involvements, and you let yourself go free to recharge your energies. You don't feel you have lost your job, lost your friends, lost your house, your car, your town, and so on. But you feel free to connect with nature, with your body in a deeper, more restorative way, your companions in a more attentive, appreciative way. Moving toward restraint of unjust entanglements with habitual lifestyle is just like adopting the vacation principle. You let yourself off from the duty to buy a new car every year. You excuse yourself from working too many long hours overtime by deciding you don't need so much more extra money. You free yourself from having to prove this or that about yourself to yourself, or to this or that friend or group. You recognize your supreme worth and value as an infinitely living person, and you feel fine just on your own. You let go of your narrow self-concerns, realizing that your well-being emerges naturally from your being more focused and concerned with others' well-being. You feel less stressed out as your time-sense expands from terminal toward infinite, and you realize that quality, not quantity, is paramount as you experience things more deeply, moment by moment. You feel less anxious about money when you recognize that it is nothing in itself, and that real value comes from leisure, relaxation, kindness, appreciation of beauty, and expanded awareness of inner reality.

The feeling of wealth is enhanced when you give, not when you take, since, subliminally, giving means you have enough to share, while taking means you may not be getting enough. Giving is a relief. Taking is a burden. This is a breakthrough discovery for American psychologists, though it is rather commonsensical for Tibetans, supporting the teaching that the cause of all unhappiness is self-concern, just as the cause of all happiness is other-concern.

This doesn't mean you need to give everything away. You might want to when you are so strong in your vision of the infinite lifestyle that you want complete freedom of time and life energy to focus on your spiritual evolution. However, in modern industrial society, with its emphasis on production and work as the basis of worth, there are not enough spiritual communities with the ability to support the bare necessities for too many persons living infinitely. You can live more justly by assessing your whole economic picture—how much you earn, how you save and spend it, what you really need for yourself and your family, what there is for your retirement, how you can economize and waste less time on trivial pursuits. You should look carefully at your personal and family habits—how you can create more quality time together; how many spiritual "vacations" you can squeeze in, not only annually on holidays, or weekly on Sunday or Friday–Saturday sabbaths, but daily in special moments, with wake-up and go-to-sleep meditations or prayers, blessings before meals, mindful naps, bath-soaks, mindful exercise sessions, massages, and so on; how you can improve your diet, occasionally fasting moderately, using less alcohol, eating less addictive, sugared foods, making sure food is organic; checking your water supplies with chemical analysis, getting filters and purifiers; checking the air quality in your environment and simply moving elsewhere if it is inadequate.

As you shift from a terminal to an infinite lifestyle, your this-life inventory is an invaluable part of living justly. If the basis of your lifestyle is disturbed by the vibrations of injustice, your contemplative practices and spiritual performances will be disturbed. You must remember that while you may remain blissfully unaware of certain contradictions and imbalances in your whole environmental nexus, your body will not be unaware, your deeper mind levels will not be unaware, and things you consciously ignore will affect you for good or ill. Everything and everyone is interconnected, and every increased awareness you develop, every good thing you do, immediately affects others, whether you tell them about it or not.

The health area is very important. If you are not confident about how your body works, what your heart, lungs, liver, pancreas, and kidneys do, how your stomach, short intestine, long intestine, gall bladder, sexual organs, and bladder work, how phlegm, bile, blood, muscle, fat, bone, ligament, marrow function, you should look into it, with a simple medical manual or reference work. The alternative medical systems—Tibetan medicine, acupuncture medicine, Ayurveda, and so forth—all have rather more readily comprehensible ways of explaining that fit well within the more complex and confusing, though highly informative, Western explanations. You should not feel dependent on "experts" about your health of body and mind, you should develop a basis of self-understanding with which to evaluate their analyses and recommendations. But you should definitely not obsess over your body: eat well, exercise, do what you enjoy, take care of yourself, but forget about super-health, super-strength, super-youth, super-beauty, all sorts of unrealistic fantasies our commercial culture tries to seduce us into based on our obsession with our bodies. Overworrying about your symptoms is in itself a source of illnesses, and forgetting about them is a source of good health. The old meditation on your own body as a corpse in various stages of decomposition can be judiciously applied as a deglamorization method that can make you feel really glad to be alive and unconcerned about small things that come and go on their own!

Whenever you gain a new level of awareness about some previously unrecognized element of injustice embedded in your life, you will feel shame, regret, remorse, perhaps even guilt. This is perfectly all right, not a problem. The problem psychologists have with guilt is not about reasonably feeling regret that you have done something or been associated with the doing of something wrong, bad, or even evil. It is about the kind of absolutist feeling that can arise in the authoritarian, religious-ideology–oppressed personality, a feeling of utter unworthiness, absolute self-condemnation, harsh self-judgment that cuts off all hope and positive inspiration. The natural shame and guilt you feel when you catch yourself in the wrong is a sign of your ethical health, your spiritual goodness. You should cultivate repentance in such moments, confessing your transgressions to yourself and all enlightened beings, who already know all about it after all; resolve never again to get involved in such things; determine to compensate for any harm caused to any other, such reparations being more important than just flagellating yourself about it. The Buddhists, like the Catholics and the secular frequenters of psychiatrists, have artful and healthy rites of confession and repentance, reform and absolution through self-transformation and other-reparation.

An important story always told in this context since ancient times is the story of Angulimala, "Finger-Garland," a serial killer who had been deceived by a malicious guru into thinking he would attain liberation if he killed a thousand people, saving his own mother for the last. The Buddha became aware of his predicament after he had killed 999 people, was wearing their fingerbones as a grisly garland, and was after his mother. The Buddha sent a magical apparition looking like his mother and caused the murderer to chase him through the jungle for miles and miles for a whole night. Finally, Angulimala wore himself out, flung himself down, and surrendered to the victim he could not catch—obviously not his mother. The Buddha then revealed himself as the Buddha, told him of his error, the weight of his sins, the nature of the suffering of the unenlightened lifestyle, and the way to freedom from that delusion, lust, and hatred. Angulimala understood the teaching, repented sincerely, applied his mind very intensely once he realized his dire evolutionary situation with so many murders on his head, and soon attained a stage near to freedom. He became a monk the rest of his life and, at death, fell into hell for a split second due to the heaviness of his evolutionary momentum, but very soon bounced back out into a celestial realm a slight step above the human, where he was able to finish his meditative process and actually did attain the sainthood of release. The moral of the story is that, if even a mass murderer could transform into a saint through powerful repentance and self-purification and eventual profound transcendent understanding, then ordinary, less heavily sinful persons have every hope of a positive outcome.

The etiquette level is important in living justly. When you eat, take a tiny portion first, a few grains of rice, a noodle, and put it beside your plate as a symbolic offering to all the hungry beings in the universe. Offer the whole meal symbolically to spiritual beings, mentors and enlightened beings, before you put it to good use in nourishing yourself to carry on your infinite lifestyle. Eat moderately and mindfully, without rushing or slobbering. The *Discipline* of the Buddhist nuns and monks has eighteen different prohibitions of eighteen different types of slurping that annoy your companions. Etiquette rules of your culture should be observed in a gracious manner. Conversations should be gentle and meaningful while eating, with not too much excitement, wild gestures, or risqué gossip.

There are a lot of artful practices that can be employed in interacting with people in public. Shantideva mentions many of them in his chapter on alertness in the *Entry to Enlightened Living.* Try not to let your eyes wander around aimlessly, taking in everything they fall upon, but when you do see something beautiful, don't let your mind get attached to it. Rejoice in the owner's possession of it, and think of your enjoyment of the sight of it as an offering to all enlightened beings. When someone asks you for directions, use your whole hand in a gesture of invitation, and think how in the future you will invite them on their way to enlightenment. When you look at another person, think how they were your mother in previous lives, and how you intend someday to repay their kindness by mothering them into their own highest evolutionary fulfillment. Be careful of course not to stare at them in the process, but look down if they gaze at you, and think how in seeing you they should instinctively sense a doorway and example for themselves to transform their own lifestyle. Don't swear or curse lightly, and don't make heated vulgar gestures. Try not to scrape the floor with chairs, slam doors, drive wildly or too aggressively. When you go through a door with another, invite them through first and make a wish to open the door for their enlightenment someday. Minimize gossip, especially if it will divide others. Don't chatter aimlessly, and don't listen to aimless chatter—which means minimize nonmeaningful TV watching, sticking to educative and inspiring programs you specially choose. As you begin to progress in replacing debilitating habits with empowering ones, don't be too judgmental of the faults of others, as especially those faults you just got the better of will seem quite irritating when you see them in another's actions.

Try not to be jealous of others' good fortune, but empathize with them as they rejoice and mentally congratulate them. When others irritate you, see their acts from their perspective, and forget about your own reactions. When negative thoughts arise in your mind, notice them and let them go, disidentify with them as yours. Be mindful of your own minor habits, and avoid nervously picking your fingernails, twitching your knees back and forth, tapping your fingers, uprooting blades of grass on lawns, or twirling rubber bands around your fingers. Become more and more self-observant and avoid letting your energy dissipate itself in such meaningless movements, which often prove annoying to your companions.

Above all, be mindful of how much thought you habitually devote to your own state, your own position in things, your own status, your own success—as if you were constantly catching yourself in the inner mirror of your concern—and once you notice self-concern arising in each moment, begin to transfer your attention to someone or something else, replace each thought with a thought of other-concern. How are they feeling? Are they comfortable in that position or seat? Do they feel respected in this moment? What are they getting out of this moment? As you make tiny baby steps in this direction, replacing self-concern with other-concern, you'll be amazed at how artful you will become in making those around you feel better, more at home, more secure, more happy. You'll be amazed at how much better you'll feel about yourself by ignoring more how you are feeling.

The justice of doing good involves active progress in the opposite of the ten negative evolutionary pathways. Remember that the three physical types of good deeds are saving lives, giving gifts, and being sexually benevolent; the four verbal are telling the truth, speaking to reconcile conflicts between others, speaking sweetly and pleasingly, and speaking meaningfully, which means giving liberating teachings; and the three mental good deeds are being detached, being loving, and being realistic.

There are many creative ways of being positive. Be mindful of your posture, how it reflects your inner feelings about yourself and the world, and accept the help of coaches and spiritual body-workers to correct inherited hunches and stoops, tightnesses and constrictions, and make your body an icon of your infinite insight and lifestyle choices. Try to relax, even about making positive progress, and don't become compulsive about virtue, concentrating on one thing at a time, making progress bit by bit. Never get all determined to make an unrealistic amount of effort in too short a time, then fail, then get disgusted with yourself and abandon all positive intention. Look carefully at everything around you and within you, using constant mindfulness, and examine your motives in everything you do.

In ancient times, Shantideva was unerring in recommending artful approaches to the positive; currently, the Vietnamese Zen Master Thich Nhat Hanh is quick to think of small things that are marvelously effective. Smile, smile, smile, he always says, be welcoming to everyone you meet, greet them and pay close attention to their needs. Recognize in everyone an ally in your progress toward buddhahood, since you need them to receive your gifts, be served by your justness, and cause you trouble to receive the fruits of your patience. Shantideva tells us to look upon them and rejoice, thinking, "I shall become enlightened depending on this being!"

Combine all your daily activities with positive aspects of the path. Look at everything you do as contributing to the creation of your buddhaverse here on earth. Associate sweeping the floor with cleansing confusion from your own and others' minds. Washing the windows empowers your removing the veil of misknowledge that blocks you from seeing the magnificence of the world as enjoyed by the awakened. Cooking a meal empowers healing others. Opening a door for a stranger becomes a magical prayer that you may have the opportunity in some future existence to open their way to liberation. Maintaining a garden resonates with making the soils of the earth fertile, eliminating poverty and famine for all beings. There is no act, no matter how seemingly mundane or insignificant, that you cannot connect to some creative action for others.

When the phone rings, bow to the person at the other end before you pick it up, and think of them as your helper on the way to buddhahood. Drive super-consciously aware of what is involved in burning petroleum products, directing a many-ton structure of metal over the ground, polluting the air and sound-realm, and be careful and gentle in your movements. When caught by a red light, don't feel impatient, but bow to it in thanks for giving you a moment to pause and rest.

Think holistically, and open your mind to being more aware of all the interconnections between things. Think of the tree that made the paper of the book you are reading. Think of the sunlight, soil, water, and air that contributed to the tree; the lumberjack who cut it down and hauled it to the plant; the machinery that turned it into pulp, the people who packaged it and transported it to the printing plant, and so on. Think of the sheep who grew the wool in the fibers of your coat, the many persons and processes involved in getting it to you as a garment to keep you warm.

Attend more to your loved ones, never be condescending. Be kind to childish people. Learn from everyone, accept their criticism gracefully, praise the good qualities of others, and ignore their faults. Above all, rejoice in their good fortune. Speak truthfully, reconcilingly, gently, and meaningfully. When you lie down, think that you are dissolving your five-sense– entangled mind into the clear light of your soul-mind, and so your rest will reinforce your sense of union with the deepest mind of all enlightened beings. When troubles come, take them as challenges and opportunities to develop patience and accelerate your evolution on the path.

The justice of accomplishing beings' aims adds to the generally meritorious positive justice of doing those special kinds of interactions with others that lead them toward their own freedom from suffering and their full enlightenment. Giving them teachings is perhaps the most important, the justice of helping them gain access to the three spiritual educations in justice, meditation, and wisdom. Just as you accomplish all your aims by developing universal compassion and transcendent wisdom, so do all beings finally want and need the same evolutionary fulfillment.

The true egalitarianism of the enlightenment traditions is grounded in this vision of each being's absolute potential to achieve the full measure of their inherent reality of infinite life. It is not that buddhas and bodhisattvas are great and other beings must depend on them forever. All beings are already infinite in that all have been beginninglessly engaged in infinite embodiments in infinite universes, infinitely interactive with infinite other beings. Unfortunately, their terminal misknowledge keeps them in a zombielike state of unawareness of this infinite inheritance they naturally possess, imprisoning them in a seemingly interminable round of suffering. Fortunately, that round of suffering is not infinite, since the infinite energies of the enlightened beings are more powerful than the infinite energies of the unenlightened sufferers, since the enlightened beings' energy springs from the need of infinite beings seeking happiness, and the unenlightened beings' energy springs from only their own single need apart from infinite others.

The living justice of the infinite lifestyle thus treats all beings with the adroitness due to beings who are soon to inherit their own freedom and bliss awareness. It is calm yet determined, transcendent yet activist, precise yet relaxed, happy yet not indifferent, confident yet intensely devoted.

Performance: Global Justice and Compassion

We modern individuals feel a sense of alienation from other beings because our culture teaches us to believe that as separate, independent entities, our lives are finite, we are on our own and existence is, in essence, futile. We compensate for our feelings of helplessness and alienation by puffing ourselves up with pride. We expend a great deal of psychological energy convincing ourselves that we're the best, because if we weren't, then life would just be too depressing. "I'm the only one whom I can count on," we tell ourselves, "so I'd better look out for myself and my own interests." This proud, self-centered attitude is the greatest enemy of compassion.

In much the same way, our society feels alienated from the rest of the world, and it compensates in a similar fashion. We identify only with our own nation, or at most only with other first-world nations, ignoring the needs and accomplishments of the rest of the world. "We are number one! America is the best!" we proclaim. We really do believe that we are superior.

It is very easy to see how this kind of prideful and solitary thinking leads to isolationism in the political arena. It prevents cooperative action. We dismiss war-torn and poverty-stricken parts of the world, considering them inferior, weak, below our standards. As people fortunate enough to have been born into wealth and stability, we believe that those in less fortunate circumstances are really inherently lazy and deserving of their fate. Why should we care if people in Africa are starving by the millions? Why should we act to free the oppressed Tibetans, even if they have been denied their political and religious freedoms by the Chinese for decades? We are just looking out for our own best interests, trying to preserve what precious little we have.

As the world draws inevitably closer together with every passing year—our destinies linked by weapons of mass destruction as much as by global commerce—we fight that reality. The rich world withdraws further and further from positive engagement with the poor world. We have left the former colonial nations of Africa, South America, and Southeast Asia, which we devastated in the first place, to their currently disastrous states of population explosion and physical underdevelopment. Yet we are unrealistic in thinking that we can isolate ourselves from the fate of other nations, especially those that continue to sink into increasingly desperate states. Our isolationism is not protecting us; it is creating the very disasters we most fear.

We learned this lesson from World War II, which was a result of isolationist policies. Most modern nations thought we could let post–World War I Germany go down the tubes. We did not realize that a desperate nation would empower a radical element, which would then turn that nation into a vicious machine focused on getting revenge. The agony, waste, and suffering that we poured into controlling the ensuing explosion of violence almost tore the world to shreds. As a result, we vowed to take a more global perspective. We founded the United Nations and began to unravel colonial imperialism. We initiated the Marshall Plan and rebuilt the societies of our former enemies. But then we lost our nerve. After just a few decades of engagement, we are now running away from reality again.

The fundamental problem with our prideful and self-centered isolationist worldview is that we think that every dollar we spend on another country is one less dollar we have to spend on our own. So we must carefully protect our resources. Every political issue is viewed in terms of "us versus them." According to this model, our money is best spent on defense, building huge walls to protect us and further our isolationism. We enact laws to prevent immigration because we presume that each additional person we let in will take away resources from our native citizens. We do everything in our power to keep ourselves "safe" from the poor, needy, and uneducated peoples and nations of the world.

We must drastically change our outlook. We return to our yoga of infinite connectivity, reminding ourselves of how everyone is our mother, how their suffering has generated in us a lifelong commitment to making their lives better. Given our inherent relatedness to all other beings, we do not fear the rest of the world nor do we feel superior to it. Instead, we embrace it and we commit to helping it.

Our modern society must adopt a global, rather than an isolationist, perspective. We must accept the fact that we are not and cannot ever be independent of our global community. We must embrace the bodhisattva spirit of enlightenment by caring for and acting on behalf of nations other than our own. I am talking about the exchange of self and other on an international scale, of transforming pride into compassion in our politics as well as in our personal lives. Where *is* our compassion? Instead of running away from the problems we all face, instead of trying to build walls to keep the rest of the world out, we must open our borders and our hearts. Out of the deep desire to ease the suffering of all humanity, each nation must take responsibility for the well-being of all nations.

When the U.S. became a welfare state under Roosevelt's leadership, we produced the greatest wealth of any nation in history. The information age has already provided us with all the resources we need in order to enact an effective plan for global assistance. By cutting back on military spending, we can provide massive aid packages without losing our necessary wealth. By sacrificing only the superfluous excess that gives us nightmares anyway, we can make drastic improvements to our quality of life, which will be greatly enriched by the happiness we have brought so many others for so many generations into the future. It is a completely win-win situation. More begets more, not less.

We must rekindle our old-fashioned American world-saving idealism and can-do optimism. Offering assistance does not only mean sharing our wealth. We must also share the sources of our wealth, which are our best qualities—our enthusiasm, our confidence, and our educated creativity.

The goal of all programs should be not just to restore the subsistence capacity of all areas of the globe, but to inspire.

We should celebrate all of life and our place in it. At first it may seem that if unenlightened life is suffering, then we have no reason to work to lessen the suffering of others by sharing with them. Shouldn't we just look out for ourselves? But as we have seen, there are harsh consequences to persisting with such an unenlightened view. Rich and poor suffer equally in the cosmic sense. Suffering is not inevitable—it comes from ignorance. By practicing the yogas of justice and compassion, we can stay focused on the happiness that results from freedom from suffering. We are motivated by the love and compassion we feel for all beings to do our best to reduce their suffering as much as possible.

As one of the wealthiest nations on earth, it is America's mission to use our resources to usher in a new era of enlightened living. We must take responsibility for bringing all of humankind out from the darkness of personal, political, and religious delusion into the light of transcendental bliss. We must lead this global evolutionary transformation. Ultimately, we cannot enjoy our ridiculously disproportionate "standard of living" unless we raise the whole planet up along with us. It is delusory to think we can raise them up materialistically. It is more realistic that our terminal lifestyle is unsustainable and too self-indulgent to be healthy, and so we should detach from some of our habitual desires and share them using generosity and justice. Then we should strive to raise up the planet's peoples through education, reinforcing their own understanding of the good life as materially sufficient but not luxurious or addictive, and spiritually balanced, satisfying, and content.

We need to unleash our sense of justice and our tremendous potential for compassion and creativity. We need to create a "Marshall Plan" for the new millennium. We must not allow ourselves to be entrapped by pride, which only leads to scarcity-fear-mongering, isolationism, and shortsighted paranoia. Remembering our intimate bond to all life, we must come to realize that our obligation is not just to ourselves or even our own society, but to the entire world.

It may seem overwhelming to take on responsibility for all peoples in all nations of the world, both through our own personal bodhisattva vows and through our global political agenda. But we must recall that we are not alone in our endeavor. Our meditations on the boundless nature of the self have led us to discover our fundamental connectedness to all life. We are one with the buddhas and bodhisattvas who have traveled this path before us and who are with us even now, so we can draw on their infinite well of positive energy. Also, we can find others in our very real and present human communities who have made a similar commitment to the good of all beings. Together, we can generate a virtuous cycle of positivity, creating an unstoppable wave of compassion that will flow out over all of humanity.

6

Patience

Preamble: Bad Habits

As we embrace the infinite life perspective, we feel empowered by our newfound freedom from our formerly domineering selves. It would be simplistic, however, to think that now we have discovered it, we can merely float happily in the boundlessness, reveling in our glowing awareness. On the contrary, the conception of the soul of enlightenment comes with attendant responsibility. Making this one significant shift in our thinking has not let us off the hook. In order to achieve evolutionary fulfillment, we must commit ourselves to the conscious development of our positive potential. In terms of everyday life, this means that we actually need to work at self-improvement. We still have plenty of bad habits to overcome.

We have already identified the worst habit of all, which is our identity instinct—our sense of having an intrinsic, absolute self that anchors our sense of being alone and separate from the rest of the universe. We have seen how it works as the primal, instinctual misknowledge, the fundamental ignorance that creates the whole world of suffering. This unrealistic worldview is the prime target of wisdom, our transcending intelligence, which can investigate it and come to understand its true nature, thereby releasing us to freedom.

Now we'll examine the dangers of the self-preoccupation habit in terms of our everyday behavior. It is our primal "I am" sense that focuses our attention on ourselves and our condition here and now: our deep "I am how?" concern; our urgent "I need what?" demand; our pervasive "I have what?" obsession. From the moment we awaken in the morning, our thoughts circle around a small enclosure of self-preoccupation, like a tiger pacing in a tiny cage. "What will I do to move ahead?" "What is hurting me?" "What is stopping me?" "What is threatening me?" "What is depriving me?" We constantly worry. This behavior seems utterly normal and natural to us; it is instinctual and habitual. And yet it is selfish, plain and simple. What's more, completely entangled with our never-ending narcissistic thoughts are the negative and evolutionarily destructive emotions of anxiety, frustration, fear, paranoia, and anger.

Foremost among these destroyers of our peace of mind—not to mention the happiness of others—is anger in its many forms, including hate, fury, wrath, malice, spite, vindictiveness, resentment, and revenge. If we want to broaden and intensify our empathetic interaction with ourselves and other sensitive beings, we first have to clear the ground by overcoming our habitual subjection to this destructive emotion. We may talk of love and compassion, kindness and peace. We may advocate glorious, benign spiritual vistas and delicious introverted practices that bring us temporary mental ease and even physical buoyancy. But if we do not recognize the fragility of our positive states, if we do not face up to our quickness to anger, our proneness to irritation, our defensive reactions to the slightest perceived offense, and our complete loss of self-control when receiving real harm from another, then we are kidding ourselves.

There are famous spiritual stories in Buddhism (and in many other religious traditions) illustrating the enduring power of anger. One such story tells of a saintly hermit who lives for years and years high up in his holy cave far away from human civilization, at peace with nature, feeling close to the divine. He believes that he is well on his way to achieving enlightenment. Then one day, circumstances require him to briefly visit the nearest village marketplace. Wandering through the town, he gets caught up in a small crowd. As he's being jostled and pushed around, a big loutish peasant tramples painfully on his fragile yogi toes. Suddenly, he squeaks indignantly, jams the fellow with his elbow in pointed outrage, turns red in the face, and starts yelling self-righteously about who he is and what does the fellow think he's doing. He loses all control and peacefulness. His anger gets the better of him and the true, hollow nature of his supposed saintliness becomes all too apparent.

To my amazement, I have witnessed similar events myself in real life. I had a friend, a skilled meditator and spiritual leader, whose saintly appearance always made me uncomfortable. Though she is not actually a monastic, she has a very silky voice and smooth manner, and is known for being calm and even holy. Anyway, she was involved in leading a conference that I was attending. Frankly, I had become quite annoyed with her because she kept refusing to recognize me during the discussions, almost as if she were acting on a policy of excluding me from the dialogue. So at one point, when another friend asked me why I wasn't participating more actively, I couldn't help myself. I replied, "I'd love to, but So-and-So won't allow me to talk. It seems she has a bug in her ear about me!" I inflected my delivery in a nasty way, knowing full well that the friend in question, standing nearby, was overhearing what I was saying.

It was a petty and rude way to speak, it showed how poor my own self-control was, and I am ashamed to tell the story. However, the reaction of the leader was an even greater shock. She rushed up to me, stuck her furious face inches from mine, and shrieked at the top of her lungs, "F———

you, Bob. F——— you. How dare you say such a thing about me! I was warned about you! They told me you would take over the discussion and make trouble all the time. F——— you!" It took quite some time for her to realize what she was doing and stop ranting in this way. As her anger exploded, all heads turned toward us. Remember, she was respected as an "enlightened" teacher, usually highly modulated in her behavior, and so everyone was truly startled to see her lose control with such intensity. I was thoroughly shaken. Though I tried to laugh it off and make light of what had happened, I could not completely let go of my own anger, either. I meanly pointed out that I had apparently been right: by her own admission there was some sort of preconceived policy to exclude me. But there was little comfort in that.

In the end, we went back into the conference deeply embarrassed with our behavior. We hadn't solved any problem with our outbursts. On the contrary, we had only charged not just our own mental space but also that of all those around us with negativity. In our self-centered outrage, we had totally failed to behave in a positive evolutionary fashion. I can assure you that we both had plenty to meditate about that day.

It's embarrassing to tell this story even today. I do so because it illustrates how difficult it is even for so-called "advanced" practitioners to rid themselves of their automatic responses to perceived threats to the precious "self." Anger is, indeed, a hard habit to break, and to overcome it and develop patience, absolute honesty with ourselves and others, is a prime necessity.

Our next step on the path to personal transformation is to come to terms with our habitual addiction to anger. We must not doom ourselves to stay locked within the sad prison of paranoia, the solitary fortress of feeling at war with the world. We must learn to control this powerful demon that grips our minds, guides our actions, and steals away our peace and happiness.

Problem: Anger

From the infinite life perspective, anger is extremely dangerous. It leads us to commit acts that will affect our happiness and the well-being of those around us not just in this lifetime, but also possibly for many lifetimes to come. Anger can do severe, long-term damage to our karma, leading us on a backward path of devolution to lower life-forms and even into hells. For this reason, the great Buddhist philosopher Shantideva (whose recommendations for overcoming anger we shall utilize throughout this chapter) said that recognizing anger as our greatest enemy is of paramount importance in conquering it.

At the very outset, however, let us be very clear about exactly what anger and hatred are. They are not mere forcefulness and aggressiveness. It is entirely possible to be lovingly forceful, as, for example, a mother will be to protect her beloved child. If her tiny daughter is about to put her finger into an electric socket, the mother will shout, "No! No!" in an extremely forceful tone while rushing to grab her child away from danger. In so doing, she does not act out of anger, but out of love.

The energetic aggressiveness that leads people to get things done, which makes many of us think that anger is a good motivator, is not really anger either. You can be energetically aggressive about playing a game, doing a job, helping a friend, saving a human life, standing up to injustice, or even criticizing pretension without becoming angry. In fact, if you do become angry in the process, you'll quickly feel frustrated with the situation, you'll be more likely to offend the people around you, and that negative edge will make your efforts less effective. Exploding in anger is not the sign of righteous resistance to oppression; it is the final capitulation to oppression, the surrender of free consciousness and controlled forcefulness to blind impulse.

It is a cardinal rule in the martial arts of kung fu, karate, and so forth that the combatant who loses control due to anger in a skilled fight against an opponent will tend to fall off-balance, overattack, overreact, and lose. The person who maintains her cool will prevail. Even their forceful gestures, wild expressions, fierce shouts, and furious movements do not constitute anger if the combatants are not actually angry. Similarly, an actor can simulate hatred that carries intense emotional energy without really being angry with anyone.

So what, then, is anger, this deadly addictive emotional poison that must be understood and then overcome to develop forbearance, tolerance, and patience? It is to be found in the innermost core of the mind. It is rooted in the deepest level of self-identity. For anger to emerge, you must perceive that someone is coming at you, threatening your precious "self." "Aha!" you say to yourself, "he, she, it, they are hurting me, stopping me, threatening me, denying me, depriving me!" Your self-interest instinct engages and you feel hurt. Then you identify the source of your injury, and are overwhelmed with the urge to remove that source. Finally, you cross over the threshold of anger when your sense of outrage and fury take you over, directing your mind and then your body to act destructively.

It may be difficult, at first, for us to recognize that *all* actions driven by anger and hatred have negative consequences. Our usual tendency is to think of anger as somehow being our friend. Remember how, as a child, you would throw a temper tantrum, allowing your rage to burst forth in tears, flailing your limbs, and perhaps even shouting nasty words at your parents such as, "I hate you!" If your parents eventually gave in to your wishes, you would feel triumphant. Expressing your anger got you what you wanted! Only later, as a mature adult, do you realize the damage that you did—how badly you made your loving parents feel, how it tortured them to see you acting out like that. And you may even see that you harmed yourself by training yourself to react to difficult situations with anger.

The key to quitting the anger habit cold turkey is to recognize that it is not at all our friend. It is addictive because it seems to bring us benefit; then when it doesn't, it fools us into thinking we need more. The alcoholic has to overcome denial and admit that the alcohol itself is destroying him. The nicotine addict has to realize that her cigarettes are killing her. We anger addicts have to face up to the reality that anger is our enemy.

When we take a closer look at reality, we see that the seemingly creative energy that comes from anger and serves to remove obstacles to our happiness is purely destructive. It can be difficult to realize this because when anger rises, it speaks to us with our own voice! When we give ourselves orders, we can only obey. When someone makes us angry, a voice within us that we feel is Chief Commander says, "That's it! I can't take it anymore! I hate it! I'll make it stop! I'll get them back!" We don't think of ourselves as "obeying" our own voice, we just think we are directing ourselves naturally. But actually, our impulse is controlling us. It is manipulating our mind, speech, and body like a child manipulates a doll. When anger rises, we do not own it—it owns us. It is not our friend or our tool. It fools us into feeling this way, and then *we* become *its* tool.

A central component of the destructiveness of anger is this feeling of helplessness you experience while you are in its grip. Just as a gun cannot resist the trigger finger that causes it to shoot, even if its barrel is obstructed and it will explode on itself when fired, so people in the grip of anger feel they cannot stop themselves from taking the actions dictated by that passion, even if they are going to destroy themselves along with their target. As long as you are in control of yourself and able to choose your responses rationally, you may seem fierce, violent, or intemperate, but you are not really angry. You are angry when you lash out blindly, when you are swept away by the feeling of utter hatred of your enemy, when you will stop at nothing less than the destruction of your target.

We are very familiar with the immediate unpleasantness of being filled with rage. Darkened with a nauseated tension, the beloved faces of our family and friends start to look ugly and evil, our delicious food tastes bad, our skin crawls, and our body trembles. If we continue to feel angry, we find that we are unable to take any interest in our usual activities, we can't sleep, and we become obsessed about vindication, revenge, and concocting strategies to cause others harm. We then become paranoid, anticipating all sorts of attacks against us, which only makes the situation worse. We get angrier and angrier, until we either act on our drives or relapse into a frustrated depression. Either way, we always hurt ourselves and often hurt others in the process.

On this topic I can speak, with much sadness, from personal experience. I somehow grew up with an explosive temper. I cannot convey in words how deeply I regret the many instances in my life when I lost control of my anger and hurt someone—sometimes a loved one, sometimes a stranger, but always myself. I accomplished only temporary goals and had to suffer the consequences of long-lasting damage to relationships, lost opportunities, and foregone happiness. Fortunately, no one died and I survived occasional suicidal impulses and self-endangering acts. Eventually, thanks to the Buddhist Dharma, I was able to see the error of my ways, and I am now much less frequently overwhelmed by anger.

Some therapists and religious counselors who work with the problem of anger believe that people should not be taught to suppress it. They think of it as a natural energy in the body-mind complex. They may also believe that if people do not release their anger toward harmful others or an oppressive environment in a cathartic way, it will turn back upon them, causing depression and corroding their physical and psychological health. Therefore, these specialists recommend giving in to anger and expressing it fully. Fortunately, even they carefully train people to scream into a pillow or hit a punching bag rather than direct their anger toward actual human targets.

There is an element of truth in this philosophy. Once you are angry, if you choose to suppress your emotions, then they can rest within you, transforming into cold malice, calculating vindictiveness, corrosive resentment, poisonous bitterness, and icy hate. Suppressing awareness of your inner feelings will erode your well-being from within, eventually causing sickness and depression. Even Buddhist lamas would agree that you must face your emotions, recognizing how you really feel and what you really think.

But the crucial difference between the philosophy of catharsis and Buddhist psychology is that Buddhists teach you never to act on your anger. You may think that as long as you avoid doing violence toward another person, your anger is doing no harm. Certainly the physical wounds caused by limbs and weapons and the verbal wounds caused by insults and abuse frequently result in spectacular injuries, maiming, psychological torment, death, and even suicide. But just the movement of the mind into anger—that alone, even if you do not act violently toward others—does tremendous damage to your body and soul. It taxes your heart and liver, your brain and endocrine system, injuring your health in this life. And it wreaks havoc on your personal karmic evolution. The only sensible thing to do is to acknowledge and accept your anger, and then completely let it go. Over time, you can learn to replace it with the positive virtues of tolerance and patience, and to channel your well-controlled aggressive, assertive, and forceful energies into creative and constructive activity.

In this context, we may think that, as modern persons, we don't need "pre-modern," "mythic" explanations of reality, such as reincarnation, former and future lives, the existence of heavens and hells, gods and demons, and so forth. Wisdom can be deepened, meditation can be perfected, virtues can be cultivated, and bliss can be experienced without resorting to old-fashioned pictures of the world. Science has discovered no soul, no proof of former or future lives, no gods, angels, or demons. Buddha's wisdom always accords with science, so why not proceed without such a fanciful context? Why do we need the infinite life context at all, just to do better in this world we can see and feel around us?

Especially in the critical work of overcoming anger, we do need the infinite life perspective. While specific details of the rebirth process need not conform exactly to any one traditional picture, we need to acknowledge the infinite continuity implied in all biologies, modern as well as ancient. We need to face the probability of the infinite consequentiality of every single thought, word, and deed. Only that infinite life context can energize our mindfulness sufficiently, and move us from awareness to really conquering anger. We have to reach down into our instincts. We can work intellectually with the conscious mind, its prejudices and habits, and make progress up to a point. But where the primal attachment to the body is concerned, when injury becomes threatening and harm severe, we will react instinctively to strike preemptively in fury, to kill and destroy, to retaliate with lethal force. The complete conquest of anger that will give us real peace is far more than a life-and-death struggle, since life-and-death struggles only concern enemies in this life, whose ultimate harm to us is the taking of our life. "If the worst that can happen to me is death pictured as mere oblivion, if the worst I can inflict on our enemy is that same oblivion, then why fear risking death to rearrange this life to my liking, why regret killing my enemy when I am merely putting him out of his misery? Though I may have ideals of kindliness and charity, when my impulse arises to destroy, why not have a go at it?"

Only when the playing field is enlarged, when the consequences of our acts will come back to haunt us beyond death in sensitive lives to come, when oblivion is not a sensible option or reasonable expectation—only then can we find the strength to combat our inner instinctual impulse to destroy when frightened or angry. The materialistic identification of the self with the body moves one's instinctual makeup out of reach. It is felt to be "hard-wired," "inalterable," natural, and inevitable. Therefore, supposedly only surface modifications of anger or greed are possible. Deeper self-transformation is considered impossible, and therefore is not attempted.

In the infinite life perspective, when we take on anger, we are taking on an enemy who has already harmed us during countless previous lives, and whose injuries in this life can afflict us endlessly in the future, even leading us to lives in hellish conditions.

To challenge anger with hope of success, we must confront this thing called "hell," what humans have imagined all over the world as the concretization of the most extreme conditions of suffering. No one can deny that anger can create hell on earth, and does so all the time. The trenches of the world wars, the fire-bombed cities, the A-bombed Hiroshima and Nagasaki, the gas chambers of Auschwitz, the torture chambers of whatever oppressor or sadistic prison warden, the genocide fields of conquistadores, communists, colonists, slave owners, Biafra, Tibet, Cambodia, Rwanda, Bosnia—these are all visible living hells, all of them created by anger. Anger has the power to create hell even on earth, so it takes an awareness of the possibility of even more drastic hells to gain the life-and-death determination really to conquer it.

The great Milarepa, twelfth-century Tibet's St. Francis of Assisi, was the first Tibetan who was considered to have transformed through spiritual evolution from an ordinary common sinner and even criminal into a perfectly enlightened buddha. As a youth, he learned the black arts of sorcery to avenge himself and his mother and sister against a wicked uncle who had usurped their inheritance and enslaved them. In a sorcerous ceremony, he raised violent spirits and had them engineer the collapse of the uncle's mansion on the heads of the whole clan assembled for a wedding, killing thirty-five people. Once he turned toward the white magic of spiritual practice, these murders anguished him with intense repentance and remorse, intensifying his positive efforts. Upon his full enlightenment, he said that the fear of falling into hells for murderers gave him the strength and the power of resolve that was indispensable for overcoming his ignorant and addicted mind.

I often encounter intense fear in those people who resist the strong possibility of their having endless future continuation as a sensitive being. They are willing to give up the infinite positive horizon of possible buddhahood in order to deny the danger of an infinite negative horizon of extreme suffering. Such a fear of the unknown after death is definitely a major cause for people succumbing to the limited life-picture and its terminal lifestyle. It makes them abandon theistic religious faith, willingly giving up hopes for some heavenly immortality in order to convince themselves that infinite negative states of pain are simply primitive myths and totally implausible. A picture of themselves quietly sinking into oblivion in nothingness is found comforting and releasing, in comparison with the intense terror images of hell can kindle. Experiencing cracking frozenness near absolute zero, searing heats of the center of suns of thousands of degrees, squashing pain under the crush of mountains, cutting pains of being sliced to ribbons, torn apart, rent limb from limb—these are the horrendous images the mind produces when hell is evoked. Going along with the physical terror are images of the most profound psychological terror, loneliness, and pain. Monotheistic people—most Hindus and Pure Land Buddhists, as well as Abrahamic believers—are afraid of hell, which makes them passively obedient to the religious institutions that maintain those doctrines. They can remain monotheistic in spite of underlying suppression by terror, because their faith in a savior, God, or Buddha, Incarnation of God, Son of God, or Prophet of God, is strong enough that they feel secure in their immunity from hell—though the underlying terror-tension tends to make the quality of their faith and personal living both rigid and fanatical. But secularists use what they consider to be the ridiculousness of doctrines of hell as a major reason to limit their horizon to this one, materially embodied life.

People avoid horrible imagery and deny the danger of a horrible fate. Yet such fears are never far below the surface. What else could explain the popularity of horror movies? They must make money or they wouldn't be produced. I personally dislike them and try to avoid them as much as I can, quickly click them off if I run into one when channel-surfing. My kids used to enjoy luring me into a horror movie, sitting me down, getting me some popcorn, and handing it to me just before the evil thing jumps out. Then they would go off in gales of laughter as I startled wildly and spilled the popcorn all over. This always annoyed the neighboring movie-goers. Such horror movies, sometimes brilliant in their special effects, are really sustained evocations of hell. Why do they appeal to a secularist audience that doesn't believe in such things? Is it that by somehow identifying with the heroines and heroes who succumb to or escape from the most horrendous, hellish treatment by the bad things, they reinforce their ability not to fear ending up in such hellish conditions ever themselves? Or is it that they still fear hell subconsciously, and they are trying to immunize themselves against that? Or do they simply want to relish the bravery in confronting terrifying imagery that comes from believing in ultimate nothingness?

If we are going to be here forever in some form or another, there is no denying we can develop toward the infinitely positive awakening of perfect wisdom, blossoming of perfect love and compassion, buddhahood with its infinite transcendent bliss. Once you can progress incrementally without limit, you can be whatever you most want to be. That infinite horizon, however, carries also the potential for infinite danger, since you can also progress incrementally toward the infinitely negative. Hell is the infinitely negative. This frightens us and makes us want to shut down our positive aspiration.

The fact remains that the alternative to commonsensical infinite continuity, the eventual entry into nothingness of our subjective consciousness, simply makes no sense. It can be wished for irrationally, we are quite good at believing in irrational things up to a point, but it cannot make sense, just from the simple meaning of the words. No matter how fanatical we may try to be, we cannot easily sustain belief in what does not make sense—our human nature is to try to make sense when it really counts. We can take advantage of the vista of the infinitely positive to inspire our positive spiritual evolution. Why should we not also take advantage of the vista of the infinitely negative?

When we get it right, fear can be a great motivator. We do not spurn its adrenaline burst when it helps us jump out of the way of a car, run from a mugger, avoid a falling tree, though we must be careful not to let it overwhelm us and paralyze us into helplessness. But healthy, cautionary fear is a powerful force in our lives, and we also need it in our spiritual development. In fact, just as to conquer anger we must learn to be angry with our anger, to defeat hate we must turn hate toward hate itself. To hate our anger we must fear our anger, we must really open up to how massively anger has, does, and can hurt us. We must recognize that a moment of anger can magnify its effects infinitely until it has created a living hell. We must fear that heartily, intensely. The intensity of that fear of hell must be turned against the intensity of the anger. Only then do we have a chance to conquer it. Only when we broaden the context of our encounter with such an entrenched instinctual force do we have a chance of uprooting it. So we should not persist in denial of some sort of hell, we should concentrate on it with the greatest care, so we can wield the laser saber power of healthy fear to skewer the demon of anger when it rears its fearsome head. While no hell or injury is ever permanent, just as no heavenly happiness is secure, anger can damage our evolutionary progress and personal state of being to an inconceivable degree. Anger constantly creates a world of pain. Therefore, the first step in conquering it is to recognize it as our foremost enemy.

It's easy to see how anger results in widespread destruction on a societal level, where it is a part of our everyday lives. We are surrounded by violence. The news media on a local level barrage us with stories of murders, rapes, beatings, and break-ins on a daily basis. And as if that weren't enough, we voluntarily expose ourselves to violent films that show all kinds of brutal acts in explicit detail. Even many of our sporting events, including boxing, football, and mock wrestling, are vehicles for modeling and reinforcing aggressive behavior.

We find violence in subtler forms, as well. We make guns easily available for purchase, and we see the effects in astronomical murder rates. The meat, cosmetics, and drug research industries treat animals horrifically, as if they were not sensitive, living beings. And at the apex of this social pyramid of violence sits the huge military establishment, the largest single line-item in the federal budget, the most gigantic collection of the machinery of destruction ever assembled in history. In fact, the Bush administration, with its "war on terrorism," is increasing this budget more and more all the time. As a result, our economy is completely entangled in the business of warfare, which is, by its very nature, the business of intolerance and hatred. Furthermore, money and human resources spent on the military is money not spent on universal education, ecological preservation, improved infrastructure, sustainable food production, health care, and other quality of life measures.

The great mass killings of the last century and the constant wars we are embarking on at the beginning of this new one have hatred as their trigger and persistent fuel. If it happened that a nuclear holocaust ended life on this planet, it would not be caused by technology or by any natural or man-made instruments; it would be caused by hate. The force that moves the hand that signs the orders to build the missiles and their deadly cargo is hate. In that final moment, the power that would move the fingers to press the buttons to launch planetary destruction would be none other than hate. Anger and hate are now armed and ready to destroy all life on Earth.

We defeat one enemy after another, only to discover that our allies in the previous fight have become our enemies in the new fight. Ultimately, we realize that the whole lifestyle based on violence and militarism is at the root of our problems. We recognize, at last, that our real enemy is anger. Then we come to the insight that the only war worth fighting is a war on anger—a war to replace hatred with tolerance, a war that will end all wars forevermore.

Practice: Developing Patience

The opposite of anger is patience: the third transcendent virtue, after generosity and justice, of the infinite lifestyle. The Sanskrit word for it is *kshānti,* which comes from the verb root *ksham,* meaning "to flow" and "to bear." It relates nicely to T. S. Eliot's favorite Sanskrit word, *shānti,* which means "peace." If we develop the ability to flow with events, to bear an injury that would make a normal individual angry, then we will be at peace. Next, if we line up the Sanskrit words for anger, hate, fury, and vengefulness, their opposites emerge as patience, tolerance, forbearance, and forgiveness. These virtues are said to constitute an invulnerable armor, a protective raiment that renders our happiness secure and our peace invulnerable. This is the great practice that we need to win our war on anger. When we have developed transcendent patience, then we will have conquered hatred, and throughout our infinite lives nothing will ever mar our happiness again.

The great Shantideva (eighth century CE), the ultimate expert on the topic of patience, gives a teaching on this topic in his *Entry to the Enlight-*

ened Life, as transmitted to me from His Holiness the Dalai Lama. I know of no better program for overcoming anger, hate, and fury, and developing tolerance and patience, than that developed by this gifted adept. I follow him in this chapter with tremendous respect and careful veneration.

Let us prepare for this practice by entering our physical and mental shrine space, as outlined in Chapter 2. You feel blessed by your mentor beings, the beings of light who inspire you by setting such a wonderful example of how to live. You spread their blessings to the host of sensitive beings around you, including your loved ones and your hated ones. Fill yourself up with calm energy, feel yourself light and buoyant, empowered to address this important issue for the sake of all life on the planet. When you are ready, turn to the practice of patience.

Shantideva asks us to begin our meditation from our decision to conquer our emotional addiction to anger. So we start by intensifying our awareness of the chain reaction that anger uses to take control of us. Remember the last time you were seized by anger and imagine that you are living that moment again. You should be able to feel the heat rising in your face, the choking sensation in your throat, your restless urge to speak or move, and the vivid, violent imagery of your fantasies projecting toward the person or harmful situation that's making you angry.

Focus on these sensations for a moment, but don't follow them through to their conclusion. Instead, try to get back to the moments just before your anger burst forth. At first, this may seem difficult because events happen too quickly—something upsetting occurs and you immediately blow up. But while in certain instances anger can arise practically instantaneously, so in other instances (for example, at a family gathering, where a particularly obnoxious relative is getting on your nerves), your feelings of frustration arise gradually and change very slowly into anger.

What you are looking for is your initial sense of frustration, that mental and physical unease that builds up during a trying situation. This sensation might have persisted as a growing tension for some time before your anger exploded. View the events leading up to the angry episode backward and forward, looking for the finer shades of transition from your preceding state of well-being to the discomfort of annoyance. When did the frustration begin to block out your feelings of good cheer? Was it a particular something a person said? Was it something in their tone or manner? Was it someone's refusal to comply with your request? Was something going on that upset you? Were you merely being reminded of another person you dislike or another time when you suffered? Try to isolate the precise moment when you lost your connection with what was actually going on and began to withdraw inward into your negative feelings. You have now entered the most effective battleground for your struggle with anger.

Next, turn your meditation to adjusting your attitude toward the events that caused you to become angry. Depart from remembering actual events and imagine instead possible alternative outcomes. Concentrate on what you could have done before you blew up in anger to change the situation. Before you withdrew in frustration, could you have excused yourself from the conversation, exited the room, cracked a joke, or enlisted someone else's help? Could you have done some special aggressive something, perhaps a bit shocking and rude even, but done it with good humor and not with anger? For instance, could you have dropped an ice cube down the obnoxious relative's shirt? Often, we have small impulses telling us to avoid a bad situation that we see coming but we ignore them, feeling obligated to follow some rules of etiquette or politeness. Instead of avoiding embarrassment, however, we only let things get worse.

Now picture yourself in scenarios in which you can do nothing to ameliorate the situation. You know that getting angry didn't help, so imagine instead doing nothing, simply walking away. You use your own inner resources to soothe your tension and divert your attention: draw deep breaths, run around the block, do some calisthenics. Visualize yourself maintaining your sense of humor and good cheer. You are extremely capable at keeping your frustration from overwhelming you, realizing that anger would only take over and cause you to lash out blindly at the situation with your body, speech, and mind.

Imagine, for example, that you are feeling frustrated because you are stuck in traffic and are going to be late for a meeting. You begin by trying to change the external situation. Can you call the person you are meeting to let her know you'll be late? Can you take an alternate route? Once you have done all that you can, you must accept that you are still stuck in traffic and you are not going to be able to change the situation. So rather than sitting in your car allowing yourself to become more and more frustrated, getting angry at the other drivers, honking and cutting people off when they try to change lanes, focus instead on changing your own perspective. Is it really so bad to be stuck in traffic? Would you rather sit in your car feeling miserable and taking your anger out on others, or would you rather enjoy this unexpected gift of free time? Use these precious minutes to phone a family member or old friend just to say, "I love you." Turn on the radio and sing along to a favorite song. Practice a meditation or breathing exercise. Think of all the reasons you have to be thankful just to be alive in this moment. Gradually, your frustration will pass. You will have successfully avoided anger altogether, creating positivity for yourself and the world around you instead.

Shantideva says, "Whatever happens, I must not allow my cheerfulness to be disturbed. Being unhappy won't fulfill my wish and will lose me all my virtues. Why be unhappy about something if it can be fixed? If it cannot be fixed, what does being unhappy do to help?" Shantideva is not suggesting that you constantly allow yourself to be stepped on like a doormat in your attempts to develop patience. Don't think that the spiritual thing to do is to swallow your feelings and be a victim. Not at all. The point is not to allow injustice, a problem you began to overcome in the previous chapter, to flourish. Doing nothing could not be more wrong. When something unjust happens, step in at once. Develop the ability to act forcefully without getting angry, be preemptive, and move beyond long-ingrained reactive patterns. So say something forceful. Get help. Be assertive. Cheerful aggressiveness is the ticket here.

Our next step is to cultivate our awareness of the predominance of suffering in the world. Picture all the inconceivable forms of violence that the living beings of this planet constantly inflict on one another, as if you were watching a nature program. I remember one time when I was working on these anger meditations, I saw on television Disney's *The Living Desert*. I became totally engrossed in watching one insect jumping on a beetle, being attacked by a snake, and finally being eaten by a spider. This was a perfect example of the suffering of "one eating another," as discussed in the Buddhist ancient texts. What a meditation I had with those images in mind! Visualizing similar types of scenarios, reflect on the many sufferings of all living beings. Think about the sufferings of human life in particular, the thousands of ways in which we can be knocked down by illness, pain, injury, sorrow, and death. Why do we take this step now? Because meditating on the prevalence of suffering helps us tolerate our pains by putting them into perspective. Often we realize how blessed we really are, relatively speaking.

Now let's turn our attention toward understanding the truth about the supposed perpetrators of harm, those people who make us angry. Visualize someone you hate or seriously dislike. Notice that just thinking about this person stirs up angry feelings within you. "What an evil person. He intentionally hurt me," you tell yourself, getting flustered and upset. Recall the harmful things this person has done to you, things that have made you suffer. Feel your hatred build and your vengeful thoughts arise.

But then use mindfulness to take a closer look at your anger. Ask yourself, "What is it that makes me hate this person so much?" You may at first answer, "Everything." Instead of fixing on the image of the whole person, however, look at him or her just one piece at a time. Is every part equally unpleasant? Focus on his hand. See it for itself. It's just a hand, isn't it? Look at his ear. It's just an ear. Look at his clothes. No problem there. Envisioning the face may bring up more negative feelings, so picture just the chin in isolation. The nose. The brow. The eye. One by one, you'll discover that none of these individual physical pieces is hateful on its own.

Now move on to other characteristics. Is this person's voice hateful? Try to recall a particular statement, perhaps an insult, which you found hurtful. "Fool! Slob! Idiot!" What do these words really mean? They anger us in certain situations but not in others. Therefore, there is nothing to hate in the words themselves. Now remember an action that enraged you. Perhaps he stole something from you. Perhaps he picked a fight with you. See the circumstances in specific detail. When you do, you'll realize that it was an impersonal process—you can't put the blame on any one isolated moment.

When you look closely, you see that this person is not filled with intrinsic hatefulness. You realize that this man was the helpless pawn of his greed; that this man was trapped in his fear; and hence he acted out toward you. But you should not hate him in return; you should feel compassion for him! Most people we perceive as "antagonists" are merely struggling individuals trapped in their bounded worldview, desperately trying to pursue their own happiness. They are lost souls in desperate need of assistance. And we are enlightening beings capable of reaching out and helping them.

Though we may bewail fate when we fall ill, we do not get angry at our life-threatening disease—we don't choose to see it as an evil demon. Instead, we see it as a natural process. When we are seized by addictive thoughts such as lust or greed, we may feel sickened, but we do not think of the thoughts themselves as intentionally wishing us ill. Rather we think of them as mental mechanisms that take over our minds. But when we think of the enemy as a willful, intentional person with an evil design upon us, we lose control and hate him absolutely. We are swept away by our anger, and our body, speech, and mind become its tools.

Shantideva says, "Everything is governed by other factors, themselves governed by others; so nothing governs itself. Understanding this, I will not hate things that are nothing but hallucinatory apparitions."

Meditating in this way, again and again, in the quiet of your mental and physical shrine space prepares you for encountering real harm and injury. But don't expect to be completely patient, tolerant, and forbearing the next time you encounter a difficult situation. If you get just a tiny bit less angry, or if your anger lasts just a little less long, or if you can intervene in the action-reaction cycle sooner, then you have made progress. As Bill Murray said in *What About Bob?* (a favorite flick for this Bob!), "Baby steps. Baby steps." In general, it is counterproductive to hype any practice. Don't suddenly make a big push in your meditation efforts and expect big results. You'll only get upset or give up in frustration when things don't work out perfectly or even seem to get worse. Just trickle your way into your practice drop by drop. Realize that every effort makes a little difference, and keep at it. There is no question that, over time, you will become freer and freer of your bondage to anger.

You now are ready to cultivate a deeper level of patience, which Shantideva calls "the patience of nonretaliation," but we may as well call simply "forgiveness." I must warn you that you will likely encounter great difficulty with this practice—you must ask yourself to do more than may seem reasonable if you still haven't fully embraced the infinite life. You are entering the realm of true heroism. You will seek not merely to diminish your anger or control yourself in harmful situations. You will adopt the aim of making patience your magic shield of invulnerability, conquering rage and hatred once and for all, making yourself the total master of your forcefulness for good.

The first phase of this meditation is to review the causality of all the injuries you have suffered and could conceivably suffer. Do this in the infinite life context, so that you include in your analysis all of your many previous deaths and the many possible ways you may die in future ones. Reflect on everything that happens to you as the product of your actions in previous lives.

Now visualize someone hitting you. You feel searing pain as you try to protect yourself from harm. The other person's muscle strength, malicious intention, and furious action are all part of the events taking place. But focus instead on yourself and your role in that situation. How may you be the cause of what is happening to you? You must have interacted with your attacker innumerable times in the past—he has beaten you and you have beaten him, as well. You must be locked in an endless vicious cycle of hurting each other. As you feel his painful blows, note how intensely you want to beat him back. Recognize that your desire for revenge will definitely result in your having the opportunity to harm him in a future life, in the same way that he now strikes you. But then realize that this will only continue the endless, vicious cycle of violence. There is nothing you can do about your attacker. But there is something you can do about yourself. You can accept the blows without anger. You can choose to gain strength from your injury, knowing that when you heal you will be stronger. And you can forgive your attacker, taking responsibility for your own causal role in events. In short, you can blame the victim, yourself, for what you must have done to your attacker in former lives.

At first you may think this thought process is simple masochism, and recoil from it. Note that reaction in your mind, but then engage in a debate with yourself. In this meditation, your heroic mind argues with your self-centered mind as follows:

Self-Centered Mind: "Why should I blame myself for being attacked? Why is it my fault that I happened to be in harm's way? How do I know that I did the same thing to my attacker in past lives? I just met the guy. This is ridiculous. Anyway, blaming the victim is the worst possible solution!"

Heroic Mind: "Of course you should never blame the victim when someone else is hurt, because that would be uncompassionate. You blame yourself in this scenario, however, in order to retrieve your power from the situation and to end the vicious cycle of violence. Since you can't do anything to your attacker besides hit back, you'll only continue to keep up the cycle. You're only ensuring that you'll be beaten over and over again in the future. Don't allow yourself to be trapped in this situation forever. When you take responsibility for your own evolutionary causality, you gain power over yourself. Take control of the harm and turn it to your advantage. Use it to break the cycle so that this never again happens in the future, neither to you nor to your enemy."

Shantideva says, "Previously I must have caused similar harm to other sensitive beings. So it is right for this harm to be returned to me who caused such injuries to others."

Meditate long and systematically about the logic just presented. Visualize yourself accepting your attacker's blows without anger or thoughts of retaliation. See how by exercising patience, you free yourself and your attacker from a vicious cycle of negative karma, turning your suffering into heroic sacrifice.

Next meditate on your soul, again viewing it within the infinite life context. Realize how your spirit cannot be killed, how it is too subtle to be obliterated by any physical death or even conscious loss of identity. Feel how there is no need to defend the life of your soul, but only to work to strengthen it, increase its openness, awareness, happiness, and connectedness to others. Shift your habitual self-identification away from your body to your soul, which is the true vehicle for your infinite personal continuity across many lives. Imagine your spirit as a golden cloud of blissful energy, permeating an ever-widening field, infusing other beings with gentle bubbles of wisdom, tolerance, and joy.

The more you are able to identify with your boundless soul, the less you need identify with who you are in this life: your body, your limited self-identity, your possessions, your jobs and successes, your ideas and images, and even your beloved friends and relations. If any of these are harmed or destroyed, then you won't be as angry with the harmer, adding to the karmic damage. You can expand your blissful soul-cloud to catch the suffering ones and steer them toward love, forgiveness, and healing.

So let's put this philosophy to the test in a difficult but valuable meditation. Imagine your loved ones being killed or hurt. Picture several different scenarios. As you did when you were visualizing yourself being harmed, distinguish between the cases in which you have some defense or recourse and those in which you have none. In the worst-case scenario, when you can do nothing but stand by and watch your loved ones die, feel the waves of nauseating sadness and disbelief wash over you. But then rehearse not hating even the most heinous perpetrator, the murderer of your beloved children. How many times throughout human history has someone killed another person's children, and then the victim has immediately turned around and killed the murderer or his children? This cycle of violence continues to grow worse and worse, often going on for generations and generations, and the victims multiply. What's more, if you get angry and feel vengeful toward the harmer, you become obsessed only with doing him violence and you forget about helping your harmed beloved. You turn unloving and withdraw from bliss, abandoning your lost loved one in a state of confused suffering, whether alive or dead and floating in the between-space before entering a new life.

Next imagine your cherished property being ruined. Vandals have come upon your lovely home. They laugh and sneer as they shoot out the windows, destroy your furniture, and trash your memorabilia. Try to imagine this scene very vividly, so that even in your meditative state you feel startled and shocked. But continue practicing until you can fully understand not reacting with hatred. Finally, imagine the vandals desecrating your most sacred image—a Jesus on the cross figure, a Buddha statue, an Allah calligraphy, a picture of your favorite mentor, or a painting of a saint. Stay with the visualization, critiquing the rising anger and sense of outrage within you. Think about how the real Buddha, Jesus, Allah, wise person or saint—none of them is even remotely destroyed by the foolish vandals' bad behavior. In fact, they themselves would not have grown angry over their own images being ruined. You will soon be able to feel sympathetic toward these poor vandals who are earning for themselves a large wave of negative evolutionary momentum.

Your meditation along these lines, your rehearsal practice for daily encounters with persons and events that habitually make you angry, will definitely progress over time. But you will know you have achieved a major breakthrough when you find it imaginable to feel sorry for the people who do you harm. Your enemies—who are under the influence of the real enemy, anger—will seem blind, their actions crippled by habit. In fact, you will even start to appreciate them for giving you the opportunity to develop your heroic armor of patience. They inspire in you the strength to build your peaceful fortress of tolerance, where nothing can disturb you. They help you fly the joyful banner of forgiveness, which articulates the bliss of your freedom from all bitterness.

A great lama whom I used to work with, Tara Tulku, once talked to me about this before I had gotten very far into my own practice of patience. He amazed me by saying, "If you really understood how to navigate your evolutionary development, then you would be much happier to come down to the kitchen table in the morning and find your worst enemy sitting there ready to harm you than you would be to find a surprise award of ten million dollars from one of those prize competitions!" I remember nodding in assent as I realized that I secretly disagreed with him. In theory I recognized the evolutionary value of having a supreme challenge to stimulate my development of patience, the ultimate opportunity to conquer my real enemy, anger itself. But at the same time, I thought I could use the ten million dollars to do so many excellent things: spread the Buddha's teachings, spend more time in meditative retreats, sponsor others in their spiritual development, and so on. My fantasies took off in that direction.

I then reminded myself to apply Shantideva's powerful practice to my thoughts. "But you'll get angry when you lose the ten million!" I scolded myself. "You'll meditate all right, but your mind will increase its attachment to this life, so it won't do you much good. Others will seek your sponsorship not for spiritual development but for personal gain. You'll become childishly attached to their praise and approval. In the end, you'll waste your precious human opportunity to transcend your involuntary instinctual habits." Later, I heard of a psychological study of people who win huge amounts of money in lotteries and publishers' competitions that verified my line of thinking. Though the winners tend to experience a burst of euphoria and excitement just after getting the money, many end up losing their stable relationships and real friends, spoiling their health, and finishing far worse off than they were before they won. So keep practicing until you would be happier to find your worst enemy at the door than the Publisher's Clearing House prize team carrying a bunch of balloons and a check for ten million dollars!

Personal Performance: Acting for Good

The more you master the practice of patience, the more you will be able to live under its protection in your daily life. The better protected you are by it, protected primarily from your true inner enemy of anger, the more powerfully you will be able to perform selfless and heroic deeds for the sake of yours and others' ongoing positive evolution.

Instead of getting upset about trying situations like you used to, use each one as an opportunity to develop your patience. Each minor incident that upsets you can serve as a training session for handling the bigger incidents that make you really angry. It's like preparing for a marathon. You lift weights and run to build your strength and endurance. Your muscles may ache and you may feel tired at times, but you know that your suffering is for a good purpose, so you don't mind. Similarly, you can train yourself to manage your anger. You may suffer a bit as you try not to react to the perceived mistreatment, but you feel your mental strength and endurance growing as you build up your patience "muscles." What was unbearable at first becomes bearable later.

Shantideva says, "There is nothing that does not become easier through custom. Becoming accustomed to small harms, I must patiently learn to tolerate greater harms."

You start by practicing not letting small irritations bother you: mosquito bites, traffic jams, long lines, grating tones in others' voices, slight hunger or fatigue. Decide that you will consciously suffer these small discomforts without getting upset about them. Then you can begin dealing with persons who annoy you. Rather than avoiding them, choose to view them as a welcome challenge, exposing yourself to them in gradually larger doses. As you do so, you'll develop greater tolerance for their annoying statements or confused ideas.

The next time you encounter an inconsiderate and imperious salesperson at a store who forces you to wait in line much longer than necessary, use the time wisely. Internally critique your attachment to your purchase. Recognize how you can find something better or don't really need it at all. When your turn comes, smile sweetly and ceremoniously hand the goods to the annoying person at the register. Thank him for taking so much time with the other customers and making you wait, since it gave you the time to realize that you didn't really need this particular thing and saved you so much money. Ask him to please put the item back on the rack when he has time, and wish him a good day!

Once you have practiced not becoming upset about anything at all, you can then move on to the next step: you can learn to rechannel the energy that builds during difficult situations into a positive force for change. Remember from our earlier discussion that avoiding an angry response doesn't mean you should become passive in your daily life, afraid to act aggressively or assert yourself. In fact, by regaining power over ourselves, we become ever so much more effective in righting wrongs and seeing to it that goodness prevails. We can help the good guys win.

Happily and cheerfully, we can intervene with lightning assertiveness in situations that we sense are going bad. We may be joyful and playful in our confrontations, or we may need to be rude and shocking at times. Either way, we should always deal with trouble before it erupts into anger. Let's say, for example, that your irritating uncle shows up at the next family Thanksgiving gathering. When he starts to rant about the worthlessness of welfare mothers and do-gooder environmentalists as he always does, upsetting you and many others at the table, leap into action at the first possible moment. Present him with a "Good Grinch" Award, read a funny poem you've written up ahead of time, or slyly put a whoopee cushion on his seat—I leave it up to your imagination. Just be sure to do something before he angers you.

You'll find innumerable opportunities like these to insert tolerance and goodwill into your own and others' lives instead of running around in a state of stress and turmoil, in danger of exploding. You will become invincible, free of any habitual response of violence. You will find yourself less fearful of others, and will be amazed at how much less they will be provoked by you. Your interventions will often be more, not less, decisive, since you will have a detachment that enables you to see events and emotions more clearly.

What about situations that require actually harming another person in order to prevent her from doing more harm to herself and others? Even Shantideva says that we sometimes may need to act forcefully in a way that may seem harmful in order to surgically prevent violence. Let's say, for example, that you are being verbally assaulted by an enraged motorist who has gotten out of his car and is walking toward you on the road. You see an oncoming vehicle rapidly approaching, and you notice that the driver is looking down at his cell phone, not paying attention to the road. As soon as you realize that the car is about to hit your assailant, you shout for him to move, but in his fury he is blind to what's going on around him. You judge that you have time to act forcefully, so you charge at him with a flying tackle, knocking both of you clear of the vehicle and saving his life. (Don't try this unless you have considerable athletic prowess as well as solid cool patience!) Your actions were aggressive, even violent. But they were ultimately beneficial in that they saved a life, and perhaps two.

A famous *Former Life Story* of the Buddha that epitomizes transcendent patience is that of the great saint "Kshantivadi," which means "Teacher of Patience." He was sitting peacefully in the forest, when a young king and his harem came to picnic at a lake nearby. The king was cavorting with his wives, eventually getting sleepy and taking a nap, his head in the lap of one wife, while others rubbed his feet and massaged his back. During his nap, his wives gently covered him and pillowed him, then went for a stroll. They met the saint and, attracted by his beauty and peaceful light, sat at his feet and questioned him about the teaching. He kindly answered their questions and gave them the teaching of patience. Soon the king awoke and was annoyed that his wives were gone. He went after them and, when he saw them at the feet of the sage, he became jealous and angry and demanded to know what the saint was doing with his wives. "Nothing special, your majesty! Your kind wives came along and began to ask me questions about my main practice, the practice of patience!" "I don't believe you," said the king, becoming more enraged. "Let's put you to the test, see how forbearing you are." He drew his sword and with a single blow hacked off the saint's arm! The saint did not even shudder in pain or fear, so advanced was he in detachment from his body. "Oh, please, your majesty, don't do this! I do forgive you, and you can see I am immune to anger over any injury or even if you kill me. But this is terribly harmful to you. Please stop!" This made the king go berserk, and he started methodically dismembering the saint, chopping him limb from limb, each time expecting cries of agony or anger. Finally he hesitated at the death blow, winded and now a bit in awe, though still his fury was unabated. Then, Kshantivadi said, "Now I must prove to your majesty the power of patience. If it is really true that I feel no anger toward your majesty, in spite of these horrible injuries, then may my body be made whole once more!" At that, his limbs were instantly rejoined to his trunk, he was as before, without a single wound. At this, it is said, the king was so shocked, he died on the spot, and was reborn in the hell of endless slicing—you can just imagine.

This story illustrates the transcendent level of patience, where its power, combined with transcendent wisdom, had become so great, the yogi was already highly enlightened. His awareness had become a golden cloud of bliss, beyond the body, able to sustain the coarse flesh-and-blood body but not solely dependent on it. The attainment of such heights of transcendence and empathy may seem utterly incredible to us, very far-fetched, and something we would never aspire to, given our indoctrination in the materialist view of evolution. But not if we open ourselves up to the infinite life perspective. Once there is no limit to the frame of reference, no predetermined restriction to the potential of continuous systematic development, anything is possible. It is like Neo in *The Matrix*. As long as he identifies himself with his coarse body in the computer-maintained illusion of the matrix, he is bound by gravity, can be killed by beating or bullets, cannot fly or disappear. But when his awareness critically cuts loose from his habitual perception and expands so he can identify with the matrix itself or any part of it on any scale, as well as return to identify with the "digital residual self-image" that is his matrix body, he can perform what those indoctrinated in the matrix reality consider miraculous feats. Whether such a vision of the quantum reality of our world is realistic or not, it is important to acknowledge that many people in other cultures with other reality views have held such a vision, and accordingly have cultivated death-transcending patience and have become capable of great heroism. We now have the opening in our worldview coming from quantum physics in the form of the uncertainty principle, the wave-particle paradox, probability theory, and so forth, though this has not yet broadly loosened the rigidity of popular materialism. We now can adopt the infinite life perspective, at first experimentally and eventually matter-of-factly, and we also can fully free ourselves from anger. We can embody transcendent patience. Along the way, we can develop baby-step heroism, feeling better with each little step. In our overstressed daily lives, any degree of patience is its own immediate reward.

As much as I am in awe of this story of Kshantivadi, both incredulous and yet admiring, I am critical of one aspect. He is impeccable in his practice of patience, but problematic in his performance of it. Why did he let the king destroy himself like that? Why did he not feel more sorry for the king, recognize him as a helpless victim of his own anger, and manifest his forbearance by pre-empting the violent deeds that landed the king in hell? Why did Kshantivadi not use martial art and simply avoid the king's blows? Or let him lop off just one limb, then magically perform his "act of truth," and make himself whole, and after that dodge the blows while calming the king down? Once we have practiced, when we perform our patience, we should not show it off and provoke our enemies even more. Using it internally to stay cool, we should use our heroism to pre-empt the enemy's self-destructive actions. At least, this is how we should aim our aspiration.

Societal Performance: Transforming Militarism

We have already discussed the ways in which violence pervades our modern society. In the "Justice" chapter, we even dove into a major exploration and acknowledgment of the atrocities that occur every day. The questions we must answer now are, "How can we use our practice of patience to diminish our glamorization of and dependence on violence? How can our society move from militarism to pacifism?"

As we have seen in terms of our personal transformation from anger to patience, the first thing we must do is overcome hatred. At a societal level, this means adopting a policy of nonviolence. In modern times, we've been taught that nonviolence is unrealistic and impractical. But nonviolence is not weak. On the contrary, it is more forceful than violence, and it is far preferable in terms of its consequences on individuals and nations.

Gandhi provides an excellent example of the power of nonviolence, as he used it successfully to make the British imperialists withdraw from their "jewel in the crown," their most prized colonial possession and greatest economic resource, entirely without the use of military force. Gandhi was inspired by his mother's Jain tradition, the Buddhist nonviolence ethos that permeated Indian civilization as part of Hinduism, Jesus'

"Turn the other cheek," and Tolstoy's nonviolent Christian philosophy. Martin Luther King, Jr., learned from Gandhi's success and applied nonviolent principles to the civil rights movement in the U.S. Currently, His Holiness the Dalai Lama offers a prime example of nonviolent resistance in action, as he struggles patiently and peacefully against the Chinese occupation, colonization, and genocide of Tibet. He has succeeded in generating support from millions of peaceful people the world over.

Nonviolence is not simply the surrender to evil. Gandhi taught that there are three possible levels of response to evil. The least recommended response is to surrender to evil, doing its bidding in passive acceptance. A better response is to fight evil with evil, to oppose it violently. I call this "hot" heroism. It can succeed in the short run, but is ultimately ineffective, since it also surrenders to evil by itself turning evil, adopting violent means and using hatred as its fuel. By far the best response is nonviolent resistance, fighting evil without adopting evil motivation or tactics. It takes the greatest heroic effort of all, combined with unwavering intelligence and compassion, to stand up against evil without becoming angry or violent. But it is also the most effective method. I call it "cool heroism," and you can only perform it when armed with patience, tolerance, forbearance, and forgiveness. You must not personalize the situation or demonize the evildoer. You must see them as they really are—in the grip of hatred and delusion. You feel compassion for them but still oppose them actively. Your goal is to liberate them from the hatred and confusion that drive them, so that they see the truth of the situation and the justice of your stance.

Gandhi advocated a nonviolent response even to the Nazis. He insisted that peaceful, unarmed warriors could have stood en masse in the streets, braving tanks and firing squads, letting themselves be killed rather than either obeying orders or fighting back. He hoped that this action would eventually force the German soldiers to realize the fact that they were not fighting an enemy, but were in fact committing atrocities against decent human beings. They would then be forced to question their evil leaders, who had raised themselves up with fear. All violent authority structures would eventually crumble and the war would truly end. Gandhi admitted that this nonviolent battle would involve allowing many casualties to occur before the enemy would relent. But he countered that violent fighting also would result in huge numbers of casualties, and he was proven right. Not only were millions of people on both sides of the battle killed during the war, but also tens of millions more were killed in the gulags and proxy wars that broke out across the globe as a result of the Cold War after World War II. All combatants, motivated by anger and fear, had become accustomed to solving problems with violence and killing.

If 1945 had instead been the year when nonviolent resistance triumphed over violent aggression, an age of true peace might have dawned on Earth. Swords would have been hammered into ploughshares. The massive amounts of money and resources committed to warfare by the victorious nations, who became the planet's leading arms dealers, could have been poured into creating a viable lifestyle for all the world's suffering people. Public health measures could have been instituted and diseases vastly curtailed. Women and men could have been better educated. Population explosions could have been controlled. Environmental degradation could have been slowed. There would still be normal deaths caused by natural disasters, famines, droughts, diseases, and other unforeseen problems. But human destructiveness would have been enormously decreased as organized militarism was discredited. Human creativity would have been unleashed in a new way, inpiring us to reach a new kind of cool heroism, and our planet could have become a veritable paradise.

So, what can you do? There are many ways you, as an individual, can work to cultivate nonviolence on the local, national, and even global levels. In any social transformation, the most important step you can take is to secure your own personal transformation. You can have an enormous impact on the world around you simply by learning to replace hatred with patience in your own life. When you finally banish anger, always acting with patience toward others, you help not just yourself but everyone around you. Perform the transcendent patience practice offered in this chapter frequently, and you will see the waves of peace spread around you.

On the social level, you can find nonviolent ways to fight oppression, and in so doing help others to develop tolerance. An extraordinary man named Bo Lozoff teaches yoga to convicts, providing inmates with the chance to use their long-enforced retreat as an opportunity to retune their bodies and minds, so that they may emerge better people than they were before they went into prison. A former gang member, Monster Cody, works in Los Angeles to help other gang members find their way out of gang violence. Cesar Chavez, a migrant worker, organized farmworkers in nonviolent protests to secure a decent living and humane working conditions. Cornel West writes and speaks about overcoming the tradition of violence that has grown out of difficult race relations in the United States. His Holiness the Dalai Lama uses nonviolence in his international truth campaign against the oppression of the Tibetan people by the Chinese. And there are many, many more examples of people who have shown us how to practice nonviolence in an extremely effective manner, even in a violent world.

You don't have to be world-famous to make a difference, either. You can volunteer for or simply donate money and time to nongovernmental organizations around the globe that work to protect human rights, protest government oppression, and maintain peace. You can become a social activist, petitioning your local representatives in Congress and organizing rallies to support nonviolent policies. You can teach tolerance to those around you, leading by example. You can reach out in thousands of ways to members of your local community, spreading the message that has been sent by so many prophets, religious, and political leaders for thousands of years: Love accomplishes more than hate. We can only conquer violence with nonviolence.

Now that we have the determination to free ourselves from the slavery of hatred and anger, we can move to a new level of freedom. We have seen how patience is an immensely powerful force. It allows us to maintain control so that we do not risk harming others. We can mobilize all our energy, emotional and intellectual resources toward compassion because we realize just how much we can accomplish this way. Tolerance is strength. Patience is cheerfulness. Forgiveness is calm, calculated responsiveness to negativity, joyful in the security of total resilience. Hate can only harm us by infiltrating us and making us feel more hate. But we have learned how to resist the temptation to react with anger by depersonalizing our attacker. Instead, we view our "enemies" as unenlightened victims who have succumbed to hate. We embrace them and soothe them with the cool water of our immense well of compassion for all beings.

Our newfound perspective allows us to dream of a world in which individuals and even entire societies vow to transform their hatred into tolerance. It is entirely possible for us to achieve widespread nonviolence, lack of warfare, decreased military spending, and global cooperation—not just at some distant and unimaginable point in the future but now, in this century. We should never surrender our reasonable expectation of humanity's capability to awaken from its addiction to violence. One of the key psychological lynchpins of a militaristic system is the prejudice that violence is inevitable: Even if we try to be peaceful, others will attack and destroy us. And yet, when we contemplate the nature of reality, we see that the advantages of nonviolence are obvious. Pacifism benefits humans as well as animals and the natural environment.

Overcoming anger with patience is not at all unrealistic idealism, but rather indispensable to life itself. We can replace the vicious cycle of violence with the virtuous cycle of peace. We must be optimistic. We must believe passionately, as for centuries the buddhas have predicted, that we can create a better world—a world without violence or hatred, a world overflowing with love, a buddhaverse here on Earth.

7

Creativity

Preamble: Nonduality

Now that you have tasted the reality of infinite life, you can entertain the possibility that you already have a buddha nature—the potential, even the inevitability, of becoming a buddha in this or a future life. You *will* join the host of other beneficent, omnipresent beings who have achieved enlightenment. In fact, from these buddhas' perspectives, you already have. If you could hear them, they would tell you, "You *are* liberated! You *are* perfection! You *are* buddhahood itself!" Time as we habitually perceive it—as a linear continuity of moments with each one separate from and following the next—is illusory. Your future enjoyment of liberation is just as immediately present for buddhas as is your current subjective experience of ignorance and alienation. For buddhas, the freedom from involuntary rebirth that is nirvana and the engagement in the cycle of life that is the samsara of others' suffering are indivisible.

This may seem confusing because the ambiguity remains; you must still work in this lifetime to improve yourself and your world. You must engage in meditation and put your practice into action in your everyday life. As we have seen in previous chapters, you must continuously seek selflessness by challenging your familiar, old, self-centered worldview, strive to live by your personal code of ethics in the midst of injustice, and overcome your anger habit by developing forebearance. So you must not now confuse the infinite lifestyle with some sort of complacent feeling of already being perfect and enlightened. You must respect your current state of being, your slowly evolving level of awareness, while at the same time striving to improve it. This is where things get complicated as we try to grasp the elusive and sometimes frustrating concept of nonduality and develop the tolerance of ambiguity.

A sort of false hope or unrealistic excitement can come from the spiritual misunderstanding of the statement that, "Everything in the world, including you, is perfect." When it collapses, we can be overcome by despair and disillusionment. The fact is that despite our buddha natures, we do not feel blissful at all times in no matter what circumstances. On the contrary, we most often feel anxious and uncomfortable, stressed out and dissatisfied, and we know all too well that any major mishap could still cause us great suffering and grief. Our distress becomes even more acute when we examine the state of our planet. Perhaps, while at a retreat or in the presence of a master, we can successfully, if temporarily, convince ourselves that everything is for the best, everything is perfect. But soon enough we look around us, as we did in our meditations in the last two chapters, and see atrocious happenings occurring. We scan the horrors of the past, we fearfully anticipate the future, and we know that something's wrong. We cannot accept that this reality is simultaneously horrible and perfect.

We are not the only ones who have struggled with nonduality. *The Teaching of Vimalakirti Sutra,* an Indian Buddhist scripture from thousands of years ago, tells the story of five hundred noble youths who journeyed from the great metropolis of Vaishali out into the Indian countryside to visit the Buddha. "Lord," they said to him, "we have already embarked on the quest for enlightenment. But we have a question: How can we bodhisattvas make our world beautiful? How do we turn it into the perfect buddha world?"

The Buddha welcomed the question. He gave the well-meaning group a discourse on the good qualities cultivated during the long evolution of the bodhisattva savior: wisdom, generosity, justice, tolerance, creativity, and contemplation. He explained how these qualities become the very substance of the bodhisattva. He showed how the quest for buddhahood is a quest to create a new world of boundless happiness not just for oneself, but for oneself and all other beings. He ended by telling the youths, "Ultimately, the perfection and beauty of the buddha world reflect the perfection and beauty of the bodhisattva's mind!"

After listening to this discourse, the great, enlightened apostle Shariputra felt doubt and confusion. He thought to himself, "If such are the qualities of a buddha world, and they reflect the transcendent perfection of the bodhisattva's mind, then what happened to the mind of this Buddha right here? Far from being a perfect world of wisdom, generosity, and so on, his world looks like an absolute mess!"

Poor Shariputra! The Buddha read his thoughts and immediately challenged him. "Is it the fault of the sun and moon that the blind do not see them?"

"Oh no, Lord," replied the embarrassed sage.

"Just so, Shariputra, it is not the fault of my buddha world that you see it as imperfect," the Buddha explained. "It is perfect for its purpose, which is to provide the optimal environment for the evolutionary development of all the beings in it. But you are too focused on imperfection to see it."

To demonstrate his point, the Buddha planted his toe on the ground in a ceremonious manner. For a moment, Shariputra and all the others present in the audience saw a vision of a buddha world, which this Earth truly is, in the experience of the enlightened. It appeared to them as a perfect realm of enlightenment. Everything seemed jewellike and exquisite, and they saw each being as situated in the ideal evolutionary position for their particular stage of development. The Buddha asked Shariputra how he liked it, and the monk replied with great awe that it was indeed beautiful. Brahma, the Creator God in general Indian belief in that day, was present in that assembly and chided Shariputra, saying how he always saw the buddha-world perfection in this world. Then the Buddha lifted his toe and everyone's vision returned to "normal." They were again fully aware of the imperfections of the world they were living in.

This story evokes the very paradox we face now. Infinite numbers of fabulous heroic beings have already become perfect buddhas, and they are interfused with every atom of our universe. They exist in every cell and molecule of our own bodies. They provide an all-encompassing envelope or interpenetrating field of blissful energy, love, and support to all of us as-yet-unenlightened beings. But still we have little faith in their vast presence. Still we are not fully enlightened ourselves. Still we do not feel satisfied. Still we only catch brief glimpses of the beautiful perfection that surrounds and fills us all the time.

It is essential for us that we feel the underlying positive energy of the universe to be real, whether we choose to perceive it as infinite clouds of buddhas or the omnipresence of a God or gods in any form—Yahweh, Jehovah, Allah, Vishnu, Shiva, Mother Earth, the Tao, or simply a force for good. It makes us feel encouraged, hopeful, and inspires us to awaken to joy. On the other hand, in order to develop insight and compassion, we must also stay realistic within our relative, conventional experience of imperfection. If we ignore the reality of the world we live in, then we will have no motivation to improve it. We won't strive to develop our own positive virtues of wisdom, generosity, justice, and patience. We won't resolve to turn the imperfect world we see into a buddha world, to help all beings escape suffering by achieving enlightenment, no matter how infinitely long it takes, no matter how many lives we must devote to the effort.

One of my favorite movies, *Groundhog Day,* illustrates very well our position as human beings on this planet. The insight we gain from the infinite life perspective is that we have infinite time in which to get things done, just as Bill Murray's character realizes when he keeps waking up to the same day over and over again in the film. This doesn't mean, however, that we can sit back and relax in this lifetime, but rather that we must work to improve our world and ourselves until we finally get things right. Otherwise, we will keep repeating our frustrations and failures over the course of many lives, just like Bill Murray's character keeps fouling up his relationships. The good news is that as we open our awareness further, betting on infinite life, infinite evolution, and infinite opportunity, we find more energy and creativity, enabling us finally to succeed where we had failed before again and again.

And so we absolutely must embrace at the same time both the known perfection of the buddha-world and the perceived imperfection of our habitual world. We must accept that both realities can and do exist simultaneously, that in fact they each rely upon the other. Without an imperfect world, we would have no way of achieving enlightenment. Without the buddha world, we would have no reason to believe that we could do so, and so no motivation to try. Once we accept the creative ambiguity of this ultimate nonduality, we can enter sensibly our next phase of personal development, which involves cultivating our vision of the buddhaverse and our confidence in our ability to help create it here on this earth.

We might as well devote our infinite lives to such a magnificent enterprise—we're going to live them anyway! It is absolutely essential not to risk falling into inferior biological forms of life, more deeply embedded in suffering. Of course, even lower states will be impermanent and we will slowly evolve back up again into superior life-forms. But now that we have such an excellent human embodiment, why not ensure that we never again become unreflective, dumb, helpless, and vulnerable to extreme suffering? How much better to live all our future lives in as good a condition as we enjoy in our present life and, even better, to help others effectively in a joyful and creative way.

Problem: Self-Loathing

By now you have found it sensible to engage with the infinite lifestyle. You have tasted the deep wisdom of selflessness and are beginning to enjoy its vast openness. You have further felt your interconnectedness with others, recognizing your relations with them as highly determinative of your own inner state of well-being. You have begun to understand how switching your inner mental pattern from self-preoccupation to other-preoccupation is the royal road to immediate happiness and long-term freedom and enlightenment. You have embarked bravely on the path to developing the transcendent virtues of wisdom, generosity, justice, and forebearance through practice and performance. In your practice of altruism, you have developed the will to give all goodness to others, the sensitivity that makes you correct and gracious with them, and even the precious ability to be free from anger, using even experiences of harm and injury as tools to help you on the path of positive evolution. Now you must focus on overcoming your addiction to your remaining bad habits: laziness, addiction, self-loathing, and despair.

These four habits constitute the problem that creativity must solve. Each reinforces the other, so that together they create a paralyzing vicious circle. Perhaps self-loathing is the most interesting habit, in that it is the most distinctively modern and the most destructive. You may be surprised at this statement since modern people, Americans especially, are supposedly so proud and vain, self-important and self-centered. How could people such as we secretly feel contempt for our precious selves? We tend to underestimate the power of our worldviews, of the world- and self-pictures we carry in our heads, which maintain the world in which we walk around day and night, fall asleep and expect to wake up. As soon as we examine our worldviews, which structure our perceived reality, we realize their negative power. How do our worldviews make us despise ourselves and therefore feel depression and despair, lacking the inspiration to accomplish anything for good? Let's take a closer look.

First, recall our discussion from Chapter 1, "The Nature of Reality," about the two dominant, bounded worldviews: spiritualistic absolutism and nihilistic materialism. We'll start by examining the impact of spiritualistic absolutism on our opinion of ourselves. According to this predominant interpretation of the monotheistic religions, God created us out of nothing and we are saturated with sinfulness and evil proclivities. Even if we can have some hope for relief in heaven after we die, we still feel totally undeserving of such grace. So deep down, we really believe that we are worthless.

On the other hand, even if we reject this religious put-down, we are saturated with another worldview that is almost as depreciative. According to the nihilistic materialist doctrine, we are the product of a completely involuntary, utterly purposeless evolution started by the chance explosion of a random collection of elements. Our personal sensitivity is therefore nothing but an accident and an illusion. Our lives are utterly meaningless, since at any second we could die and disappear back into the totally uncaring nothingness that is assumed to be our fundamental reality. Whatever happens, we are just as worthless as the spiritualistic absolutists think we are, but in this case we don't even have the hope of ending up in heaven!

Added to these disheartening worldviews is our bleak and uninspiring vision of the cosmos. We see ourselves as billions of germs crawling on the wafer-thin skin of a boiling rock, in a tiny envelope of earth, water, and air. We are composed of imperceptible particles zipping around with nauseating unpredictability, themselves somehow sustained by subatomic waves or elusive particles that are mere vibrations or probabilities. All this somehow holds together to form an illusory consciousness for our terminal selves, and there apparently are no other such beings throughout what we perceive as an infinite, cold, mostly dark, and impersonal universe.

Small wonder depression is our dominant mood! Small wonder we suppress our natural, joyful creativity, since whatever we could do to improve the world would be ultimately pointless! Small wonder that we secretly long for death and oblivion, thinking of it subliminally as restful, deep, dreamless sleep, a welcome escape from this untenable situation! Small wonder that we secretly loathe ourselves, considering human beings an unfortunate accident, badly made machines ill-suited for a heartless environment! Small wonder we fear expressing any sensitivity for other beings, who also have no incentive to show us kindness! Small wonder we are too lazy to engage in a meaningful way with our surroundings! Filled with such a powerful poison of crippling self-loathing and paralyzing depression, how does our innately human creativity stand the slightest chance of emerging?

On a day-to-day basis, we cannot confront our miserable reality of hopeless despair, so we unconsciously enter a state of denial. In order to maintain this state, we find ourselves seeking constant distraction. But distraction is a double-edged sword: at the same time that we divert our attention away from the hollowness of our worldviews, we also divert it away from the healing conscience, the moving remorse, and the fundamental desire for goodness that lie within us.

Our chief distraction is self-importance, the idea that we are the center of the universe. As long as we must suffer living, we should be able to get hold of whomever and whatever we want and get rid of whomever and whatever we don't want. There is no reason to deny ourselves instant gratification. We quickly become addicted to entertainment that helps us escape reality, cosmetics and clothes that flatter us, and superficial pleasures that make us forget for a moment where we are. We confuse our superficial self-importance with true self-confidence based on a realistic, positive worldview. We confuse the superficial addictive pleasure of egocentric entertainments—loveless sex, thrill-seeking, violent sports, alcohol and drugs—with the real pleasures of self-transcendence, melting the rigid boundaries between ourselves and others through loving orgasm, the absorbing beauty of nature and art, creative playfulness, and altruistic labor. But the temporary solutions only bring us more dissatisfaction, thereby intensifying our addictions and our unhappiness. We become totally absorbed in maintaining our seductive self-images and destructive habits.

So we go through life half-dead, never feeling secure except when we're sound asleep, never truly self-confident or satisfied, and never free from laziness, anxiety, and despair. Our sad state of mind resonates with the mind patterns of our fellow human beings around the world, creating a planetary community on the brink of a destructive apocalypse. We seem stuck in a rut that will inevitably lead us to doomsday, so we try our best to simply withdraw.

If we have been clinically diagnosed as suffering from depression, our therapists have likely helped us to blame our parents. Perhaps, in their own despair, they drank too much, denied us adequate affection, were psychologically or physically abusive, or brought us into their own depression. But they also are the victims of this unhappy dominant cultural complex. They are no more to blame for their beliefs and behaviors than we are. Nevertheless, that does not provide us with an excuse to wallow in our misery. We must take responsibility for our own state of existence.

The good news is that even our usually debilitating self-preoccupation can be turned to help us question and eventually escape our negative worldviews. When we realize just how dissatisfied we are with our lives, we can either choose to accept the unfortunate hand we've been dealt in life or seek happier alternatives. We should discard the provincial, frog-in-the-well idea that our own culture is the only or the best one available. There are other civilizations more sensible and humane than ours whose traditions can help us break free of our self-loathing and despair to awaken to a more positive vision of reality. Certainly we should feel curious to learn more about them, if not to totally embrace them as our own.

It is never too late to change. We can liberate ourselves from laziness and despair with creativity, overcome self-loathing with true self-confidence, and get inspired to eliminate our addictions by finding deep-seated satisfaction in a new, inspiring, empowering worldview. Once we make this transition within, nothing can stop us from creating the buddhaverse we long for. We needn't feel any stress about this task, for there's no reason to hurry: we have infinite life and infinite time and space to transform ourselves and our world, since death is no obstacle. Filled with joy and inner peace, we can be energetically creative in building a realm of love and happiness.

Practice: Creativity Yoga

Our next step on the path to evolution is to develop the transcendent virtue of heroic creativity. The Sanskrit word for it, *virya,* roughly translates as "effort," "striving," "vigor," "energy," and "diligence." It is associated with *vira,* the Sanskrit word for "hero." Creativity is defined in various ways as enterprise, joy in doing good, enthusiasm, unshakable self-confidence, and positive inspiration. It is the antidote of the four negative habits discussed above—laziness, addiction, self-loathing, and despair. The three transcendences we've just worked on—generosity, justice, and tolerance—are primarily altruistic and other-fulfilling. Wisdom, our first transcendence, and contemplation, our next, are primarily self-interested and self-fulfilling. The creativity transcendence is considered the root of all the transforming virtues, since without it none of the others can be accomplished.

The practice and subsequent performance of creativity yoga involves fully embracing the inherent goodness of the universe. No outside force—God, gods, philosophical or political system—dominates us. No scientific measurements "proving" the reality of our nothingness have any validity. You must open to the possibility that we human beings are not doomed to failure, but rather that we absolutely have the opportunity to create a better world.

I have, in fact, developed a patented formula for why good is more powerful than evil. It came to me based on many conversations that I used to have with a friend who worked for most of his career on political campaigns in America and around the world. Whenever we would meet and celebrate together, at some point in the evening he would invariably come back to the issue that troubled him most deeply. "Really, Bob, from the enlightened point of view, is there really any way for good to conquer evil?" he would ask. Though I had answered this question many times already, both for myself and for him and other students, hearing it from my friend always got me thinking more carefully about the response.

So after many years, I finally came up with my patented, mathematically precise formula to prove the triumph of good over evil. An infinite number of beings act badly, since they view the world in an unenlightened manner as a hopeless place of pain, suffering, and endless inadequacy. But there are also infinitely many others who act benevolently, engaged in manifesting an enlightened world of bliss and freedom. The unenlightened and evil are defined by self-centeredness, whereas the enlightened and good are defined by other-centeredness. Self-centered beings are driven by their individual desires and aversions, delusions and fears. In their battle against what they perceive as a hostile world, they must draw on the emotional energies and needs of just one single being. Therefore, however many bad things such beings may do to others, they are soon exhausted since their drive is based only on their own appetite and will. Other-centered beings, to the contrary, are driven by the desires and aversions of an infinite number of beings. In their efforts to make the world a better place, they can draw on the emotional energies and needs of infinite others. Therefore, other-centered beings will always last longer and perform more capably, since their source of energy is so much greater than that of self-centered beings. The formula thus is: infinity times one (that is, evil) is *infinitely* less powerful than infinity times infinity (that is, good).

You must open your heart to the Buddha's discoveries about the nature of reality and to your own greatness. Reflect for a moment on the relative and unproven assertions of the worldviews that originally made you think you were a worthless being. Now open your imagination to other possibilities. Consider the teachings of the Buddha and many other world sages who, over the course of many centuries, have investigated and contemplated the nature of life. They do not make use of dogmatic assertions, as do the spiritualistic absolutists and nihilistic materialists. They claim to understand our reality perfectly well, but they also admit that its complexity cannot be reduced to any formula or set of rules; it must be understood by means of direct, individual experience. All verbal descriptions, therefore, are in some sense hypothetical: they can be useful guides to critical analysis, but in the end only critical wisdom can generate enlightened awareness. It's now time to put your critical wisdom to work.

Think about times when you have felt really blissful. Remember how intense the experience was, and how each time you so were amazed that you could feel that good. Recognize that there's no limit to your blissfulness, since bliss is the feeling you experience when you burst your habitual "self" boundaries and emerge into the joyous space of infinite life. True, the thrill can be a little scary, but it is also immensely fulfilling.

Now meditate on your own greatness. What a marvelous being you are! You are so free and multipurpose, creative and inventive. You are self-aware and analytical, plus you have language and the vast store of knowledge gathered in books and computers that allow you to share the collective memory of millions of other humans. You have imagination and can reach out experimentally to experience the still unknown. You have a natural sense of justice and empathy. Kindness, love, and generosity come easily to you. Finally, you have the ability to transcend your weaknesses in order to make the world a better place for all living things.

You have so much to enjoy and so much joy to share with others. Less evolved animals have a much more limited capacity to feel and to share. How pleasurable does a crocodile's caress feel to either party? They also have little time and energy left from their constant struggle to survive to devote to seeking happiness. Many humans are equally unfortunate: they fear and suppress their own bliss, develop theologies that it is diabolical, and react violently against others who claim that they have found the way to achieve a lifelong, joyous energy. Or, they simply live in conditions that prevent them from exploring themselves and their life-views: poverty, famine, warfare, slavery, and societal violence, controlling theologies or state systems. Look at how fortunate you are by comparison! You live in a free country where you can thoughtfully choose to believe whatever you like. You have the leisure time and the opportunity to read this book and to practice new methods of spiritual development. You are capable of imagining total liberation from suffering and the enjoyment of lasting happiness. How rare and precious is your special human life-situation, endowed as you are with intelligence, liberty, and opportunity!

Count your blessings in this way over and over again, especially within the context of having the ability and opportunity to attain full enlightenment. You are like a CEO who makes hundreds of millions of dollars a year and so considers his or her time worth tens of thousands of dollars a minute. Your precious time in this blessed human life-form is worth far more than that. To get where you are now, you have worked so hard and accomplished so much over your millions of lifetimes. It would be utterly foolish to waste these valuable moments of your human awareness and abilities to engage in nonevolutionary or even downright devolutionary activities.

Appreciating your own greatness in this way, from an evolutionary and spiritual perspective, builds up a genuine and beneficial self-confidence. It renders you immune to the superficial self-importance that comes from thinking that the most important things in life are money, fame, and status. As you make progress in this direction, you realize how astonishingly good it feels to consider yourself naturally great—not great because you did, have, or are something, but great because of the huge success you have already achieved to become the kind of human that you are. When you do, however, you realize that you are too great to waste your efforts on childish ambitions. You must invest your preciousness wisely in the only meaningful enterprise there is: that of becoming a Buddha or bodhisattva, a truly awakened, fully blossomed, human flower.

Next, meditate upon your death in this life. Begin by focusing on the certainty that you will die. As you do, you'll notice that your normal thinking is just the opposite—you regularly operate on the assumption that you'll go on living for some time. You postpone doing things, taking for granted that you can do them later. You invest in your pension assuming that you will be able to enjoy your retirement years. You hesitate to pass on your property to your offspring, thinking that you will always need it. But carefully consider the fact that there is no certainty about when you will die. Young people sometimes die before older ones. Healthy people sometimes die before sick ones. People living in peaceful countries sometimes die before people living in war-torn ones. Truly realizing that your life could come to an end at any moment generates a sense of urgency. Built upon the foundation of the valid self-esteem you've just established, this becomes a powerful source of energy and a fount of creativity.

When you really concentrate on the certain yet unpredictable nature of your death, it slowly dawns on you that at some point you will cease to exist in this human form that you currently identify as your "self." Press down further into this awareness and feel the layers of superficial concerns and obsessions that usually encumber you fall away. As they do, you feel free to focus on what should be your greatest concern—your journey into infinity beyond this life.

In order to do this, we'll be using a process described in the *Tibetan Book of the Dead,* more properly called *"The Book of Natural Liberation Through Understanding in the Between-State."* Picture yourself dying. Imagine yourself losing control of your motor functions, becoming unable to move your limbs, fingers and toes, head and facial muscles. Your senses fade: first sight, then hearing, then smell, taste, and touch. Next, your awareness enters an inner realm of vision as your eyes fill with hallucinatory shimmering and spinning patterns, like flitting fireflies or raindrops falling on a watery surface. These images blur until all that remains is a candle-flamelike light.

Now you lose the sense of being in an inner world or in the presence of your body at all, and your awareness becomes space itself. It's as if you were an open sky flooded with pale white moonlight that has no apparent source. Your awareness tries to resolidify itself but fails, and as it does, its energy intensifies and you change into an open sky filled with bright orange sunlight. Your energy calms in its infinity and your brightness disappears, leaving you an open sky of pure black darkness. You feel as if you are about to lose all consciousness, but as you release, you instead go right through the dark and become aware of self and other, of infinite subjects and objects as inconceivably interwoven, as a spacious state of pure transparency known as "clear light," like glass or diamond. Your awareness seems to be everywhere, as does everyone else's, and the realm of discrete objects is also simultaneously nonobstructive and discernibly present. Meditate on your blissful awareness of your ecstatic union with all beings and things.

Then meditate on what it would take to return to rebirth as a single being separate from the infinity you now feel as your selfless self. Note how it would involve withdrawing and solidifying as a subjectivity behind an array of sense organs looking, hearing, smelling, tasting, and touching the separate objects around you. The surge to feel yourself as distinct in retreat from infinite bliss involves going back through the states in reverse order, back through darklight into sunlight, through sunlight into moonlight, through moonlight into still flame, from flame into sparks and fireflies, through that swirl into smoke and clouds, and then into spinning visual patterns. Through the spinning patterns you perceive vast numbers of human couples in sexual union, melting into each other in various stages. Pick a couple you find the most exceedingly beautiful. Decide whether you want embodiment as female or male, imagine yourself as being like the partner you wish to resemble, and let yourself feel powerful desire for the other partner. As you melt orgasmically into their union, you lose consciousness down again through the same stages very rapidly and bounce back up from transparency equally rapidly, and dimly begin awareness in material form as a human embryo.

You can see how cultivating subtle mindfulness in this life before you reach the death transition will help you remain aware and calm throughout the actual process once it arrives. Simulating the process in visualizing your death helps to make you more aware of its immediacy. More important, it makes you realize that you have nothing to fear, because your innermost wisdom and mindfulness will see you through the transition in a conscious and creative way. You can't take your money with you, you can't take your friends and family with you, you can't take your body with you. You can only take with you that which you have integrated into your deepest being of the liberating wisdom of the Dharma, the true reality that releases you through understanding and opens you to the loving energy of compassion.

Meditating in this way on the preciousness of your human life and the virtual immediacy of your death transition gives you the powerful self-confidence you need to overcome self-loathing and the intensity of energy you need to overcome laziness. It propels your transcendent creativity into overdrive.

Do not rest complacently even in your intensity of creativity, your joyous energy aiming at the positive development of self and others. Focus your imagination and visualize yourself manifesting in streams of embodiments around the world, saving lives on a massive scale, giving huge gifts, restraining all sexual abuse, and supporting the positive entwinement of all beings, bringing the light of truth to all, reconciling all conflicts, speaking delightfully and entertainingly to all in all settings, and teaching humans so that they can understand how to transform their lives from sadness to happiness as you have done. Meditate that your mind becomes a giant turbine wheel of generous rejoicing in the fortunes of all beings, a wheel of loving energy even for your former enemies and for beings you don't even know, and a wheel of clarity and realism for all.

Visualize yourself as radiating from your innermost heart of free wisdom myriad rainbow light rays of positive energy that explode throughout the imagined universe and unimaginable buddhaverse. See these rays solidify into embodiments of beings, sounds, and images, which manifest exactly what each other sensitive beings need to take the next step into their own release and flow of happiness. Be specific in visualizing, approach specific beings and manifest appropriately and graciously to each. See gentle beings and manifest to them in radiantly beautiful forms, become works of art that open them to imagine their own higher experiences of bliss and peace. See fierce beings and manifest to them as even fiercer beings and things, whom they cannot hope to dominate yet who do not simply crush or devour them but amaze them by exercise of restraint and compassion, and so turn their attention to the superiority of gentleness and harmony.

Here you can use the recorded visions of the world's mystics or their mother lode in the Buddhist Universalist Mahayana Sutra literature to help you envision a world of positivity. Your creativity here needs to imagine the buddhaverse, the best of all possible worlds, as a palpable realm, the real nature of the environment of Mother Earth, visible to imagination and so truly possible, the kind of realm you become more and more determined to join all buddhas to create. Your flow of meditative creativity needs the inspiration and reinforcement of the magnificent positive imagination developed so expansively in the glorious spiritual civilization of ancient India. Nowhere is this imagination more evident than in the *Garland Sutra,* a very elaborate Buddhist Universalist Mahayana Sutra, also called *The Inconceivable Liberation Sutra.* You can use the vividly imaginative passages of this sutra to help develop your creativity. I quote a small section of it for your contemplation.[1] Such sutra passages from this Universalist spiritual literature should be read fre-

---

[1]*Garland Sutra* (Sanskrit in *Gandavyuuha Sutra,* P. L. Vaidya, ed., Darbhanga 1960, pp. 220, ff.), passage parallel to T. Cleary translation from the Chinese, *Flower Ornament Sutra,* Shambhala, Boston, 1993, pp. 1329 ff.

quently to inspire the contemplative imagination that releases the virtue of creativity.

In the following passage, a young Indian gentleman by the name of Sudhana, who bravely journeys to seek enlightenment from many teachers, meets a female bodhisattva savior called Prashantaruta Sagaravati, which means "living ocean of superbly peaceful voices." She tells him about her attainment, practice, and performance of the "enlightening liberation of each moment of consciousness producing oceans of energies of infinite joy." I quote her ecstatic description of her liberation at some length to enable you to taste its reading as a meditation practice, to let your mind flow through its visionary passages, to see the rich world of spiritual imagery it reveals. Vairochana Buddha is a cosmic Buddha whom this sutra considers the source of the emanation of the embodiment we know in the history of this planet as Shakyamuni Buddha.

I, noble son, have attained equanimity by purifying the ocean of mental aspirations. I have totally attained indestructible beauty of manifestation undefiled by flaws of all worldly desires. My mind is unregressing and unswerving in its initiative. My mind is unwavering, adorned with virtues like a mountain of jewels. My mind is free of location and free of static foundation. My mind is determined to totally liberate all beings. My mind is never satiated in seeing all oceans of buddhas. My mind is pure in aspiring to the powers of all bodhisattva saviors. My mind lives in the ocean of awareness of the luminous manifestations of universal knowledge. I am suffused with the creativity to free all beings from sorrow and sadness. I am intensely dedicated to eliminating all beings' pain and anguish. I am determined to eliminate all beings' immersion in the ocean of names, forms, sounds, scents, tastes, and textures. I am certain to extinguish beings' suffering caused by losing their loved ones and meeting their enemies. I am determined to prevent all beings' sufferings that come from confusions arising from objects and situations. I serve as a refuge for all fallen beings. I am determined to show all beings the way out of the miseries of living in the life cycle. I am concerned to prevent all sensitive beings' sadness, anguish, suffering, depression, and sorrow occasioned by birth, aging, and death. I have undertaken to infuse all beings with the supreme bliss of the transcendent buddhas. I find satisfaction in dispensing happiness to all beings in all villages, towns, cities, regions, countries, and kingdoms. I provide them with Dharmic spiritual protection, and I gradually develop them toward omniscience. That is to say, I inspire disillusionment in people who live in great palaces and mansions, and I take away their various kinds of anguish, and then I teach them the facts of reality, in order to extricate them from all unrealistic preoccupations and cause them to understand well the true nature of things. I teach true realities to those people who have long-standing habits of affection for and involvement with their mothers, fathers, brothers, sisters, friends, and acquaintances, in order to help them become involved with buddhas and bodhisattva saviors. I teach true realities to people who are deeply involved with their spouses and children in order to free them from craving self-centered pleasures, to develop their equanimity toward all beings, and to help them develop universal compassion. I teach true realities to people who are preoccupied with business in the markets, to help them meet, get to know, and take advantage of the noble community and the enlightened buddhas. I teach true realities to people who are addicted to consumer pleasures in order to help them develop transcendent detachment. I teach reality to people obsessed with the delights of concerts, plays, and dances, to help them find the joys of spiritual entertainments. I teach realities to people greedy for enjoyment of sense objects, to help them reach the sphere of the enlightened. I teach reality to people who are filled with anger, in order to lead them to transcendent patience. I teach reality to people who are depressed, in order to perfect their transcendent creativity. I teach reality to people whose minds are confused, to help them attain the transcendent meditation of realized buddhas. I teach reality to people trapped in the thicket of unrealistic views and fallen into the gloom of unknowing, in order to free them from the trap of convictions and the darkness of ignorance. I teach reality to people who are unintelligent, that they may acquire transcendent wisdom. I teach reality to people attached to the threefold cosmos of desire, form, and formlessness, that they may escape from the sufferings of the life cycle. I teach reality to people with lowly ambitions, that they may fulfill the vow of transcendent saviors. I teach reality to people preoccupied with their own benefit, that they may accomplish the vow to bring benefit to all sensitive beings. I teach reality to people with feeble determinations, that they may perfect the transcendent power of bodhisattva saviors. I teach reality to people whose minds are darkened by ignorance, to perfect their transcendent bodhisattva intuition. I teach reality to people who are ill-formed, to help them perfect their beautiful buddha bodies. I teach reality to people whose bodies are unreliable, so that they may perfect the unexcelled reality body of buddhas. I teach reality to people who have bad complexions, so that by the beauty of the subtle golden complexion of enlightenment, they can perfect their embodiment in touch with the heavenly bliss of buddhas. I teach reality to people who suffer, that they may attain the supreme bliss of transcendent lords. I teach reality to people who are happy, that they may attain the bliss of omniscience. I teach reality to people who are prey to disease, that they may enjoy the reflection-like bodhisattva body. I teach reality to people who are addicted to various pleasures, that they may know the joy of the bodhisattva life. I teach reality to poor people, so they may obtain the spiritual treasury of bodhisattva saviors. I teach reality to people in parks and gardens, in order to cause them to strive to seek the enlightenment teaching. I teach reality to people on the road, so that they set out on the road to omniscience. I teach reality to beings in villages, that they may escape from the entire threefold universe. I teach reality to people in many countries, in or-

der to lead them beyond the paths of disciples and hermit buddhas and establish them on the stage of buddhahood. I teach reality to people in cities, in order to illuminate the city ruled by reality. I teach reality to people caught in directions, that they may attain knowledge of the equality of past, present, and future. I teach reality to people in the four quarters, so they may realize full knowledge of all things. I teach reality to people whose behavior is governed solely by lust, to stop their craving for all self-centered pleasures through the contemplation of impurity. I teach reality to people who act on hatred, that they may enter the ocean of ways of universal love. I teach reality to people who act on delusion, so that they may achieve insight through the critical understanding of all things. I teach reality to people who act on lust, hatred, and delusion in equal measure, so that they may distinguish themselves in the ocean of ways of the vows of all vehicles. I teach reality to people who are inclined to enjoyment of unsatisfying mundane objects, so as to lead them away from such inclinations. I teach reality to people who are touched by all the miseries of the life cycle, to protect them from such sufferings. I teach reality to people who are able to be tamed by the enlightened, to illuminate for them the unborn state. I teach reality to people who are attached to physical abodes, so they may live free in the realm of ungrounded reality. I teach reality to cowards, to show them the distinctive beauty of the path of enlightenment. For those who are conceited, I elucidate the tolerance of the equality of all things. For those who are inclined to the realm of deceit and guile, I elucidate the purity of the intention of bodhisattva saviors.

In this way, noble one, I take care of all sentient beings by the gift of teaching them reality. With a variety of arts, I turn them away from all paths of sufferings and miserable states, show them the consummate happiness of humans and gods, free them from the dominion of the threefold realm, establish them in omniscience, and bring them to maturity. Thus having attained the realization of the oceans of energies of universal love, I rejoice, I am ecstatic, and I become glad at heart.

Further, noble one, as I survey in all directions the oceans of the assemblies of bodhisattva saviors, I totally bring forth oceans of energies of universal joy, for the bodhisattvas who live up to their various vows, who variously purify their bodies, variously array themselves with spheres of light, radiate spheres of light rays of infinite colors, variously shine with knowledge that releases oceans of ways to omniscience, plunge into oceans of various concentrations, manifest various occult powers, speak in oceans of various voices and languages, manifest variously adorned beautiful bodies, immerse themselves in the various ways of enlightenment, embody themselves in releasing and flowing into oceans of various buddha-lands, immerse themselves in various oceans of buddhas, immerse themselves in oceans of various intellectual capacities, realized of the realm of the knowledge of the various liberations of buddhas, encompass oceans of various knowledges, dwell in various oceans of methods of concentration, freely deploy various teachings, liberations, and disciplines, approach various doors to omniscience, variously array the sky of the reality realm, suffuse the sky with clouds of various beautiful arrays, survey the oceans of various assemblies, gather together in various worlds with the force of joy, create and visit the various buddhaworlds, gather together in various regions of oceans, are emissaries of various buddhas, depart the presence of various buddhas, in company with groups of bodhisattva saviors, shower forth clouds of various beautiful arrays, enter the systems of various buddhas, contemplate the oceans of teachings of various buddhas, plunge into various regions of oceans, and take their seats in the midst of various magnificent arrays. Those bodhisattvas, born of the oceans of the force of various joys, enter the ocean of the assemblies of the buddhas, behold them, and contemplate them; as they meditate on the infinity of the powers of the buddhas, oceans of the energies of universal joy arise in them.

Furthermore, noble one, perceiving the inconceivable purity of the form body of the Lord Buddha Vairochana, adorned by the marks of universal greatness, I experience vast joy, serene faith, and exaltation. Observing his sphere of light, vast as the realm of reality, moment by moment, manifesting infinitely varied oceans of colors, in each moment of joyful consciousness I experience oceans of universal joy.

Also, noble one, seeing as many oceans of great rays of light as atoms in infinite buddhaworlds emanate from each pore of Buddha Vairochana's body, each ray of light accompanied by as many oceans of light rays as atoms in infinite buddhaworlds, filling all buddhaworlds and alleviating the sufferings of all beings, in each moment of consciousness, I experience oceans of energies of universal joy.

Also, noble one, seeing clouds of mountains of lights of all jewels, as many as the atoms in all buddhaverses, emerging from Vairochana's head, from moment to moment pervading all universes, in each moment of consciousness I feel oceans of energies of universal joy.

Also, seeing clouds of light rays of various fragrances, as numerous as atoms in all buddha-worlds, emanating from each pore of Vairochana's body in each moment of thought, in each moment of consciousness I experience oceans of energies of universal joy.

Also, as I observe Vairochana's body, seeing clouds of buddhas adorned with the marks of greatness, as numerous as atoms in all buddhaworlds, emanating from each of the buddhas' marks of greatness in each moment of thought, in each moment of consciousness I experience oceans of energies of universal joy.

Also, seeing clouds of magically manifested buddhas, shining with the eighty signs of greatness as numerous as atoms in all buddhaworlds, emanating from each of the buddhas' physical beauties in each moment of thought, in each moment of consciousness I experience oceans of energies of universal joy. . . .

And so I attained what I never attained before, understood what I never understood before, encompassed what I never encompassed before, absorbed what I never absorbed before, saw what I never saw before, and heard what I never heard before. For what reason? All things are to be completely understood as marked by the nature of reality, as having one characteristic at all times while still appearing as all things in their endless variety.

This is the illumination of the ocean of means of the bodhisattva liberation of the beautiful array of each moment of thought producing immense oceans of energies of joy. This liberation is infinite because it enters the oceans of facts of the reality realm. This liberation is inexhaustible because it is inseparable from the conception of the will to omniscience. This liberation is endless because it is seen only by the vision of bodhisattvas. This liberation is peerless because it suffuses the whole realm of reality. This liberation is omni-faceted because it enfolds all miracles in each object. This liberation is not in vain, because it lives in the nonduality of all embodiments of reality. This liberation is unborn because its practice is like magic.... This liberation is like the great earth because it is the refuge of all sensitive beings. This liberation is like water because it pours great compassion upon all sensitive beings. This liberation is like fire because it limits the cravings and addictions of all sensitive beings. This liberation is like wind because it directs all sensitive beings to omniscience. This liberation is like the ocean because it is a treasury of the ornaments of the virtues of all sensitive beings.... This liberation is like a great cloud, showering the rain of the cloud of the teaching upon all sensitive beings. This liberation is like the sun, dispelling the darkness of the misknowledge of all sensitive beings. This liberation is like the moon, infused with an ocean of goodness and knowledge. This liberation is like the arrival at Thusness, accessible everywhere.... This liberation is like a great tree, flowering with miracles of all buddhas. This liberation is like a diamond, its nature unbreakable. This liberation is like a wish-fulfilling jewel, accomplishing an endless variety of miracles. . . . This liberation is like a jewel of happiness, equally giving voice to the teaching of all buddhas. This liberation is illustrated by countless such similes.

Meditate on this passage. This *Garland Sutra, The Inconceivable Liberation Sutra,* is the greatest resource I have ever found for meditation to develop the imagination and inspiration of heroic creativity. We should not be too proud or ethnocentric to reach for such resources from other civilizations. Let me emphasize again that you do not have to become a "Buddhist" to read enlightening texts such as these. You can enjoy the *Sutra*'s images of the dedicated bodhisattva and her flowering universe while remaining loyal to your religion, allowing the description simply to broaden your imagination.

All the meditations used in this creativity practice have two main purposes: To help you overcome self-loathing and the false self-importance it generates by developing true self-confidence; and to help you overcome despair by envisioning the flawless perfection of the buddha-world. When you drop your superficial narcissism and enjoy the realistic pride of the bodhisattva savior, your healthy confidence empowers you to accomplish great improvements for the sake of all beings. When you replace despair with a positive view of what may be, you feel inspired to work creatively for positive change. In both cases, you realize that your thoughts and acts are meaningful, and will inevitably succeed. You understand that there is such a thing as a buddha-world, a world as envisioned by enlightened beings, a world of happiness, and that it does in fact exist right now. But at the same time you understand, with your appreciation of nonduality, that you must work to make that buddha-world a reality for all living beings. You must not waste your great potential as a human being. You must spur your imagination to realize and achieve what is possible.

Personal Performance: Graciousness

The *Garland Sutra* and other Indian works reveal an infinite universe or multiverse sparkling with benevolent life-forms, extraordinary heroic beings whose sole purpose is to save others from suffering. Knowing that they are there, and that we have an infinite number of lifetimes to join them, transforms the context within which we approach our thoughts, words, and deeds of virtue. In our habitual doom-filled worldview, when we give a gift, act with true justice, or behave in a heroically tolerant and creative manner, we're doing something with little hope of long-term benefit. Rather, we feel ourselves to be operating against a tide of selfishness, disaster, and danger. We feel we are being foolish even when we are kind. In the enlightenment-envisioned reality, on the other hand, even our tiniest acts of virtue are empowered by the supportive energy of countless enlightened, divine, and angelic beings. We have already seen, with our creative imaginations, the perfect buddha-world filled with floods of joy that we are working to help build. Our every thought, word, and action contributes to the positive evolution of ourselves and all other beings. We are, therefore, immensely motivated to make each moment of this human lifetime count by putting our virtues into practice in our daily lives.

Performing the transcendent virtue of creativity does not necessarily involve rushing out and getting involved with all the activist causes you can find. In fact, some people work as activists for a good cause out of purely egocentric motives, as part of a strategy of denial, deploying all sorts of negative emotions in the process. Often, the failure of such causes results from this negativity—the people participating in them do not have the proper other-centered motives. In order to operate based on true, transcendent creativity, you must maintain the sense of selflessness that comes from your infinite life perspective. This means that you work without expectation of reward and without selfishly demanding credit for your good deeds. You are determined to be successful, but have no desire to personally appropriate the success as your own.

When I was a child, I used to listen to *The Lone Ranger* on the radio (that gives you a hint of my age!). After the hero had saved the victims of evil and injustice, he had a way of quickly disappearing before people got around to thanking him and celebrating him for his achievements. The last phrase of the show was, "Who is that masked man?" And the answer would come back, "Why, that's the Lone Ranger!" (Never mind that he never could have managed to accomplish his good deeds without the help of his Native American friend, Tonto!) Then you would hear, "Hi-ho, Silver, away!" The great thing about that show was that it laid down the principle of not fighting injustice simply to aggrandize oneself. It taught us American radio fans the lesson of the Dharma: "To perform good deeds for the benefit of others without expectation of reward."

Thus, as with all the transcendent virtues, constructing your attitude and motivation with wisdom is the first exercise in performance. Your comfort in selflessness will also make you feel more relaxed, more energized, and more joyful as you engage your creativity in the world. Your imaginative energy is the natural overflow of your joy in having found the freedom and promise of enlightenment. You feel the presence of a better world not just as a possibility but as a reality, and, in your selfless desire to make such a world available to others, your creativity flows out of you like a ray of sunshine.

Everything you think, say, and do now becomes a work of art. You become mindful of every little gesture that could perpetuate a fearful and depressing worldview rather than a magnificently hopeful one. Confucius was extremely refined in his understanding of these levels of creativity. His concept of *li,* usually mistranslated as "propriety," emphasized how people should be extremely conscious of their every gesture, as well as artful in making the gestures as meaningful and gracious as possible. He created a model for interpersonal behavior that continues to help make life in society more harmonious even today. I call this sense of rightness and artfulness in common behavior "graciousness," in that it brings a sense of divine "grace" into our everyday lives. So we express our transcendent creativity with graciousness, conveying in every way we can the presence of the gracious blissfulness of the buddhaverse, calming the fears and worries of unenlightened beings and encouraging them to open themselves to the wonders of infinite life.

First and foremost, you can focus on your gestures and body language, which communicate a great deal. They either reinforce a sense of alienation or inspire people to be more aware of and open to others. You should always adjust your behavior to suit the person you are dealing with, being sensitive to their needs. For example, if your handshake is too vigorous, you may unintentionally cause the other person to withdraw from your aggression. If your handshake is too limp and wimpy, however, you may make another person feel that you are only pretending to reach out to him when really you want to avoid making contact. With your transcendent creativity in action, you focus all your goodwill into that handshake, holding the other's hand in just the right way to give him the most encouragement, signaling your utmost kindness and concern.

The way you make eye contact also deserves constant mindfulness. If you glare too brightly at others, they may shrink away, feeling intimidated by you. If you avoid their eyes altogether, they may mistake your motive and think you are furtive or unfriendly. You can focus on how your eyes should serve as windows for others to see the infinite life worldview. Use your eye contact as an artful way of conveying your happier version of reality.

Shantideva, the great teacher who guided us in our forebearance practice, also has advice on the subject of graciousness. He reminds us to focus our mindfulness on our hands when we speak. We should not gesticulate wildly when talking, since that will agitate us and those we are conversing with. When asked directions, we should never point in a bossy way with one finger, as if commanding the other person, but rather should move our whole arm invitingly, as if ushering them on their way. He asks us to vow not to spit or clear our throats too loudly, and not to eat noisily or greedily. He then moves beyond basic gestures, reminding us that we should dress well and keep ourselves clean and beautiful so that our appearance serves as an inspiration to others. We should strive always to portray warmth in our facial expressions. Shantideva himself even chose his name, which literally means "God of Peace," so that anyone who hears it will feel peace and happiness.

The art of speaking is perhaps even more important as a channel of creativity than are your gestures, facial expressions, and general appearance. After all, it is through our speech that we share our minds with each other, as I discussed at the beginning of Chapter 2. The ground rules for speech are to speak always in a truthful, reconciling, sweet, and meaningful way.

"Speaking truthfully" means that you may need to speak critically at times, not accepting others' pretensions or delusional ideas. In our current era of mass media brainwashing, many people repeat popular ideas with no thought as to their accuracy. The prevalent attitude is, "If 'they' say so, then it must be true." So, truthful speech challenges ideas and stimulates dialogue with others in order to help them think more critically about what they are told. My wife used to trouble our children (and sometimes myself) by talking back to the announcer of the news, challenging certain statements they made. She'd ask, "Why is that the case?" or "How do you know that for sure?" when various facts were declared. However, we all got used to her behavior over time. Definitely, our children and I became more involved and clear-minded, less passive and depressed in our TV viewing than if we had all sat quietly accepting whatever was said. My wife has the intuitive wisdom and tireless creativity to engage consistently in truthful speech, even with people present only through an electronic device!

"Speaking in a reconciling manner" means that you should always be mindful about the impact of your words on others. When we gossip together with friends, we say mean things about third parties, sometimes knowing full well that we are poisoning our friends' minds. We tend to think that we can draw closer to our friends by separating them from other friends, as if sharing negative information about others in this way would make them like us more. In fact, this is exactly what makes gossip so harmful. We are certainly not making our relationships any better. On the contrary, we are creating tensions between people, and making our friends and ourselves feel tenser in the process. If we speak in a reconciling manner, on the other hand, we refrain from such negativity. In so doing, we improve the relationships of all parties involved, making them feel happier. They sense us as a source of relaxation and acceptance, and draw closer to us in trust and appreciation.

"Speaking sweetly" means speaking artfully. You modulate your vocal tones, talk from your heart, and even speak in poetry or burst into song if necessary to kindle the lights in others' minds. Your eloquence, adorned with amazing sweetness, serves to open others to enlightened insights. This behavior is highly valued in the Buddhist tradition, as it should be. Manjushri, the wisdom archangel, was said to speak in a voice having sixty dulcet qualities. Sarasvati, the goddess of art, dwells in the heart of bodhisattvas, sending out sonic rays of enchanting music within their speech.

"Speaking meaningfully" means communicating the nature of reality to others. When you speak meaningfully, you open doors in your listeners' minds, turning their attention toward the wisdom of selflessness, freedom, insight, and compassion. You encourage their sense of being present in the infinite now, of choosing love and goodness always and in every way.

The monastic *vinaya* discipline of Buddhism similarly details the comportment of monks and nuns in very particular ways, creating a world of graciousness and other-consideration within the creative, enlightenment-seeking *sangha,* or community. Most of the injunctions are directed at the refinement of speech and behavior, but even actions of the mind are included. For example, one must not refuse a gift while secretly wishing that the donor would give you something more valuable. This is called "sideways begging." It clouds the air, spoils the joy of both the giver and the receiver, and blocks the creativity of making a monastic donation. You can think of many other examples of how to align your thoughts in such a way that you are not just performing good deeds, but also performing them for the right reason.

Joyful buddhaverse-building is an essential element of your creativity transcendence. In *The Teaching of Vimalakirti Sutra,* the Buddha tells the Licchavi youth Ratnakara and his comrades that the bodhisattva knows that it is impossible to build or adorn a buddhaverse, since all things are like empty space and anyone knows that it is impossible to build a world in empty space. Nonetheless, the bodhisattva still determines to build and beautify a buddhaverse, out of her overwhelming love for sensitive beings. Joyful creativity transcendence thus exuberantly determines to perform the impossible, to dare to do what no one can do. This makes her creativity transcendent, since it flows forth in deed, word, and thought without any expectation of result, without impatience about any seeming obstacle, without concern for interference, and without appropriating any accomplishment.

In fact, through transcendent wisdom, the bodhisattva knows that *nothing is impossible, all things are possible,* since the frame of reference is the infinite, meaning all certainties about the relative state of things in the infinite are only relative, never absolute. The bodhisattva begins from the expanded awareness that ultimately there is no difference between him and all sensitive beings and all insensitive things, they are one body of infinite life, measureless in space, and beginningless and endless in time. Transcendent transformation of the self is transcendent transformation of the world. Your becoming a buddha, thought of initially as an ultimate mutation into pure goodness of your personal continuum of body, speech, and mind, is the same as the universe's becoming a buddhaverse. Along with you, every other interconnected being must become liberated from suffering and exalted in bliss. Sensitive beings stuck in the reification of a present moment separate from the past and the future, stuck in the reification of their present physicality, boundaried off apart from all other beings and things, may feel that the universe is still a universe, even though perhaps some other being has become divine or "buddhine," and that must be respected as part of the enlightened infinite oneness—their sense of noninfinity and the suffering of alienation is also still part of the oneness. They cannot be transformed by force—from the outside, so to speak. They only can transform themselves from within, by reaching a deeper understanding.

Your bodhisattva's transcendent creativity rises joyfully to the challenge and lovingly surrounds and permeates the lost and lonely sensitive beings with every possible scientific clue and artistic indication of their buddha-potential, their right to freedom and the reality of happiness. This comes from your supreme self-confidence grounded securely in groundlessness, drawn invulnerably from infinity, from the transcendent wisdom that experiences absolute selflessness as universal connectedness, that loves irresistibly, like a fountain that gushes forth an ocean, inexhaustible. The transcendent bodhisattva savior you intend to be is utterly free of any trace of self-importance, since bodhisattvas know that they cannot even find themselves as a thing apart if they look with all their might. They feel buoyed by the loving infinite energy of infinite numbers of other buddhas and bodhisattvas. If they were not there, that infinite love would still be there, so they need no insecure sort of self-importance. On the other hand, they are indestructibly there, since they *are* that infinite love; all buddhas are indivisibly connected to their infinite love, securely infinite and inexhaustible.

Your joyful creativity tirelessly and delightedly builds and beautifies the impossible buddhaverse. Not only is it impossible to build it because ultimately nothing can be built since nothing is produced with any sort of intrinsic reality, but also it is impossible to build it relatively, since all buddhas have already built it infinitely everywhere, and wherever one is inspired to create a new buddhaverse of the substance of one's generosity, justice, tolerance, creativity, serenity, and wisdom, one finds that all buddhas have already created infinite numbers of such buddhaverses. There are infinite numbers of infinite buddhaverses in every subatomic energy wave, or particle, so creating, in a sense, is merely rediscovering. Shakyamuni never lets down sensitive beings. Neither do any of the infinite buddhas ever let us down. We are enfolded in their inexhaustible creativity and have always been so. We are merely given our own time to come to experience our own fulfillment, though there are also many doors for accelerated paths, powerful machines created to hurtle us more rapidly beyond all suffering.

The Kalachakra, "Time Wheel" or "Time Machine" manifestation of buddhahood, is the most extraordinary and exquisite cosmic revelation of the enlightened beings' astronomical permeation of all time and space. Here the buddhas take Great Time and transform it into a field of compassion, a mansion for the evolution of sensitive beings into freedom and bliss. Time is universally thought of by the unenlightened as the Great Destroyer, since all created things are impermanent. Having come together of components, they inevitably fall apart. Birth ends in old age and death. Buildings decay and crumble. Suns burn out, explode, and fizzle. Planets evolve and are destroyed. Even heavens expand to receive those who have won godhood through their merits and virtues, but then they also withdraw their havens, and the once divine fall into lower births again. So gods and humans fear Great Time above all.

Enlightenment breaks free from time into timelessness, into infinite life and infinite love. Yet enlightened wisdom understands that time is needed still by beings to evolve into their own fullest bliss. Too much bliss surging into too weak a vessel would burst the vessel, and the consciousness-continuum would form itself into more and more tightly guarded vessel forms, into ever greater enclosure and alienation. So the buddha beings manifest their infinite bodies of love and bliss into a benevolent embodiment of time, all-knowingly looking in all directions to see all beings with four faces in four directions, sensitively reaching into every moment, every second with twenty-four arms, with one hundred twenty delicate fingers, and pervasively attending to every conceivable evolutionary form of being with the 721 companion manifestations of the mandala or buddhaversal mansion.

Why this intensely active emanation of total engagement in time as history and evolution, if all atoms and cells are already full of buddha energy, of buddha wisdom? Because of compassion and love. Compassion and love do arise from the endless experience of the infinite bliss of buddhas, since they feel so good themselves and so cannot tolerate that others still feel suffering. They are intensely impatient that other sensitive beings become free from suffering and endowed with happiness. Infinite bliss is not a bliss that numbs, that makes buddhas insensitive to the frustrated sensitivities of others. Instead, it empowers all creativity, all artistic manifestation, and the buddhas effortlessly but dynamically deploy their architectural and cosmic mandalas to landscape worlds, to worldscape universes, and into buddhaverses, incessantly and tirelessly.

Our performance of transcendent creativity always maintains this cosmic perspective during all our day-to-day contemplations and actions.

Societal Performance: Universal Responsibility

His Holiness the Dalai Lama calls the societal performance of creativity "universal responsibility." Since we are infinitely interconnected to one another, we must all take care of each other. Just as we have universal human rights to life, liberty, and the pursuit of happiness, so we have universal responsibilities to safeguard those rights for all people. We cannot sit back and "let someone else take care of it" because then it will never get done, and in the end we will lose what freedoms we are fortunate enough to enjoy. Only if each of us participates in making the world a better place will we, bit by bit, get the job done. As the old saying goes, "Many hands make light work!"

The nations of the world tend to operate not from a feeling of universal responsibility for other nations, but rather from an attitude of competitive defensiveness. As in our personal lives we feel jealousy toward people whom we view as more successful, so countries feel envious of the wealth and power of other countries. We Americans—who, in our superficial self-assuredness, tend to see ourselves as the best, the ultimate superpower, the most significant force in world culture and politics—fall victim to this competitive approach. We constantly fear that we are losing our position of comfortable dominance. All nations, including the richest and most powerful but also the poorest and most downtrodden, are divided and weakened by defensiveness. Class, race, religious affiliation, sexual preference, nationality, ethnicity—any characteristic can be used as an excuse to make us feel that we are separate, different, and therefore locked into battle, one against the other.

On a national level, the privileged classes fear and therefore oppress the less privileged. As a result, we enact laws against welfare, build more prisons, strip money out of the school system, and cancel affirmative action programs. On a global scale, richer nations blame poorer nations for their problems. We offer some aid packages, but we largely ignore other countries' needs, focusing instead on our own. We isolate ourselves from the rest of the world rather than embrace it.

The key to the universal responsibility transformation that our creativity virtue demands is not to fear or envy one another, but to start afresh with optimistic determination. We must develop a new set of policies and practices based on our understanding of our fundamental interconnectedness. We must base our decisions not on suspicion but on empathy. We must act toward other countries as we do toward our own—with love and compassion. His Holiness the Dalai Lama, among others, promotes this approach to world politics.

The practice of transcendent creativity unleashes our imaginations so that, for the first time, we truly see what we can do to turn the negative into the positive. And we truly see that good can triumph over evil. We vow to work not only for others' enlightenment in future lives but also for their social well-being in this life. We want to provide them with the optimal opportunity to achieve enlightenment. In order to do this, we realize, they need to be able to devote time and energy during this human lifetime to their evolutionary development. This means that they need to have their basic needs for food and shelter met, a solid education, and the chance to share in their own governance, to have power and authority over themselves.

We can adopt an overall agenda that supports cooperation rather than competition. We willingly give up some of our own extra comforts in order to ensure the well-being of all people, in our country and across the globe. We resolve not to let ourselves be fooled by the divide-and-conquer rhetoric of politicians who are interested mostly in maintaining their own self-interests. When we cut off funds for education, affordable housing, job training, drug rehabilitation, medical care and nutrition for the poor, we harm numerous infinitely precious lives. Moreover, we end up going to much greater expense punishing the disillusioned souls who commit crimes out of desperation, wasting billions of dollars on police forces, legal systems, and correctional institutions. How can these policies possibly help the ill-educated, underprivileged people who are driven to violence and self-destruction by a complete lack of positive prospects? We should instead invest our money in proactive programs to prevent people from arriving in such desperate circumstances in the first place.

In this twenty-first Common Era century, in spite of appearances to the contrary, we have come tantalizingly close to achieving a world democracy operating under global law, universally demilitarized, and prosperous in a balanced and sustainable way. But we are held back by our selfishness and fear based on the assumption that violence and scarcity will never be eradicated. We must call on our transcendent creativity to overcome these hurdles. With its help, we can free ourselves from fear, rid ourselves of despair, replace our self-centered protectionism with an other-centered view of universal responsibility, and inspire ourselves and others to work for the good of all humanity. Our creativity yoga helps us realize that, step-by-step, we can honestly accomplish anything we set our minds to.

Skeptical as we always are, we may initially feel that taking on the concerns of others will only make us more miserable. We already have plenty of our own problems and feel pretty powerless to do much about them. How much worse would it be to accept responsibility for others' problems and then also be helpless to do anything for them? We can be hopeful because transcendent creativity has become today no longer the exercise of an elite wise few who have seen the magnificence of the assumption of universal responsibility and aspire to the bodhisattva's messianic career. It has become a survival necessity in our present world.

Great dangers stalk the globe—the four horsemen of the apocalypse: war, famine, pestilence, and death. There is no mystery about them. They are self-fulfilling prophecies. War has gone nuclear, biological, and chemical, and so is no longer viable, since there can be no winners—it fulfills our paranoias and becomes self-destructive for all concerned. Famine comes from the notion of scarcity, that we must hoard and not share with others or we will not have enough for ourselves. But then others die en masse and our whole globe is poisoned, so the hoarders are dragged down too. Pestilence comes from the devastation of war and famine, from the destruction of the environment by hatred in war and greed in excessive consumption. And death comes from the failure to realize the infinity of life, the excessive clinging to this life-form only, the aims and appetites of this life only. Joyous, transcendent creativity expresses itself in the positive vision that is the key to defeat the general that commands the four horsemen—despair itself. Trust, hope, and creativity can defeat the horsemen. We must not just call for them. We must develop them step-by-step.

We must apply what we have learned about the power of our creativity. When we make the commitment to build a better world, we experience a tremendous influx of creative energy. We become beings of radiant blissfulness. As our love flows out to embrace all sensitive beings on Earth, throughout the galaxies and beyond, we come up against not only black holes of despair but also vast suns of confidence and determination. Since the universe is infinite, containing infinite beings interconnected by infinite lives, our will to happiness becomes a kind of explosion, an unstoppable force to create a universe of enlightenment that works to liberate all souls.

8

Contemplation

Preamble: Relativity

Throughout the past five chapters, you have been working to transform your life through the use of specific meditations. What then, you may be wondering, are you doing reading a chapter called "Contemplation" now, at the end of the book? It seems backwards. Trust me, it is not. Contemplation transcendence comes from cultivating concentration and meditation. Meditation is a tool that we use to intensify our awareness of the world, increase our wisdom to understand it more deeply, and adjust our thought patterns in order to build a better reality for ourselves and others. It enhances our ability to understand and practice the critical transcendent virtues we've discussed so far: wisdom, generosity, justice, patience, and creativity.

Here, we view contemplation itself as a transcendent virtue. When we do not merely master it as a tool to enhance other virtues, but enter into it as an end in itself, we become capable of fully embodying the infinite lifestyle, entering into higher states of awareness, and developing advanced accomplishments and powers. As a result, we are even better able to perform all of the other virtues and, therefore, to achieve our goal of buddhahood, the ultimate freedom and full evolution of our minds and bodies and total transformation of our environment.

"Contemplation" (*dhyāna*) is chosen most importantly for the transcendent virtue in the list of six or ten of them, and for the four contemplative states that correspond to the four "divine abodes" (*brahmavihāra*) of Indian yogic cosmology. These divine abodes are realms of pure and measureless love, compassion, joy, and impartiality. Together, they constitute the sixteen levels of the "realm of pure form" (*rūpadhātu*).

A mistake that is often made, however, by many Buddhists and followers of other contemplative religious traditions, is to think that learning to reach deep states of serene contemplation and mental discipline means advancing their meditative mastery of altered states of consciousness to such an extent that they can achieve a release defined as the final departure from this miserable world. If contemplators become completely entranced with being in such states, they may actually abandon their human embodiment, initially going out of body and leaving it in a state of cataleptic trance and finally discarding it into physical death, as their minds enter into the subtle energy-embodiment of one of the divine states. When they do this, they experience intense joy of body and mind that seems like a final positive destiny, their bodies becoming pure light and energy, expressing in their subtle and boundless form the pure feelings of love, compassion, joy, or impartiality

As delightful as this may seem, they have unintentionally slowed their evolutionary progress toward real buddahood, because they have become trapped and suspended in a kind of divine stasis, an ecstasy that has not transcended self-centeredness. They still have the awareness of what they erroneously sense to be their real self, boundless-seeming or not, and so they still feel separate from other beings and things, though they are ecstatic enough to love them all without discrimination. So they are still caught in the deepest suffering of all, known as the suffering of selfish creation, since they are still composite beings who are limited and impermanent, perceiving themselves as being within a composite universe and so subconsciously aware of and still anxious about their divine mortality.

The subtle discomfort of both contemplators and deities in these states is evidenced by their tendency to abandon in turn the measureless divine abodes of the form realm and move toward even subtler states of mind, into the four absorptions that constitute the "formless realm" (*ārūpyadhātu*), the absorptions of infinite space, infinite consciousness, absolute nothingness, and neither-conscious-nor-unconsciousness. These states result from the powerful deep urge to obliterate the sense of separate and alienated self. The positive drive toward infinite life liberation gets diverted toward self-obliteration through linear mind-control development. One loses one's aim for the supreme experience of bliss-void nonduality through critical wisdom's dissolution of the delusion of selfhood through infinitely deepened understanding.[2] One settles instead for a divine rest, a tranquil aloofness, a seemingly absolute withdrawal from relations.

When the divine beings who were accomplished yogis previously, after eons of static quiescence, eventually emerge from such absolutely tranquil states, there is no guarantee they will return automatically to a human life-form. They will not recognize where they are or remember where they've been, their critical mind will be extremely dull and easily confused, they will feel tremendously oversensitive in any more con-

---

[2]It is helpful here to put these eight altered states accessible to contemplators in a table of the three realms, to give a quick overview of the contemplative cosmology.

Desire realm: Lower realms, human realm, titan and humanoid god realms, such as the Olympian realm

Form realm: Four measureless divine abodes of love, compassion, joy, and equanimity, subdivided into three, three, three, and seven divine embodiment heavens, respectively

Formless realms: Realms of infinite space, infinite consciousness, absolute nothingness, and beyond consciousness and unconsciousness

cretized embodiment. They may have to start all over again in the quest for understanding reality, in the development of the intelligence and wisdom that are the only faculties that lead to full enlightenment. So the enlightenment contemplative tradition does not consider such heavenly attainments to be desirable at all.

Therefore, it is never advisable to merely launch into deep contemplation for its own sake, simply to attain mental stability: it often ends up reinforcing our egocentrism. We must watch out for our by-now familiar addiction to selfishness. If we gain certain skills without first conceiving the spirit of enlightenment—the dynamic altruism of true compassion—we can be sure that they will only serve to inflate our self-preoccupation. Our motivation will not move beyond, "What taste of nirvana can I get during this session? How much can I attain? Will I know more things, gain more powers, experience more bliss?"

Expanding selfishness into cosmic experiences is dangerous to our spiritual evolution, as it leads us strongly into the realm of temptation. Supernormal awareness and expanded mental powers such as clairvoyance, telepathy, memory of former lives, and telekinesis are said to come naturally with the mastery of deep contemplation. They could all be used to pursue the egocentric ends of power and fame if we were to lose sight of our enlightenment goals. Selfishness is the real cause of suffering in the unenlightened universe. There is no point in arming it with contemplative power, as this will only increase our suffering.

I think it was for this exact reason—to prevent me from achieving success in deep contemplation before I was ready for it—that my original teacher, Geshe Wangyal, was always trying to prevent me from practicing it. When he translated for me the first Tibetan Buddhist book I ever read (an excellent summary of the entire Dharma teaching that presented the four noble truths in a powerful way that I have never forgotten) as the prescription for overcoming suffering, he skipped hastily over the verses and commentary on contemplation transcendence. I read it anyway and was intent upon implementing it. "Who does not desire to develop the prowess of extreme mental focus and stability?" I thought, still highly involved in my self-centeredness.

But Geshe-la had an uncanny ability to tell, whether night or day, when I was experimenting with the serenity meditation, and he never failed to distract me. After concentrating with all my might, sitting stock-still in meditation in my darkened room, my focus would begin to break free of strain, to float into spacious realms. Just as I was starting to think I'd achieved some sort of release and entered an effortless trance, just when I'd reached the threshold of feeling like I was getting somewhere, Geshe-la would show up. He'd knock at the door and invite me to the kitchen for a late-night cup of tea or bowl of yoghurt while he told me stories. Or if it were daytime, he'd ask me to work on a project in the temple or in the garden. I began to get the message he was sending that he didn't want me to meditate, or at least succeed in meditating, toward these advanced stages.

At one point when I was very close to experiencing a major breakthrough in spite of his attempted diversions, Geshe-la finally told me why he had been trying to stop me. He launched into a discourse about how a true bodhisattva does not develop strong meditative prowess *at the wrong time.* He told me that the abilities you attain with deep contemplation—the abilities to isolate oneself from relationships, to deaden the emotions, to withdraw when encountering obstructions, to palliate suffering with genuine detachment—can make you stick at a level of self-centeredness that stunts your spiritual growth. I since learned that this is the general Tibetan Buddhist teaching method. It insists that the practitioner obtain a certain level of learning and critical, reflective understanding—of wisdom, in fact—before launching into sustained meditation practice. Rather than belying an excessive focus on scholasticism, as some have thought, it is a sign of a truly healthy respect for the power of the mind. After all, a materialist can be extra devil-may-care about plunging into mental states due to his subliminal misconception that the mind is just the brain, doesn't really exist in itself, is not really a force in nature and therefore cannot have any serious disturbing effects on one's long-term state of being.

The danger of deep contemplation, even for advanced practitioners, lies in the fact that the experience seems to be unquestionably absolute in its reality. Imagine yourself as having achieved such a state. You move through a series of overwhelming experiences: into boundless love intensifying into compassion as you become more aware of the interconnectedness of life; into joy as you feel every molecule in the universe suffused with beneficent divine presence; into impartiality as your feelings extend to all beings without exception; into vast spaciousness as all objective and subjective boundaries dissolve; into restfulness and oblivion as it seems so crude and unnecessary to remain conscious at all; and finally into a subtle semiconscious state of infinitely distributed self-presence.

Perhaps you have read or heard about mystic experiences in which people achieve "union with the absolute." If so, you may recognize similar qualities in the standard description, provided above, of world-transcending states given by the Buddha and many of his successors. The key difference is that some mystics think of these advanced contemplative states as true realizations of ultimate reality, and their attainment of them as true liberation. The buddhas, on the other hand, describe such states as *relative* experiences of divine joy, bliss, and peace—fabulous beyond all earthly compare, yet still dualistic, still not freeing you from the prison of self-involvement, still not allowing you to open yourself to living infinitely.

"But when buddhas reach nirvana, don't they absolutely escape the cycle of life that is samsara?" you might ask. Indeed, even within the institutional borders of Buddhism there is an accepted understanding of nirvana as a passing away into an alternative state of being and a final extinction of any discriminative perception of the world. All branches of Buddhism offer ample descriptions of adepts having transcendent experiences that are made to sound like liberation. Yet it turns out that such descriptions are provided only as allegories to inspire the unenlightened, and are not intended as true interpretations of nirvana.

In *The White Lotus Sutra,* another ancient Universalist Buddhist Mahayana scripture, Shariputra, the apostle we already met who had attained advanced meditative states of seeming extinction and therefore considered himself liberated, questions the Buddha on this very subject. Shariputra hears the Buddha discussing the nonduality of nirvana, ultimate liberation, and samsara, the cycle of instinctual life, and he confesses that he feels doubt. "Didn't the Buddha tell his disciples many times that nirvana is *freedom from* samsara, the cycle of life?" he worries. "If so, then how can the two coexist nondually?" The Buddha admits that he allowed Shariputra and others to think of nirvana as a state beyond the world, a place of extinction, and an abode of uttermost peace, just in order to inspire them to achieve it.

The Buddha then illustrates his point by telling a parable about a skillful caravan leader with magical powers. His passengers are exhausted during a long desert crossing; they are low on water and provisions, having traveled across a wasteland for weeks. The leader knows there is an oasis two days away, just past a low ridge, but he realizes that his followers do not believe him. They're conspiring to revolt and turn back to the fertile regions they left behind long ago. The leader knows they will surely die if they do so, but he cannot persuade them that he is right, since they have lost faith in him. So he conjures up an illusory oasis, just out of reach but seemingly an easy morning's journey from where they are. They are delighted to see it, and feel greatly encouraged. They regain their faith in their leader, drink their last water, and settle down to rest. The next morning, they proceed to the oasis only to find that it has disappeared. At first they are angry with their leader for fooling them, but then they realize that from where they now stand they can see the real oasis beyond the ridge. Since they have no more water now and know for certain that they would have died if they had turned back, they gladly continue on. The next day they reach the oasis safely, and soon after, they joyfully complete their journey.

The Buddha asks Shariputra if he thinks the caravan leader's magic trick was a reprehensible act. "Certainly not," replies Shariputra. "Without it, the people never would have found their way to safety."

"Exactly! So that is the kind of trick I played on you all," says the Buddha. "I knew you would be discouraged if I told you that nirvana is nothing more than the selfless understanding of samsara. It would seem to you impossible that you could achieve complete freedom for yourself while remaining engaged with the bondages of others. So I let you think that nirvana was supreme isolation, a final haven for the freedom-seeking, selfish "self" you felt bound up with at the time. When you then truly did achieve enlightenment, you were able to understand it as the obliteration only of this *selfish* self rather than the sheer obliteration of the whole self-and-other condition. You were then ready to take responsibility for your unbounded, relative, *selfless* self as infinitely, blissfully, and freely present within the world of suffering other beings."

Finally, the Buddha ends by telling the famous parable of the burning house. A kind father tells his many children, who are frolicking unawares inside of a burning house, that he has carts for them to play with outside, letting each one think it is the cart they love best, a deer cart, a horse cart, or a bullock cart. After they have run outside, they find only bullock carts, since that is all he has. They feel disappointed, but not for long. They soon realize why their father misled them when they turn around and see the burning house they've just escaped collapsing in flames.

The key to mastering advanced levels of mind control while avoiding the danger of entrancement, then, is to further develop your wisdom. You must use your reason to remind yourself that these cannot, in fact, be absolute states. *Everything is relative:* you with your sense of a fixed self, your perception of the world as being a certain way, even your sense of having found true joy and happiness in a deep meditative trance. If you, a relational being, encounter something, then it must also be relational, even if it appears to be absolute, since you have related to it! So any seeming absolute can only be a relative absolute, including these supposedly "absolute" nirvanalike states of serenity and bliss that you can experience through deep contemplation.

We thus need to develop contemplation transcendence, but only when harnessed specifically to the magical leader, the kind father, the great mother, that is our wisdom transcendence. Wisdom helps us stay grounded in our practice by making us remember that everything is relative. It keeps us from getting caught up in the feeling that we've escaped to a new and absolute reality, which is dangerous to our spiritual development. With both these transcendences working together, we can achieve an intelligent, balanced, serene insight that moves us toward a vast and complete understanding of ourselves, other beings, and the universe we all exist in together.

Problem: Stress

Our modern lives are far from serene. We are constantly preoccupied to the point where we feel that we don't have a single moment to spare. Every second of every day is booked, if not double-booked. I should know—I certainly live this way! All the while, our minds are going crazy with a nonstop, chaotic jumble of emotions, memories, fantasies, and worried anticipations that rush through us at lightning speed, like images flashing by outside the window of a high-speed train, leaving us feeling rattled and even a little motion sick. We're overwhelmed with obligations and responsibilities, needs and desires.

Our sense of having insufficient time to do all that we must do is, in fact, what is called *stress.* It is a heavy and unhealthy burden that causes us much suffering, massively shortening our precious human lifespan by years. We find some blessed relief from it only during deep sleep, although even our dreams are often filled with anxiety.

The primary reason for our high levels of stress is attachment. We are attached to our own bodies, and so feel terrified of even the slightest hurt or disease. We are attached to our vanity, youth, and strength, and so spend a tremendous amount of time and money on products and processes designed to improve our appearance. We are possessive about clothes, furniture, art objects, decorations, dwellings, vehicles, tools, sports equipment, and even experiences, which we madly seek to accumulate in a never-ending game of "keeping up with the Joneses." And we are even overly attached to our friends and family members, thinking that we could never survive without them, devoting much of our time to worrying about whether they still love us and are loyal to us.

As a result of all our attachments, we have a very difficult time being quiet and calm. We can't stop thinking about what we don't have, what could happen to us if something were to go wrong, and what we could have, get, or do next to make our lives better. These types of negative, worthless thoughts dominate our awareness for most of our waking hours. And yet we know now, from our meditations so far in this book, that we will never—can never—be satisfied. As long as we embrace attachment, our selfish "I" will always demand more.

In order to practice deep contemplation, we must develop detachment from our obsessions. We have to learn to enjoy serene solitude. But we quickly find that this is easier said than done. The moment we try to settle down alone for a minute of peaceful meditation, removing ourselves from all immediate distractions, our thought flow immediately returns to its familiar attachments: our body, others' bodies, pleasures, possessions, and experiences. Our mind simply will not stop running over memories, anticipating situations in every possible variation, and launching into outright fantasy. We cannot stop thinking about ourselves.

Yet despite our seemingly high level of involvement in what's going on around us, when we carefully inventory our lives, we begin to realize how it can feel as if years have gone by without our even noticing. New Year's to New Year's, birthday to birthday, time passes without our perceiving much change in any deep sense. Perhaps a few disasters stand out in our memory, such as an accident involving a loved one, the loss of a job, a health crisis, or a divorce. We might also happily recall a few extraordinary events, such as the birth of a child, a promotion, or a particularly enjoyable vacation. But for the most part, our lives are just one big blur.

What explains this paradox of simultaneous stressful overcommitment and lack of involvement? The reality is that, caught up as we are in our stressful day-to-day existences, we mostly just let life blindly pass us by. We devote hardly any significant, meaningful time on a regular basis to contemplation. When do we write "meditation" into our busy schedules? When do we make time for considering the really important issues in our lives? Who we are, what we want to become, what we should be doing to take advantage of this brief human lifetime, and how we can best serve ourselves and others?

In truth, for the most part anyway, we don't *want* to contemplate reality or our place in it. We don't want to add one more item to our "to do" list, one more worry to our long catalogue of concerns. We blame our busy, stressful existence for our problems, when really we are responsible for them. We are not passive victims of the modern lifestyle; we are active participants in it.

In order to prove this point, let's conduct a simple mathematical calculation to determine how much free time we really have at our disposal that we could be using for contemplation and personal development:

- There are 24 hours in a day.
- We should spend 8 hours a day asleep. Often we don't get that much rest, and authorities from traditional and modern medicine agree that we suffer serious health problems as a result. But let's say that between sleep and illness, we average about 8 hours in bed per day. Subtract that from 24 and we're down to 16 hours of awareness.
- Now, we spend at least 8 hours a day at work, five days of the week. We're supposed to have time off for weekends and vacations, but we also tend to work extra hours in evenings, take home tasks on weekends, volunteer for community projects, even do two jobs, and so on. So let's say that we really do work about 6 hours per day on average. Subtract that from our previous total, and we're down to 10 hours of time free each day.
- We spend several hours a day buying, preparing, and eating food, then cleaning up afterward, or waiting around in restaurants for someone else to serve us. Let's say that averages out to 2 hours per day. Subtract that, and we've got 8 hours left.
- Should we allow half an hour or a full hour a day for the bathroom? Let's just give it half an hour. But then let's add on another 30 minutes for showering, brushing our teeth, and getting ready. That's one more hour off, leaving us 7 free hours per day.
- Surely we spend at least 3 hours a day on miscellaneous tasks such as commuting, doing household chores, making phone calls, pay-

> ing bills, shopping, catching up with friends, taking care of family members, having sex, and perhaps working out. So we subtract 3 hours for those odds and ends, and we're down to 4 hours of free time while awake per day.

Actually, four hours per day of free time doesn't seem that bad at all! See, you do have time to contemplate. You can make achieving serenity a priority in your life.

The problem is that most of us, rather than taking our problems on, seek to avoid them. We feel that we are in desperate need of escaping from our tortured minds, so we distract ourselves with forceful stimuli—media, sex, drugs, alcohol, violence—that drown out our troubling, divergent thought flows, enabling us to enter a trancelike state of seeming contentment. But this contentment is merely an illusion; it has not solved any of our problems. It is also only temporary. As soon as we walk away from the distractions, we find ourselves back where we started, living our hectic existences in our miserable and confused minds. And so we can see that our primary response to stress, distraction, does us no good at all.

The ultimate distraction machine is the television. Going back to our mathematical calculation of our daily time for awareness, we get a very disturbing picture. We concluded that, in general, we have about four hours free a day. But do you know how many hours of TV Americans watch per day on average? Four hours! That's right. On the whole, we spend every precious moment we have to do with as we please distracting ourselves in front of the television set. The number of hours is even higher for children, who have more free time. This waste of our human potential is simply tragic.

Unfortunately, most of us avoid using what could be excellent, aware time at work as a distraction, as well. We daydream minutes and even hours away without realizing it, spend time surfing the Internet, take as many coffee breaks and as long lunches as we can, engage in useless or harmful gossip with colleagues, and generally don't use our time effectively.

We must learn to treat work not as a distraction or a duty, but rather as another opportunity for personal development. We could focus better on our work without letting our minds divide between routine tasks and inner fantasy life. We could also choose our work more carefully, doing less of what we do not believe in, but instead finding meaningful work that we love and enjoy. Our work should express our creativity, not just be a means of earning money and passing time away. Studies have shown that meaningfulness in work is crucial to our health, while doing meaningless work that you hate just to make money is a surefire prescription for an early heart attack, not to mention daily misery. The preferred time for such heart attacks, by the way, is around 8:30 a.m. on Monday morning!

If we didn't own a television and enjoyed our work, thinking of it as a gift rather than a burden, then we would have many more hours a day to spend on the personal development of our own minds. Every minute we take back from mindless distraction and devote to purposeful contemplation is a minute of our precious human lifetime spent turning away from addictive bondage, subjugation, dissatisfaction and anxiety, and turning toward our own positive evolution, toward freedom, power, and happiness.

The mind is the most powerful controller in the whole universe. It determines not just what you do, but how you interpret what you do. It determines how you make decisions, what you choose to remember, and how you plan for the future. The mind is responsible for all of your experiences, bad and good. If your mind is addicted to attachment and scattered by distractions, as most of our minds are, you will not move forward in a positive evolutionary direction. An ancient Tibetan proverb says, "If you want to know what your future life will be like, no need to consult a fortuneteller—just look at the condition of your mind right now!" If your mind is a chaotic nightmare, then you cannot expect to improve your state of being going forward. If your mind is frustrated all the time, then you will lack motivation. If your mind is dull and sleepy, barely reacting to anything but the most obvious stimuli, then you can expect a long sojourn in the animal kingdom in your next life. If your mind is filled with rage and jealousy, you will always be doing battle with yourself and others. If your mind is blissed out in a complacent way, focused solely on pleasure while ignoring the condition of the world around you, then you must anticipate an eventual horrible and depressing fall.

So value your human mind—fragile and volatile, curious and quick, strongly motivated to find out what's what—with a view to creating a positive future for yourself and those you love. The time to make your mind more powerful by intensifying your ability to control it is now. This step is only dangerous if your wisdom and compassion are not developed enough for you to resist the temptation to use your soon-to-be-manifested power selfishly, which inevitably proves self-destructive. But you have already cultivated the spirit of enlightenment by contemplating the nature of selflessness, the interconnectedness of all beings, and your ultimate responsibility for your own life and your place in it. Therefore, I believe, you should be ready to begin this critical and high-impact practice. You can begin transforming your stress into serenity today.

Practice: Deep Contemplation

The Sanskrit word for contemplation, *dhyāna* (which is the source of the Japanese term *zen*), refers to a state of one-pointed concentration, wherein the mind can focus on a chosen object or objective without veering away into distracting thought flows or sensory preoccupations. It should not be confused with "meditation," which is a far broader term used to describe all types of inward-looking activities.

There are two main types of meditations, those of insight (*vipashyana*) and those of serenity (*shamatha*). So far in this book we have been focused mainly on the former—meditation as critical insight (*vipashyana*). Within this category, there are two primary subtypes. There are those meditations by which you seek to cultivate a particular attitude or frame of mind, such as tolerance or compassion, and there are those by which you seek to understand reality through critical investigation, such as when meditating on the impermanence of all things or the nature of selflessness.

In this chapter, however, we will engage in the serenity type of meditation (*shamatha*), which is contemplation. Contemplation is a transcendent virtue that permits you to make your mind ever more stable and substantial. It in fact leads to the highest level of awareness, best enhancing your ability to perform positive thoughts and deeds for the sake of yourself and others. Deep contemplation practice involves interrupting all flows of thought in order to reach a rapturous state wherein your mind stays effortlessly focused on any object you choose. It enables you to completely harness the power of the mind.

In addition to the evolutionary dangers of misdirected contemplation discussed above, there is a more mundane danger, namely that the power developed through deep contemplation can be put to bad ends, not only good ends. For example, an army commander who wants his soldiers to become single-mindedly focused on their hatred and desire to destroy the enemy will use meditative methods of conditioning to cultivate their intense and unquestioning engagement. He will train his troops to ignore any distractions coming from their fear of losing their lives or from their compassion for the enemy. This is precisely why we come to this transcendent virtue last: we know that we, with our solid basis of understanding of selflessness, grounding in compassion, and desire to ensure our positive evolution, will only put our mind powers to good use.

Throughout your journey here into infinite life, you have already been using meditation to develop the other five transcendent virtues. In each instance, you have used your own version of a shrine space in which to practice. You have created an inspirational physical and mental setting for yourself, one where you are able to optimally open yourself to your own special heritage and your immense potential for progress and understanding. By now, this space should hold great comfort and meaning for you.

However, since now you seek meditative contemplation itself as a transcendence, you need to make an additional effort. You need to go on a slightly sustained retreat for more continuous practice. For this practice, you might need a new place to serve as a special refuge. The contemplative tradition urges you to seek solitude in a beautiful place in nature, in the company of gentle animals and singing birds, with protective trees, clear water, and a modest but comfortable shelter filled with ample provisions. Ideally, you can also bring along a contemplatively inclined assistant to look out for you, seeing to it that you have what you need without intruding on your solitude. Or you can go on a group retreat that offers this kind of support to participants. Don't worry about being too ascetical on such retreats. There is no point in making yourself suffer, intensifying too much your physical or mental pain. Find a relaxing, pleasant place to practice where you truly enjoy being.

If you cannot find the time to take a meditation retreat, don't despair. You can do a miniature version of this practice in the midst of your daily life (taking back some of that stolen time from TV!), preferably in the evening before you are too tired, or in the morning before you are too stressed. But at some point you will need to take longer, more sustained retreats in order to make quantum progress in detachment, serenity, and concentration.

Even if you do go on a meditation retreat, each of your contemplation sessions should last no more than ten to twenty minutes. Don't set yourself the goal of accomplishing hour-long sessions, since your focus will only dull and the practice will become more and more unpleasant for you. Short bursts of focused attention are the key to success with this practice.

Joy is another secret to successful deep contemplation. You will find energy and bliss in freeing your mind from addictive, involuntary thoughts. Joy will come to you effortlessly as you forget about wanting it and stop seeking it. And joy will sustain you as you persevere through obstacles such as boredom, sleepiness, and agitated nervous frenzy.

Now you are truly ready to begin. First, select an object that will be the focus of your meditation. If you already have a strong understanding of selflessness and can engage in the process of looking for the self, turning back on it until you are spinning, dissolving, disappearing, and reappearing, and sustain the nonfinding of it, then you can select the "self" as your object of concentration. It is the most subtle, difficult, and rewarding meditative object, leading to the most liberating, integrated practice of serenity and insight. But it can also prove extremely challenging, even to skilled practitioners. Therefore, I recommend choosing a more palpable object, such as a round ball or a piece of fabric. Or it can be particularly auspicious to use an object of spiritual significance to you, such as an icon of the Buddha, a Christ or Madonna sculpture, Allah prayer calligraphy, a dancing Krishna statue, a yin-yang symbol, a Mother Earth goddess figurine, or whatever you prefer. Although any object can serve your purpose, one representing your highest ideal will, as a side benefit, become deeply imprinted in your mind as you devote much time and effort to mastering this unimaginably intensified concentration.

When you are ready to begin your practice, take the object and hold it in your hands. Stare at it for some time, until you are able to visualize it in every detail. Now close your eyes and picture it floating a short distance in front of your forehead, in front of your third eye. It is radiating golden light, shining and alive. Once you catch a glimpse of this image in your mind's eye, focus on it and let all your other thoughts and images go. Acknowledge them as they arise, but then let them float away, bringing your mind always back to the image in front of you.

Don't be alarmed if at first you can barely sustain the image in your mind's eye for more than a few seconds. You'll find that it immediately slips away. You'll hear your selfish voice nagging you at the same time as other flows of thought start to invade. Suddenly, you'll find your mind moving down an entirely different thought-path—remembering the past, imagining other possible presents, and anticipating the future. Become mindful of these swerves, but don't get too upset about them. If you allow yourself to become frustrated, you will only impede your progress. Remind yourself that digressions are natural, and quietly come back to the picture of your object. Continue in this way for the entire time you've allotted for your practice session.

Along the way to attaining the full-fledged serenity of deep contemplation, you will encounter five main obstacles: laziness, forgetfulness, boredom, nonreacting, and overreacting. Take a look at the descriptions of these obstacles and their remedies, provided below, to properly prepare yourself for the challenges that lie ahead.

The first obstacle is laziness, a kind of mental inertia that makes it very difficult for you even to begin your contemplation practice. You can overcome it by cultivating your faith in the importance and power of serenity. Reflect on its great virtues—how it magnifies the power of the mind by sharpening concentration, stabilizing thought patterns, and energizing you with joy and bliss. It also heightens your intelligence. You may believe that mental aptitude is fixed from birth, and that education can only add information and instrumental skills to your brain. But the truth is that intelligence is fluid, constantly growing through challenging times or atrophying during times of disuse. So by practicing intense concentration, you can systematically increase your brainpower.

Once you have confidence in the desirability of serenity, you naturally develop a strong ambition to achieve it. You become determined to cultivate a mind that will do what *you* want and need, rather than allowing the mind to which you are habituated use *you* for *its* own inscrutable purposes. You can, therefore, easily overcome the inertia of mental laziness and make your serenity practice happen.

The second obstacle to contemplation—forgetfulness—is overcome by mindfulness. When you catch yourself forgetting your object or even that you are practicing one-pointed serenity contemplation, you should focus all of your attention on remembering the object of your meditation in detail, holding your mindfulness firmly on it, and staying alert for oncoming distractions.

You overcome the third obstacle, boredom, with alertness. This resembles the subtle mental watchfulness you use to slyly observe your "I" during the selflessness meditation. While the main part of your awareness concentrates on the meditation object, keep another part of your mind secretly engaged in watching out for signs of sinking into boredom, like a spy. When it sees you starting to lose interest in the meditation—yawning, shifting your body position, or allowing your thoughts to wander to daily concerns—Secret Agent Alertness recharges you by reminding you of the benefits of serenity listed above.

The fourth obstacle to achieving deep serenity is nonreacting. When this happens, the object of your meditation gets lost in a fog and you find yourself unmoved by your contemplations of bliss, joy, and serenity. You feel totally blasé. In order to overcome such nonreacting, you must go back to some of your most basic motivational meditations and rekindle your interest in enlightenment. Engage in the preparatory practice, wherein you envision yourself receiving the blessings of your mentor beings. Rediscover your insight into the preciousness of human life. Count your blessings for having already accomplished so much good and for being able to enjoy this opportunity to further impact your positive evolution. Feel grateful for the vast accomplishments of other enlightened beings. Remember the wisdom of the Buddha, the beauty of the

Dharma, and the reliability of the sangha community. Think about whatever makes you feel joyful. Then, when your mind is refreshed, return your awareness to the object of your meditation. If you still suffer from nonreacting, then take a break. Go outside for some exercise, wash your face with cold water, or do some yoga postures. Return to the meditation only when you feel reinspired.

The fifth obstacle to contemplation, overreacting, is overcome by equal-mindedness. You must introduce moderation and balance into all your mental efforts, so that you do not allow yourself to become overstimulated. If your excitement has gone too far, so that you do not feel serene but rather want to jump out of your meditative state, try to relax. The most efficient way to do this is to think about suffering, death, and the dreadful situations of so many living beings. Remind yourself of the terrible events occurring all the time in the world: warfare, epidemics, famines, poverty, murder, and so on. Doing so will stabilize your mind by making you feel more serious. If that doesn't work, try counting your in-out breath cycles up to ten, twenty-one, or one hundred and eight if necessary. Keep on repeating the counting until you reach the target number without distraction. Calm and collected again, you can then return your attention to your meditation object.

The brief description of deep contemplation that I've given above provides you with a framework or scaffolding upon which you can build your own state of mental serenity. Once you have a sense of your mind as a powerful entity at your service, energized by faith and ambition, shepherded by mindfulness, guarded by alertness, and properly balanced, you can begin to really deepen your contemplation to the point of achieving great calm and control. Eventually, you reach full-fledged serenity. You'll find the power of your mind magnified immeasurably. Attaining states of one-pointedness opens up areas of your mind and brain that you previously would have considered completely inaccessible. Your selfless, infinite being is totally saturated with bliss, and at the same time your mind remains completely undisturbed in its focus on your chosen object. And so you truly experience nonduality: you are simultaneously aware of the boundless joy and absolute freedom of the buddha-world, while maintaining a thorough grasp on your relative self and the world that surrounds it. At this point, deep contemplation becomes effortless.

It is important, however, that you not become complacent once you attain this advanced level of serenity. As you frequent this contemplative state more often, developing greater and greater mental powers, you'll become far more capable of helping others than you ever were before. Keep yourself in check by continuing to develop your wisdom practice at the same time. As you mature, you must vow ever more fervently to put your amazing abilities to work for the benefit of all living beings.

Personal Performance: Self-Improvement

Once you are familiar with all the elements of contemplation practice, you can implement it as a transcendent virtue step by step. It usually takes quite a long time to reach full-fledged serenity. Those who are prepared to withdraw totally from their habitual lifestyles and go on a long retreat should be able to attain serenity within about six months. This estimate presumes that contemplators are fully prepared for their adventure, totally supported in their efforts, and able to engage in the retreat in an excellent location relatively free from distraction. Some Tibetans, such as my mentor Tara Tulku, worry that even the very air in a place such as America is so inherently full of distractions such as microwaves, radio signals, electrical energy, and airplanes, that serenity concentration will not come easily to anyone. Regardless of whether or not this is actually the case, you get the point: You can't expect to achieve advanced states of meditation quickly and easily. You must work at it.

Does this mean that once you have the confident aim and powerful inspiration to achieve this goal of deep contemplation, you must withdraw from your current life situation for a while and devote yourself full-time to its pursuit? Yes, to be blunt about it—ideally, at least.

You willingly give several years of your life to college for an education, and possibly many more to graduate school. You start out in a lowly position at your company and work there for maybe a decade to learn the business before climbing to a high-salary job in the home office. You go to boot camp in the military before you can serve as a soldier. You willingly attend seminars to further your professional training. You go away to health spas when you get cancer or want to lose weight. You happily engage in all these "retreats" of various kinds in order to improve your life in one way or another. So why shouldn't you be willing to withdraw from everyday life for six months or so to master your mind? The serenity and insight you'll certainly develop will likely be the most significant, deeply life-changing, powerfully beneficial changes you can make, helping you live up to the full potential of your infinite life.

So go on a retreat. However, if you feel that you cannot manage a retreat right now, or for the next few years or even decades (even though you can never be certain of how many years you have left in your present human form), then there are still many other essential and progressive steps you can take. An excellent start would be to commit to doing two, twenty-minute meditation sessions a day—one in the morning, and one in the evening.

While you'll find your new meditation habit beneficial in many ways, don't expect it to revolutionize your life. It's unlikely that you'll make enormous sudden changes. Don't announce to yourself, your family, and friends that a huge transformation is coming. Also, don't spend so much time in your shrine space that you let other duties, relationships, and activities suffer. Remember our now-familiar mantra: "Baby steps, baby steps." If you try to accomplish too much at once, then you'll only stress yourself out. After a short time, if you haven't met your ambitious goals, you may feel that you have gained too little for all your sacrifice and decide that the whole exercise is useless. Thus misguided, you will fall back even more seriously into all your old bad habits, now feeling cynical about even having attempted any kind of spiritual discipline.

So set realistic expectations. Tell yourself you're just meditating to remind yourself of what you must have done in previous lives, and what you will try to do better in this and future lives. Work on one piece of your contemplation practice each day, such as balancing your reactions or overcoming boredom. Each time you are able to count a few more breaths without distraction, see the image of your object a bit more clearly, or experience slightly deeper focus, congratulate yourself for the excellent work you've done. You're making steady progress! Keep up your practice every single day, but if you're tired or overstressed, don't push yourself. Always quit the session a bit sooner than you want to, so that you take the break while you are still enjoying yourself. That way, you'll be eager to return to your practice the following day.

You should also take advantage of as many day-to-day activities as you can to practice contemplation. When you mow the lawn, think of it as a metaphor for clearing away delusion so that you can see reality. When you sweep the floor, think of it as a metaphor for removing spiritual defilements and material addictions. When you wash the dishes, think of it as a metaphor for cleansing your unconscious mind of all negative drives. When someone asks you for something and you give it, think of yourself as joyfully sharing the greatest gift of all, the Dharma.

The incredibly wise Vietnamese Buddhist teacher, Thich Nhat Hanh, is a master of combining everyday activities with deep contemplation in this way. He tells us, "peace is every step." One of my favorite lessons that he shares is how to react to the phone when it rings. You should never pick it up right away, he says. Use the first ringing sound as an opportunity to stop whatever you are doing and become mindful of the fact that there is another sensitive being on the other end of the line. On the second ring, make ready to provide the person with a doorway to higher awareness through whatever you say in conversation. Now answer the phone on the third ring. Pack all your love and kindness, your patience, creativity, serenity, and wisdom into your first "Hello!" Whatever else happens, the quality of your phone time—not to mention your interpersonal relationships—will vastly improve.

Thich Nhat Hanh also teaches us how to contemplate even when waiting in traffic at a red light! Instead of becoming impatient, take a deep breath, turn in your seat, and make a little bow to the light. Thank it for giving you a moment of rest and mindfulness. Then imagine all that goes into a car—making it, transporting it, fueling it, maintaining it, and so forth. Think of its weight and power, the gas it wastes, and its potential destructiveness if misdirected. Renew your resolve to be cautious while driving. After trying this a few times, you will get so that you almost regret when the light turns green and you must move ahead once more!

Integrating even a little sliver of the contemplative lifestyle into your daily life in this way has an enormous cumulative positive impact on your health, your happiness, your relationships, and your overall state of being. You feel less driven, less torn, less tempted by distraction, and less agitated by attachment. You don't want to watch TV anymore. You are easily able to sublimate your cravings for pleasures of food, drink, and sexual experiences, as well as physical possessions, power, and fame. You more frequently remember to recognize the demon of self-preoccupation and the angel of other-preoccupation at work in your own mind. When you are feeling depressed, you can instantly conjure up the image of the joyful refuge you've created in your mental shrine space, seeing yourself surrounded by enlightened beings who are radiating luminous energy and blessings. When bad experiences happen, you remind yourself that everything is relative. You remain inwardly cheerful, thinking about how such challenges give you the opportunity to strengthen your shield of invulnerable tolerance, tireless forbearance, and ingenious forgiveness. As you look at people around you, even strangers, you reflect on the infinite interconnectedness of all beings and naturally practice compassion and tolerance with them. You are able to keep your current existence in its infinite context and let go of your fear of death, recalling that it is nothing more than a widthless line between one life and the next.

Aware that you are responsible for generating the negative or positive karma that will determine the direction of your personal evolution, you are minutely careful of your slightest thought, word, and deed. You make an effort to keep even your fantasies loving, positive, and beautiful, remembering that whatever you wish for will eventually come true. Everything in your life gains higher significance and meaningfulness.

Societal Performance: Transforming Conformism

If self-improvement is the action we take to implement contemplation on an individual level, then societal improvement is the action we take on a global level. We must help all people to gain time away from distractions and learn how to release themselves from their attachments in order to realize their own true natures, their exceptional capabilities. We must facilitate meditation practice for every single member of our society, because otherwise they will just go along with what others tell them, never even giving themselves the opportunity to discover how much happier their lives could be.

We Americans believe that we are the greatest individualists of all time. After all, we won our independence from England and wrote a constitution guaranteeing every individual's right to political freedom and personal happiness. No one tells us what to do. We make up our own minds, act according to our own desires, and don't let anyone boss us around. We are fully engaged in our lives and our world. We don't need to change. Or so we think.

Unfortunately, this version of reality is merely fantasy. It's good that we have it, because believing that we are individualists helps us feel some self-confidence, at least on a superficial level. But the truth is that our culture is based on conformism rather than individualism. Schools establish obedience as a cardinal virtue. Even those adolescents brave enough to resist authority end up conforming to the rebel youth code of their peers. In most religious institutions, we are told to surrender to a God whose edicts and priests we are supposed to obey unquestioningly. We are conditioned to rely on experts for everything—we never dare challenge scientists, doctors, lawyers, priests, or politicians. Our government uses fear, in the form of police and military presence, to control people in our own and other countries. We nervously watch TV newscasters, pollsters, magazines, and opinion-makers to decide what to think about things, whom to vote for, what to say, and what to wear. As a result, we feel uncertain about who we are and what is our place in the world. We do not trust ourselves.

We do not realize the extent to which we are passive conformists. After all, we certainly enjoy some individuality in our modern lifestyle, especially compared to the even more oppressed traditional or totalitarian collectives around the world: We choose whom we marry, what jobs we do, where we live. But, as sociologist David Riesman pointed out, we also herd together in mindless "other-directedness": We wear the same uniforms of dark suits and briefcases, we seek the same status symbols, and we establish the same overall life patterns. As we move steadily forward on the path society tells us to follow—go to school, get a job, get married, have children, produce materialistic wealth, retire, die—we very rarely question who we are or where we are going. Charlie Chaplin's movie *Modern Times* aptly depicts us as cogs in a machine, in spite of all our intellectual aspirations to individualism.

Because our authoritarian culture makes us feel that we must conform, that we must not trust ourselves, we are unable to participate in a true democracy. We are afraid to be kings and queens ourselves; hence we project kingly ability onto others who often only pretend to have the necessary knowledge, ability, and compassion. This can prove extremely dangerous. Such evildoers as Hitler, Stalin, and Mao were kept in power by the forms of authoritarianism and conformity prevalent in their cultures.

You may find it ironic that we have worked throughout this whole book to destroy our sense of absolute self and attendant selfishness, and yet in the end it seems we're trying to build it up. How do we reconcile our need to accept the reality of selflessness and discover release from selfishness with our quest for confident, empowering individuality? It seems like a controversial step. But there is no actual contradiction. Buddhism fundamentally celebrates individualism: Though metaphysically there is nothing indivisible, the highest cause in the relative, social world is the individual. It's true that you do not exist as a fixed entity, that you are selfless, but at the same time the only way for you to achieve enlightenment is to begin by discovering the truth yourself. An entire society will only reach enlightenment when each of its citizens reaches enlightenment.

Truly enlightenment-oriented societies are never authoritarian. Rather than encouraging conformity, as people in the West commonly misperceive Eastern cultures to be doing, Buddhism fully encourages individuality. The entire social and spiritual system is set up to offer every person the optimal opportunity for personal development, with the understanding that only by each person achieving insights through contemplation will the entire society be able to progress. Look at the model of Siddhartha, the young prince and soon-to-be Buddha: he abandoned his expected role in life to go into the woods and become an adept. The most honored citizens in Tibet are monks and nuns, people who have given up all responsibility for contributing to society in some materialistic sense in order to pursue their spiritual goals.

While it may seem that a society of true individualists would be chaotic, each after only his or her own best interests, this is simply not the case. You work toward your own goal of truth-seeking, but because you are selfless, your interests *are* the interests of the entire society. The more you become your selfless self, the more you become one with all beings. Therefore, by definition, you work for the good of all beings. You do not end up with a society of thieving, lying, stealing, heartless individuals, nor do you end up with a society of self-centered religious fanatics wandering off to the forest. Not at all! You end up with followers who not only study and practice to achieve the soul of enlightenment in infinite future lives, but also seek to make a difference in this life. They enter into the community to build schools, hospitals, and retreat centers, to educate and heal the sick, to enlighten us all.

Luckily, those of us who have awakened enough to see that our inherited culture is not the inevitable way to experience life can work for change. We need not settle for a self-condemning, conformist outlook. We can help everyone in our society develop a healthy individuality, and a powerful and responsible creativity, through contemplation.

In order to accomplish this societal goal, we should work to ensure that meditation retreats are considered a normal part of everyone's education. An educated person should be defined not only as one who can read, write, calculate, and think critically and skillfully, with a wide range of accurate information about the world at her disposal, but also as one who can control her own mental functions, concentrate effectively on any task, understand how her mind and emotions work, and be deeply insightful about her real nature.

We should also help build a true social support system for monasticism in our country. Rather than looking at those who choose to devote their lives to the pursuit of enlightenment as burdens on the rest of us, we should learn to enjoy their presence, vicariously accepting the blessings of their higher level of mental freedom. By cultivating contemplative serenity, they are helping not just themselves but every single one of us along the slow but steady path to enlightenment.

Contemplation is the essential balm we can use to heal ourselves, to restore our sense of purpose and meaning while acknowledging the liberation of infinite life. Once we learn to control our minds, we can recreate ourselves as happier, more evolved beings—individuals free from self-preoccupation, greed, immorality, anger, despair, distraction, and attachment; individuals full of self-confidence, compassion, goodness, tolerance, creativity, serenity—and, above all, love. Contemplative serenity enables us to make the most of our infinite life, being present and aware to the full, moment by moment for all time.

9

The Art of Infinite Living

Preamble: Activating the Spirit of Enlightenment

Having tasted the six transcendences through the previous six chapters, you have already begun to enjoy a new reality. There is no going back to your former, bounded lifestyle now. You have no doubt that you will continue to exist beyond this life in some new transformation.

The question you face now becomes: What will you do to ensure that your future unfolds the way you want it to? When you become aware that your existence is eternal, you realize that there are ongoing consequences to everything you do, say, and even think. You feel the weight of your life's new significance. Like Nietzsche's Zarathustra, you don't want to do a single thing that you would not be willing to repeat endlessly. Yet you also realize that you've vastly improved your chances of success at finding happiness since you have immeasurably intensified your loving care for yourself and others. Your worries dissolve as you revel in the freedom of eternity. You joyously assume responsibility for creating the best possible life for all living beings. Furthermore, you understand that you are completely capable of transforming yourself into the liberated, compassionate, change-effecting person you want to be.

Infinite living is pure art, and you are an artist. With your transcendent *wisdom,* you grasp your true nature as a selfless being, free from the bonds of this body, this world, and this reality. Through your *generosity,* you are mentally (if not necessarily physically) able to let go of your attachment to things, ideas, and even people. Realizing that nothing is really "yours" anyway, you share material comforts, protection from harm, and the Dharma with others. With *justice,* you vow to behave with the uttermost graciousness and fairness toward other beings in order to increase their happiness as well as your own. You fortify yourself against injury and aggression by means of your patient *forebearance,* absorbing all negativity, then allowing it to dissolve into the infinite void. You make the world more beautiful with your *creativity.* As your joy bubbles over with its crystal waters of enthusiasm, it transforms your surroundings into a blissful buddhaverse. Then you stabilize and secure these changes with the power of your serene *contemplation.*

Once you have opened yourself to experiencing each and every moment in this way, you have already started on the path to infinite life. This book has served its purpose. You are now ready to move on to more advanced readings and meditation practices, and perhaps also to finding yourself a mentor and a community of like-minded thinkers with whom to interact.

But I want to offer you just a bit more material, one last challenge before we part company. I want to show you the full process for becoming a bodhisattva. Once I've explained what this means, I'll give you the opportunity to conclude the chapter and the book by taking the bodhisattva vow. In so doing, you will take universal responsibility for exerting maximum effort to bring the spirit of enlightenment's love and compassion to all sensitive beings.

Infinite life has a daunting implication that I hinted at but did not fully explain in Chapter 1, "The Nature of Reality." I thought you might not be prepared for it yet. Now, I believe, you are ready for its unrestricted elaboration.

At the start of this book, I asked you to accept the simple premise that life is infinite—you have always been and always will continue to be alive, and death, therefore, is nothing more than a swift transition from one existence to the next. I also asked you to accept the logical corollary of the infinite life perspective, which is infinite interconnection—you are deeply and undeniably linked with all other beings. If all of them have been living for innumerable lifetimes, just like you, and all of them will continue to be reborn endlessly, just like you, then your existences must be deeply entwined. We are all linked together by a vast network of past, present, and future shared relationships, entwining us like a spider's web that's been woven around the Earth for millions of years.

The powerful implication that I'd like you to embrace now is that, since we are so bound together, *we can only attain happiness when all beings attain happiness.* Therefore we must decide, even though we have not yet fully experienced the bliss of awakening ourselves, that we will awaken the whole world along with us. If we are one with all life, then we must take responsibility for it. It's not that we would innately resist attaining nirvana alone, but rather that we recognize how the unhappiness of any single other being would spoil our blissful state. When we understand the realism of this attitude, we naturally *want* to help. Our motive is no longer to liberate just our own minds from unenlightened suffering; it is to liberate all minds.

When you have conceived the spirit of enlightenment in this way, you are ready to take the bodhisattva vow. You have awakened your soul to an awareness of its oneness with all other souls. You are ready to become a dedicated world-savior, a messiah—one who is determined to help the entire community of sensitive beings attain the blissful state of enlightenment.

I want to empower you as much as possible in your new mission. I want to help you overcome self-doubt once and for all, to optimize your altruism. You have already opened yourself to the wisdom of selflessness, and in so doing transcended many of the obsessions of the terminal lifestyle. You have already assumed a compassionate commitment to improving the lives of others. Now I'm going to help you take the next step of becoming a true bodhisattva savior. In order to assist you, I'm going to give you a look at esoteric Buddhist psychology, which demonstrates the ultimate artistry of self- and world-creation. This artistry is accessible only to the infinitely alive. It is not generally taught to the uninitiated. Taking this next step requires that you be free enough from the old habits of your rigid self-sense to allow yourself to become a work of art in progress.

This chapter is dedicated to those of you who have released yourselves from the bonds of your previously constricting worldviews, who have dared to tread delicately in the boundless moonlight of freedom, who have stepped bravely into the sunlight of the infinite life expanse. I want to leave you with an invitation to a *mandala*—an inspired realm of self-creation. I want you to find encouragement in the knowledge that there are arts available to you, the infinitely alive, of which terminal beings do not even dream.

Problem: Cowardice

We have already begun to conquer many of our greatest problems—misknowledge, stinginess, injustice, anger, self-loathing, and distractedness—by mastering the first six transcendences. Most of us, however, still have untapped depths to explore, and residues of our problems are therefore still blocking our path to the life of transcendent art. The greatest remaining issue is our hesitancy to become as fantastically great people as we can be, as we in fact already *are.* With true courage, we would be totally prepared to take on our bodhisattva roles, here and now. And yet something is holding us back. We are afraid.

The great Indian sage and saint Arya Asanga said that our buddhanature, our human inheritance, is our recognition of our "supreme self of selflessness" (*nairātmyā-paramātma*). Hopefully, you now know this selflessness from firsthand experience. Your practice and performance of wisdom, even at the initial level of reasoned intellectual understanding, has opened your mind to it. You can tolerate the cognitive dissonance that arises from realizing that you have no fixed, unchanging, independent, terminal "self," the self you most identified with in the past. You discover absolute freedom in your new, relative self, a self that is flexible, interconnected, evolving, and ongoing—a self that is *supreme!*

Why is this relative self "supreme"? Because it is the eternally engaged self of universal compassion that flows out to relieve the suffering of all sensitive beings. This self is far superior to any blindly self-centered self, which erroneously thinks it is disconnected from others and therefore suffers in a state of stressful competition with the universe. The relative self knows that you, in your interconnectedness, are the sum of all beings, far more powerful, wise, and enduring than a fixed self, which perceives itself as just one being, separate and alone. Clearly the relative self is supreme: the unenlightened ones are so alienated and miserable!

The problem is that we feel intimidated by the idea of being "supreme." Ironically, when we exist in a selfish state of ignorance, we secretly harbor fantasies of superiority, such being the tendency of egotism. But actually, even then we seek to avoid it because we're afraid, we innately dread being placed in a "superior" position because we know that we'll attract the jealousy, hatred, and competitive aggression of those around us. And even as we work to achieve a newly enlightened state through the various yogas presented in this book, still we lack courage. We secretly identify with Neo in *The Matrix,* who hopes that he is not really "the One," as everyone seems to think. We prefer to hide in mediocrity, and thereby avoid assuming the immense and intimidating responsibility of the bodhisattva savior that comes with being "supreme."

We are cowards because we think we are not good enough for such a task. "Not *me,*" we tell ourselves, "*I'm* not capable of helping others. I'm barely even capable of helping myself!" We don't honestly believe that we have the power to radically change our own perspectives and habits, much less anyone else's. We tend to think of art as something another, more gifted person is fortunate enough to produce, and we feel helpless and apathetic in comparison. We don't have confidence in our innate capacity for creating good. And yet we must develop it.

You must never, ever think that being selfless means avoiding feeling good about yourself. Quite the contrary, you cannot even get started along the evolutionary path until you recognize your own breathtakingly awesome achievement at already having become a human being. How marvelous you are to have progressed to such an advanced life-form over the course of countless existences! You must be filled with gentleness, compassion, intelligence, and self-awareness to have reached such heights. You are a magnificent creature!

Furthermore, if you have braved the odds and bet on infinity with me at the beginning of this book, if you have therefore renounced the terminal lifestyle, then you are realizing your full human potential right now. You are already sawing away merrily on the imprisoning bars of fearful anxiety and self-loathing. You are discovering, through your own experiences, the vast sunny horizons of self-confidence, positive change, and sheer joy that lie beyond the walls of your previously constraining cell.

So you are ready for the role of the bodhisattva savior. As an interconnected and enlightened being, it is your responsibility, your calling, and your ultimate challenge, but also the key to your happiness. Let me share with you the whole magnificent, outrageous, fantastic vision of the infinite life of transcendent art. Taste of it to whatever extent you choose, but know that if you embrace it fully, it will empower you to reach levels of "supreme" living surpassing anything you've ever experienced before.

Practice: Self-Creation

We come now to the seventh transcendence: art. This virtue represents the indomitable will of the bodhisattva to spread happiness to the minds, hearts, and bodies of all sensitive beings. The *Garland Sutra,*[2] that marvelous piece of Buddhist literature that I introduced you to in Chapter 7: "Creativity," describes transcendent art as follows:

Bodhisattva saviors in this seventh stage enter the infinite realms of beings. They engage in the infinite evolutionary actions of fortunate buddhas that discipline and mature beings. They enter infinite world systems and pure

---

[2]*Garland Sutra* (Sanskrit in *Dashabhumika Sutra,* P. L., Vaidya, ed., Darbhanga 1967, pp. 36 ff.), passage parallel to T. Cleary translation from the Chinese, *Flower Ornament Sutra,* Shambhala, Boston, 1993, pp. 755; 789 ff.

fields of enlightened buddhas. They engage in the infinite variedness of things. They engage in the infinite enlightened knowledge of the lord buddhas. They engage in the infinite presence of the buddhas in countless eons. They engage in the buddhas' immeasurable awareness of past, present, and future. They engage in the infinite differences in interests of beings. They enter the infinite variety of form bodies of lord buddhas. They engage in the infinite variety of inclinations and abilities of beings. They engage in the infinite satisfaction of beings that results from voices of the buddhas. They engage in the infinite variety of minds and actions of beings. . . . They engage in the infinite teachings of the paths. They engage in the lord buddhas' infinite teaching and living in the door of wisdom, and in the bodhisattva's application to the bodhisattva practices.

Art springs from the freedom of selflessness and the power of compassion. But in order to fully achieve the virtue of transcendent art, in order to become true bodhisattva saviors, we need to change the setting in which we exist. To do this, we need the inspiration of the ancient Indian Buddhist imagination, a yoga to help prepare us for our critical role. That yoga is the self-creation practice.

Self-creation begins with the mantra: "OM—Divine energy in me! I am the one whose real nature is the diamond, the intuitive knowledge of freedom!" Try saying these sentences out loud. They are quite powerful. With this mantra, you let go of your habitual sense of self, as you have learned to do in previous meditations throughout this book. You let your body and mind dissolve down through the darkness of unconsciousness and into the realm of clear light. You surrender any hold you have on being or owning anything; you let go of all words and thoughts, forms, sounds, smells, tastes, and textures; you abandon even the sense of sinking into the absence of these things. You affirm the foundation of your being in the unbreakable, absolute knowledge of selflessness, and here you find infinite life. Filling with the power of your true self, you experience the energy of total bliss. As you continue with self-creation yoga, it is crucial that you maintain this sensation, which is absolutely secure in its groundlessness.

In this vast and peaceful realm of selflessness, you do not feel isolated from other beings. On the contrary, you feel you are present with and inseparable from the deepest hearts of all buddhas, gods, goddesses, humans, and other beings throughout the universe. You joyously and lovingly consider every single cell and thought of every single being, feeling them as no different from yourself. You recognize that most beings delude themselves, and your universal compassion moves you to help them experience the freedom and bliss that they deserve. The more powerful your empathy becomes, the more intense is your will to provide for others' happiness. Conventional social or material actions seem too slow and feeble. For your love to accomplish its will, you need a higher technology.

Following these meditation methods established by the great adepts, you reimagine yourself and your environment. Tapping into artistic creativity usually bound up in routine fantasy, you envision the world as a place of beauty and security, a sacred and exquisite mandala palace free from suffering. You see yourself as a fount of wisdom, streaming with perfect love and goodness.

Begin by visualizing your ideal universe, shaped in any way you wish, arising out of the spacious void as elements of energy, fire, water, and earth. You stabilize those elements in a cosmic pattern that feels secure to you, and you surround it with an impenetrable protective force field. You bring all beings together on a planet that is perfect for coping with their needs.

Do not picture yourself as a concrete embodiment separate from these beings, but rather as an all-encompassing, cloudlike awareness. Your boundless joy and compassion cradle them, your vast wisdom and serenity sustain them. When they suffer, you put them at ease, open them up, and make them wish to connect with others in a positive way. You are a vast teaching machine.

You always know the best way to respond to individual beings by taking different forms. Whether your normal body is male or female, you can manifest yourself as male if that will elicit the most positive reaction from someone, or female if that works better. While you are human, you can also appear as any type of animal if that would benefit a person most. For example, if you wanted to confront a frightening, evil person who would usually meet you with great hostility if you approached him in human form, you could instead appear as a cat, horse, or dog. Then, he might let down his guard and pet you, taking pleasure in your gentle form.

Next, dissolve your sense of self in any ordinary form and visualize yourself as a buddha, a being with supreme self-confidence and total commitment to the immediate happiness of all beings. When you float in this buddha-identity, you don't have to think about your virtue, power, insight, and energy, because you absolutely embody them. You are invulnerable in the face of terror, death, and pain. You are time itself. That is, you are manifest not only in the here and now, but are infinitely present throughout time as well as space. All beings sense your existence. Even those who feel doomed to a horrible life find hope in seeing you: You assure them of future relief from their suffering. You feel immense compassion for every living thing, and your desire for their happiness holds enormous transformational potential. All of them look to you for guidance and security as they float through the maelstrom of life. You tolerate no misery or meanness. Evil beings melt into goodness just from looking at you.

You are surrounded by a giant mandala palace, such as the Taj Mahal times a thousand, which stands in the center of a magnificent garden filled with gods and goddesses dancing in endless and exquisite bliss. You draw all beings toward this blissful place, establishing each of them in the most exalted situation imaginable. You feel ecstatic joy as they overcome their delusions, fear, pain, and anxiety, and relax into peace and joy, understanding their own lack of a fixed self in a static reality. They return back into their original environments contented, virtuous, benevolent, and a source of help and happiness to others. They begin working to create an enlightened self and enlightened societies, using the yogas you have learned here, until they also radiate wisdom and bliss.

Meditate from within this feeling of ecstasy, from within this architecture of sublime power and connectedness, joyously surveying your ideal universe. Your body is interconnected with the bodies of every buddha and enlightened being that has ever been, including all the deities of every culture on the planet. You resonate with them, and then you send them out to purify the environment, to bless the minds of all beings and give them relief.

When you feel adequately filled with the energy and determination to eventually make these magical visions a reality, you can begin to slowly dissolve back into your subtle, selfless essence. You arise in your normal body in this life and return to your habitual circumstances. But you now have imagined the ideal of what you can achieve. The security and power you have discovered remains within you, alive and active, a source of inspiration and self-confidence that gives you the courage to go forth and change the world.

To conclude your meditation on art, I'm going to take you for another swim in the visionary world of the *Garland Sutra.*[3] I quote it at length because I know of no better way to jump-start your imagination. Consider this passage carefully, picturing yourself in the role of the "bodhisattva savior," and it will open you up to the sci fi–like reality vouchsafed to us by numerous buddhas and bodhisattvas:

---

[3]*Dashabhumika Sutra, op cit.*, pp. 55 ff.

There appears to the bodhisattva savior an immeasurable lotus made of great royal jewels, larger than ten billion-world universes, inlaid with all kinds of jewels, surpassing objects of all worlds, produced form transmundane roots of goodness, perfected in the realm of the nature of magic, appearing as well established in the reality realm, surpassing any divine object. It has a great sapphire wish-granting jewel stem, a pericarp of incomparable royal sandalwood, and a fringe of great emeralds with leaves of shining rosy gold. Its body blooms with limitless rays of light, its inner chamber completely filled with a profusion of all the most precious jewels. It is surrounded by as many other great jewel lotuses as there are atoms in ten billion world-universes.

The savior bodhisattva stands present there, his or her body corresponding to that form, and, once anointed by the supreme wisdom of omniscience, appears seated on the great royal jewel lotus, bent forward in concentration. As soon as the bodhisattva is seated there on the great royal jewel lotus, on as many great royal jewel lotuses as surround that great royal jewel lotus, that many bodhisattvas appear and take their seats there, assembling from their world systems in all ten directions. Each becomes entranced in a million samadhi concentrations while gazing on the anointed bodhisattva. As soon as all of them are thus entranced, all world systems begin to quake, and all realms of horror are pacified, all realms of reality shine with the light of realization, all worlds are purified, the names of all buddhaverses are automatically pronounced, all harmoniously living bodhisattvas assemble there, all worlds' divine and human music and chanting sound forth, all sensitive beings are filled with bliss, and there is the manifestation of inconceivable profusions of offerings to all real and perfect buddhas.

What is the reason for that? Thus, Oh you buddha-children, as soon as that bodhisattva world-savior sits there on that great royal jewel lotus, countless millions of light rays shine downward from the soles of her feet and illuminate all the beings in hells and put an end to their sufferings. Countless millions of light rays are shining from the discs of her knees, which extinguish the sufferings of all beings living as animals. Countless millions of light rays shine forth from the sphere of her navel, which extinguish the sufferings of all beings in the hungry ghost realms. Countless millions of light rays shine forth from her left and right sides, which extinguish the suffering of all humans. Countless millions of light rays shine forth from both her hands, which extinguish the sufferings of the gods and titans. Countless millions of light rays shine forth from her shoulders, which illuminate followers of the disciple vehicle and open their door of entry into the light of reality. Countless millions of light rays shine forth from the back of his neck, which illuminate hermit buddhas and open their way to enter quiescent concentration. Countless millions of light rays shine forth from her face, which illuminate all bodhisattvas, from those who have conceived the spirit of enlightenment up to those on the ninth bodhisattva stage, and present them with many ways to develop their proficiency in wisdom and art. Countless millions of light rays shine forth from the circle of hair between his brows, which illuminate all the abodes of devils in the ten directions and, opening their minds, introduce them among all anointed bodhisattvas. Countless millions of light rays as numerous as atoms in billions of universes shine forth from the top of her head, which illuminate all the assemblies of realized buddhas throughout the ten directions of the realm of reality, fill up all the realms of space, and, having circumambulated all the ten kinds of worlds, stand still and form a sphere of networks of great rays of light, manifesting a great arrangement of offerings to all transcendent buddhas called "Ultimate Illumination."

From that great sphere of networks of light rays there gush forth, in all real universes in every direction, manifestations of flowers, incense, garlands, perfumes, aromatic powders, umbrellas, banners, pennants, clothing, ornaments, wish-granting jewels, and more, all beyond the scope of all worlds, produced from transmundane roots of goodness, endowed with every excellence, and sustained by the inconceivable power of nirvana, as from a great cloud, pours down a great rain of jewels of various beauties on each and every transcendent buddha. Whosoever witnesses and acknowledges those offerings becomes finally predestined for unexcelled perfect enlightenment. Then those light rays, having made their offerings, having circumambulated all the transcendent buddhas, disappear into the soles of the feet of all those saintly, transcendent buddhas in their assemblies in all the worlds and directions of all universes. Thence it is announced that "this bodhisattva who has attained, who has practiced and performed her bodhisattva deeds, has now reached the time of her anointment."

Then, Oh buddha-children, from the limitless universes of the ten directions comes a measureless host of countless ninth-stage bodhisattvas, who surround the bodhisattva, make great offerings to her and, gazing upon her alone, entrance themselves in millions of samadhi concentrations. Then from all the bodies of the bodhisattvas on the tenth stage, from their wellness ornaments, from each of their diamond wellness signs, a great light ray called "Triumph over All Devil Enemies," each surrounded by countless millions of light rays, shines forth, illuminating the ten directions and manifesting limitless miracles, and dissolves into the wellness symbol on the brow of the anointed bodhisattva. As soon as the light rays disappear there, the bodhisattva's power and strength increase immeasurably.

Then, Oh buddha-children, there shines forth from the tuft of white hair between the eyebrows of each of the transcendent buddhas a light ray called "holder of the superknowledge of omniscience," surrounded by countless light rays. These illumine all universes and circumambulate the ten kinds of worlds, manifest the great magical transformations of all transcendent buddhas, inspire many hundreds of trillions of bodhisattvas to achieve full enlightenment, shake up all buddhaverses in six ways, terminate all death-migrations into bad states, eclipse all abodes of devils, manifest all the buddhahoods of all transcendent buddhas, present magical arrays of beauty for all buddha assemblies, suffuse all the reaches of space with liberating illumination, and then come back to the assembly of bodhisattvas, serving and circumambulating. The light rays finally dissolve into the top of the bodhisattva's head, and all the surrounded light rays dissolve into the heads of all the surrounding bodhisattvas' heads. As soon as this happens, those attending bodhisattvas attain millions of samadhi concentrations they had never attained before. Then the light rays also dissolve into the head of the central bodhisattva. And that is when that bodhisattva is said to have been truly anointed, in the realm of truly perfect buddhas. The bodhisattva then wields the ten powers and is called a "truly perfect buddha."

The purpose of this yoga of extravagant imagination is to provide you with a playful, magical way to experience creative self-confidence. Grounded in the safety net of absolute freedom from a fixated ego-self, you cultivate a broad sense of pride, not to serve any selfish purpose but only to intensify your confident love and benevolence. You feel yourself as a true bodhisattva within the endless multidimensional universes that are the fabric of your reality. Universal good emanates from your heroic actions and out into the world.

Personal Performance: Becoming a Bodhisattva

You are now ready to put the spirit of enlightenment into practice in your own life by taking the Bodhisattva Vow. This is the most powerful step you can take in terms of making a commitment to developing the transcendent virtues detailed in this book for the good of all beings, including yourself.

Here, then, is our wise mentor Shantideva's version of the vow. I will take you through each verse of his classic formulation of the messianic spirit with a short explanation. I encourage you to read slowly, and then meditate carefully on the meaning of the vow. It's crucial that you truly grasp the significance of the spirit of enlightenment for yourself, personally, in your own life. If you ever reach a sense of stability in the infinite lifestyle, the security of full openness that makes you confident you will really never turn back, then you can turn your reading into a solemn undertaking of the vow. You then transform from being moved by the *aspiring* spirit of enlightenment to living in the *activated* spirit of enlightenment. Once that happens, Shantideva says that your positive evolutionary merit and momentum intensifies immeasurably all the time, even when you are asleep. When you get formal, or even when you anticipate the glorious rebirth of your soul, you should go out and buy a profusion of flowers, fruits, cakes, and other beautiful offerings, array them in your shrine space, visualize vast clouds of magnificent inconceivable offerings, and concentrate on invoking the refuge tree field of enlightened beings, so that you read or make the great vow that opens up your infinite heart in their luminous and delightful presence.

Shantideva's Bodhisattva Vow[4]

For all sick beings in the world,
May I be the doctor and the medicine,
And may I be the nurse
Until every single one is healed!

Begin your vow here, considering the welfare of all sensitive beings, not only humans. In previous meditations, you have already spent many

---

[4]*Entry to the Enlightened Life*, III, 8–34 (my translation).

moments visualizing sick beings and responding in detail to their specific ailments and agonies. In this verse, you express your unswerving commitment to helping each and every one of them.

May a rain of food and drink descend on all
To clear away the pain of thirst and hunger,
And during the great eon of famine
May I turn myself into food and drink!

The "eon of famine" mentioned in this verse refers to a period imagined in Buddhist cosmology when the entire planet runs out of food and water, a situation that threatens us today due to the reality of population growth and environmental degradation. Picture such a doomsday scenario, and visualize yourself transforming your own body into delicious food and life-sustaining fluid to help all beings suffering from thirst and starvation.

May I become an inexhaustible treasure
For those who are poor and destitute;
May I turn into all things they could need,
And may these be placed close beside them!

Be specific as you think of offering particular beings with special needs exactly the things they need. You create these things for them from the substance of your imagination, the magic of your love, and the power of your compassion. Have faith that eventually you will be able to make this vision real.

Without any sense of loss,
I shall give up my body and possessions,

And all my virtues of past, present, and future
For the sake of the supreme benefit of all.

You vow that someday you will achieve the highest level of transcendent generosity, nonpossessively giving way even your own physical embodiment. This attitude comes from being vividly aware of the essentially dreamlike nature of physicality. Immersing yourself in relativity, you are able to blissfully let go of your "self" and glide like an ecstatic skydiver or an impassioned dancer.

By giving away all, all pain is transcended
And my mind realizes the sorrowless Nirvana.
So best that I (now) give all to all beings
Just as I shall have to give it up (at every death).

You reinforce the idea that letting go opens the door to the full bliss of nirvana. You remember how many times you have already let go of everything—your body, your mind, your physical possessions—every time you died, an infinite number of times throughout an infinite number of past existences. Here you resolve to make your life a gift, once and for all, so you never again need encounter death as severance and suffering.

Having given my body away
For the pleasure of all beings,
Abusing, beating, and even killing it—
May they always do whatever they want!

Although they may play with my body
And make it a butt of jokes and taunts,

Since I have given it away to them
What's the use of holding it so precious?

You return to your practice of transcendent tolerance from Chapter 6. You vow to transcend any remote mental vestige of attachment to your embodied self, soaring away completely from identifying with it. Furthermore, you vow not to become upset if beings choose to abuse you. Think of yourself as an antelope that has just been chased and killed by lions. As they rip and tear at the delicate flesh of the broken corpse that used to constrain you, you do not grow angry or fearful. Rather, you ignore the behavior of the tiny pride below as you leap into the vast sky in a freer, subtler, soul-form, laughing in relief, and wish them "*Bon appetit!*"

Therefore I shall let them do anything to it
That does not cause them any harm,
And when any encounter me,
May it never be meaningless for them!

You formalize in this verse your determination to exchange your self for others, replacing your self-concern with altruistic thoughts and behavior. As you abandon your self-centeredness, you become a special kind of "other" for sensitive beings, a part of their universe that gives itself to them, becomes food for them, pleasure for them, and life for them. In so doing, you subliminally erode their clinging to the false opposition they imagine exists between themselves and the universe, and you release them to some tiny but significant degree from their own self-centeredness.

If in all those who encounter me
Faithful or angry thoughts arise,

May they constantly become the source
For fulfilling all their wishes!

You vow here to steel yourself against all blows and turn all negativity into positivity. Love and forgiveness become your second nature.

May all who say bad things to me
Or cause me any other harm,
And those who mock and insult me,
Have the destiny fully to awaken!

You further celebrate your resplendent armor of patient tolerance, the limitless resource of your forgiveness. You become truly artful in creating a world sufficient to meet the needs of all beings.

At this point in your vow, you commit to exchanging equally your self and others. You abandon looking out of your own eyes and enter others' perspectives, seeing yourself and the world as they do. You become especially helpful to them now, since they can subliminally feel your open, loving energy embracing them, and so they relax ever so slightly. Your presence introduces them, however imperceptibly, to the upwelling power of peace.

May I be a protector for those without one,
A guide for all travelers on the way!
May I be a bridge, a ship, and a little boat,
For all who wish to cross (the water)!

May I be an island for those who seek one
And a lamp for those desiring light!
May I be a bed for all who wish to rest
And a slave for all who want a slave!

May I be a wishing jewel, a magic vase,
Powerful mantras and great medicines!
May I become a wish-fulfilling tree,
And a cow of plenty for the world!

You vow to explode like a volcano of good things, a cornucopia of wish fulfillment, for the benefit of all beings.

Just like space and prime elements
Of earth, water, fire, and air,
May I always sustain the lives
Of all the infinite beings!

And until they pass away from pain,
May I also be the energy of life
For all the worlds of various beings
That reach unto the ends of space!

Here you embrace existence to such a vast extent that you become unified with the very elements of embodied life: the earth that offers loving sustenance, the water that soothes the pain of nonexistent boundaries, the fire that warms the numbness of isolation with joy, the wind that blows with the truth of our ultimate freedom, and the infinite space that lets it all happen. This verse just happens to be the favorite verse of His Holiness the Dalai Lama, which he recites with passionate intensity every single day.

Just as the previous Lords of Bliss
Brought forth this soul of enlightenment,
And just as they subsequently lived
The bodhisattva savior code of action—

So for the sake of all sensitive beings
Do I bring forth my soul of enlightenment,
And so shall I too subsequently
Live up to the bodhisattva ethic!

Here you fully accept your universal responsibility. You vow to share your infinite life with all beings, providing them the energy to evolve and awaken into their own enlightenment. You and they together become the creative force, the infinite art, that builds an exquisite buddhaverse to nurture, educate, and exalt all beings.

Last, in this final part of the Bodhisattva Vow, Shantideva instructs us to rejoice. You should congratulate yourself, take pride in the magnificence of your fantasy, appreciate your courage, and enjoy your wisdom.

In order to further increase it from now on,
The genius who has clearly conceived
The enlightenment spirit in this way,
Should celebrate it along these lines:

"Today my life has become fruitful!
I fortunately won my birth in this human life,
And now I'm born again in the buddha-family!
Now I'm among the buddha-children!

"Whatever deeds I perform from now on
Must be in tune with my buddha-clan,
Never shall I disgrace or corrupt
This noble, impeccable family!

"Just like a blind man who discovers
A precious jewel in a trash heap,
By some good fortune I have found
The enlightening soul within me!

"This is the supreme elixir
That overthrows the rule of death!
This is the inexhaustible treasure
That ends all poverty in the world!

"This is the ultimate medicine
That cures all the world's diseases,
The tree that shades all beings who roam
Sadly on the road of terminal lives!

"This is the universal bridge that crosses over
To real freedom from unhappy states of life!
This is the rising moon of the mind
That cools the torture of addictions!

"This is the great sun that burns away
The mist of the world's misknowledge!
This is the quintessential butter
Churned from the milk of Dharma!

"This satisfies with joy all my guests,
Who now roam the road of terminal lives,
Who wish to enjoy the wealth of happiness—
It actually lifts them unto supreme bliss!

"Today in the presence of all the saviors,
I invite all the world to be my guests
At the festival of temporary and ultimate delight—
May gods, titans, and all beings rejoice!"

After you have carefully studied the meaning of each verse to ensure full understanding, speak the Bodhisattva Vow aloud. Make concrete your commitment to deliver all beings from suffering.

You have now taken on responsibility for the happiness of every being. Does the magnitude of your task overwhelm you? Do you not feel "supreme" enough for it? Is this all too much? No! As you put the vow into practice and dare to perform the infinite lifestyle to its fullest extent, becoming more and more helpful to others, you will grow more magnificent, powerful, and blissful. The more lofty your aim, the more glorious your dedication, the more connected you feel, the more peaceful, happy, and hence capable, you become. No wonder you can feel the healthy pride, the realistic self-appreciation, the invulnerable self-confidence of the wise that comes from within, needing no reassurance from external validation or petty domination.

If reality had an intrinsic objectivity, if it could exist only in the way it appears to exist within our ordinary frame of reference, then it would be masochistic to practice such meditations and perform such vows. If there were a rigid limit to how thoroughly we could come to know reality, and hence a rigid limit to our ability to influence and transform our lives, then adopting the boundless ambition to transform all beings into a state of enlightenment would only put us under unbearable stress. But the enlightenment tradition has discovered that there is no barrier to perfect insight into the nature of reality. There is no rigid structure of things, no absolutely fixed order that makes them forever one way and never another way. Therefore the possibilities for living beings are infinite: they can all be transformed into endless, wonderful states when pushed by our positive imagination and shaped by our determination, knowledge, and love. We can feel confident in our ability to join with infinite other enlightened beings to change reality for ourselves and others. We can arise in glory and make our infinite living a supreme art.

With this final transformation, we have developed ourselves fully. We are now secure in our selfless individuality, compassionate and self-confident in our ability to aid other beings in their quest for truth. We have envisioned an enlightened society filled with joyous beings, and we know that we can make that vision a reality. Our creative art expands through our insights and practices from ourselves to other people, and more and more makes the idyllic realm of the buddhaverse on Earth a living possibility.

Societal Performance: Transforming Authoritarianism into Democracy

It is said that more than two thousand years ago in the magical kingdom of Shambhala, the wise king Yashas, an emanation of the wisdom bodhisattva Manjushri, abolished the caste system and proclaimed the total equality of all citizens. He announced that from that time on, every person would belong to what he called the *vajra,* or "diamond," class. This proclamation had great significance. It meant that everyone would possess a fragment of royal power. In other words, everyone would be, to some extent, a king or a queen. We can see the profound correlation between this idea and the concept of democracy: Every citizen in a country has authority; each helps to decide the leadership and law of the land. It is like the powerful image at the heart of Thomas Paine's *Common Sense,* in which he compares a revolution to the shattering of the royal crown of the king, and the subsequent democracy to the sharing of the gems of the diadem with all the citizens of the land, symbolizing the return of the sovereignty they had granted to the ruler such that they should assume the royal responsibility to rule society themselves in harmony with each other.

Kings and queens, like bodhisattva saviors, have the power and privilege to rule, and also the responsibility to rule well. Good leaders do what is right and best for the entire nation. As we discussed earlier in this chapter, we normally entertain secret fantasies about being powerful, and we work hard to succeed up to a certain point. But actually we fear real power and the responsibilities it carries. One of our most comforting delusions is that we have no power, and therefore what we do, say, and think, doesn't really matter. But we must overcome this delusion. We must accept responsibility for our contribution to our own and others' lives. We must develop the deeper kind of self-confidence that feels so secure and stable that it allows no ordinary pride, none of the self-inflation and self-promotion that usually arises out of feelings of insecurity.

In the mythic country of Shambhala, the king himself is a supreme adept of the Tantra, or technology, of unexcelled yoga. He conducts spiritual initiation and coronation rituals in the gardens outside his royal palace, helping each of his people envision himself or herself as the king or queen of his or her own buddhaverse. We do not live in Shambhala, and so we do not have an enlightened ruler to lead us in our practice of democracy. But we do have the powerful ideals of our founding fathers and mothers, and we still are free to work on developing our American dream of democracy, even if its implementation has been imperfect so far. It is a work in progress, and each one of us has to take responsibility for our own gem from the royal crown that our ancestors have bequeathed to us.

Philip Slater, the respected sociologist and author of *A Dream Deferred: America's Discontent and the Search for a New Democratic Ideal,* pins the decline of democracy on institutionalized submissiveness. He says that our society is really authoritarian, filled with individuals who lack true self-confidence and feel internally powerless. Their inner self-loathing causes them to conform rather than question. Fearing real freedom, they feel most secure when confined. Therefore, conformists look outside themselves for a source of strength and worthiness. Ironically, they look to those who reinforce their own sense of worthlessness: harsh superiors who seem totally sure of themselves and the correctness of their decisions. In the end, however, conformists realize that they are unhappy with being controlled by others. However, their leaders harness this frustrated energy, the power of focused hatred, and channel it against various enemy targets in order to distract people from a more healthy desire to rebel against their authoritarian imprisonment.

This is no way to live. How can we possibly hope for the enlightenment of all human beings if we continue to exist in a state of only imagined freedom? How can we find the truth if we don't operate in a society that encourages and supports our individual goals, rather than urging us to obey? We must transform our society from one that is authoritarian to one that is truly democratic, involving all people as equals.

As with every transformation in this book, societal transition begins with personal transition. The only way we will be able to transmute our political structure from authoritarian to democratic is first to realize our individual potential by replacing our self-loathing with self-respect. Thus, as we have worked on in this chapter and throughout the book, we must build true self-esteem, develop a positive self-image, and maintain total confidence in our own ability to create a better world.

Slater's brilliant analysis provides us with several recommendations for how we can begin to exercise our bit of king- or queenship and hence make our society a true democracy. We must vow to resist systems of oppression, refusing to participate in them either as the oppressor or the oppressed. We must insist on knowing and understanding everything that goes on in the governing of our country, not accepting unsolved mysteries or secrets maintained for reasons of "national security." We should trust in our own intelligence and use every effort to seek, gather, and share information—the Internet is an excellent tool in this endeavor. And we must put our frustrated energy to good use instead of bad by turning it from destruction to creation. Let us not fight wars with those who are different from us, or try to impose our own authoritarianism on them, but rather let us replace enforced structures of oppression and alienation with enlightenment-oriented systems: Education, health care, welfare, social activism, liberal democracy, equality, and freedom.

Our current political system is a democracy: Our constitution upholds the ideals of individual freedom, universal participation in government, and equality of all citizens. However, we need to admit that we are not participating in a true democracy at this moment, just because the forms and mechanisms of democratic governance surround us. Take, for example, the fact that less than half of the eligible U.S. population votes. The process of voting is more than just a ritual. It is your opportunity to express your individuality, to contribute to your government. It is your sacred responsibility. To vote is to be a king for a moment. If you take this kingly duty seriously, you learn what the candidates stand for and you make the best judgment you can. And yet how many of us really take the time to do this, to cast a thoughtful vote every chance we get?

We need to rethink our commitment to democracy. With our newfound confidence, we must embrace freedom. Rather than subordinating ourselves to group conformity or to the authoritarian power structures of big business and dominant political machines, we need to remind ourselves on a regular basis of our powerful individuality, grounded as it is in selflessness. True democracy must be recreated every day in every crisis.

We must vow to take a more active role in our community, and to encourage others to do the same. This is what it means to be a king or a queen.

Conclusion

There is nothing more to say. Live your infinite life, wondrous moment by wondrous moment. Content with everything, expand endlessly in friendliness and bliss. This book opens a door for you. Please now take a deep breath and walk on through it, out of the habitual universe and into the infinite buddhaverse. Or else, forget about it, take a break, and come back to it some other time.

About the Author

ROBERT THURMAN, a college professor and writer for thirty years, holds the first endowed chair in Indo-Tibetan Buddhist Studies in America at Columbia University. He is the cofounder and president of Tibet House New York, an organization dedicated to preserving the endangered civilization of Tibet. He was the first Western Tibetan Buddhist monk and he shares a close, thirty-five-year friendship with the Dalai Lama. He lives in New York City. Contact Professor Thurman at rthurman@tibethouse.org.